Commercial Contracts

COMMERCIAL CONTRACTS

A Practical Guide to Negotiating and Drafting

Michael Griffiths and Stuart Williams

icsa

Trust through governance

Published by
ICSA Publishing
Saffron House
6–10 Kirby Street
London EC1N 8TS

Typeset in 9½ on 12½ pt Kuenstler by Hands Fotoset, Bexhill, East Sussex
Printed in Great Britain by Hobbs the Printers Ltd, Totton, Hampshire

British Library Cataloguing in Publication Data
A catalogue record for this book is available from the British Library

ISBN 9781860724787

Contents

Preface

While there are many books on contract law, the object of writing this one was to provide a unique combination of guidance on the different stages in the lifespan of a contract and a range of key terms for inclusion in drafting contracts. Although no substitute for legal advice – there will be circumstances where proper professional advice should be taken – this book will equip you with the confidence to consider contracts yourself and provide you with a better awareness as to when such advice should be taken.

For those who have already studied the subject, this handy desktop reference is meant as a reminder. For those who have not studied the subject, it is meant as an introduction.

The book covers the full lifespan of a contract – from offer to acceptance, to discharge and everything in between. It shows you when a contract comes into existence and how to avoid a contract being brought into force inadvertently. It gives practical tips on how to make sure that what was intended is actually brought into the contract. It examines, in detail, the terms of the contract – how they may be brought into the contract by law, even though the parties have not agreed them and shows how the terms must all be agreed before the contract is actually brought into force. It also examines the effects of the terms used, including retention of title clauses.

The book also looks at when, in the eyes of the law, a contract will have been sufficiently performed as to enable the parties to consider themselves discharged from further performance, and what will happen if the contract becomes impossible to perform. The book also provides guidance on what happens if there is a breach, and how the court assesses damages.

It then moves to look at some of the key terms of commercial contracts – what are generally referred to as 'boilerplate' clauses. The expression is not used in any pejorative sense – these standard boilerplate clauses do the jobs which they are intended to do and can be very useful in drafting your own contracts. There is no point in seeking to reinvent the wheel!

We are grateful to the publishing team at ICSA Publishing, especially Emma Reitano, for her patience in dealing with us.

Stuart Williams and Michael Griffiths
July 2014

About the authors

Michael Griffiths

Michael Griffiths LLB LLM was formerly the Deputy Head of the School of Legal Studies, University of Wolverhampton. He has lectured extensively to both professional and academic organisations on company, commercial and insolvency law.

He has written and co-authored a number of books on these areas of law. He is a contributor to *Gore-Browne on Companies* and *Charleworth's Business Law* and is co-editor of *Loose and Griffiths on Liquidators*, *Weisgard and Griffiths on Company Voluntary Arrangements and Administrations* and *Loose, Griffiths and Impey on The Company Director: Powers, Duties and Liabilities*.

Stuart Williams

Stuart Williams LLB (Hons) Cert Ed, Cert TESOL was Associate Dean of the School of Legal Studies, University of Wolverhampton until his retirement in 2010. He has lectured extensively to both professional and academic organisations on aspects of the Law of Contract, Commercial Law and the Law of Consumer Credit. He was external examiner for the Institute of Credit Management (1987–1990) and for the Chartered Institute of Arbitrators (2003–2007). He is currently a freelance lecturer in law and a consultant and writer for various distance learning projects.

Stuart has written and co-authored a number of books on the law of contract, commercial law, insolvency and company law and has presented seminars to, amongst others, the Government Civil Service College and the Banking Ombudsman's Office.

PART I

1 – Introduction and offer

Most contracts can take any form. They can be made:

- in writing
- orally
- by conduct.

These are known as 'simple contracts'. In deciding whether an agreement is such a contract, the court will look at the essential elements required. These are:

- offer
- acceptance
- consideration
- certainty
- intention to create a legal relationship.

In other words, the courts look at the substance rather than the form of the agreement.

Offer

An offer must be clear, certain and must show a definite willingness to contract on particular terms. It can take any form as long as it shows a definite intention by the person making the offer (the offeror) to be bound in contract if the other party (the offeree) accepts.

There are, however, some situations where what appears to be an offer actually is not. These include:

A display of goods in a shop window

This is not an offer to sell but rather an invitation to customers to go into the shop and make an offer to buy. The shopkeeper can then accept or reject that offer. Such a display is known as an invitation to treat (to treat meaning to bargain).

The same principle applies to the display of goods on a supermarket shelf. The customer selects the goods and makes the offer at the checkout.

In *Fisher v Bell [1961] 1 QB 394*, a flick knife was displayed in a shop window. Under the Sale of Offensive Weapons Act 1959, it was an offence to sell such weapons. The court held that displaying the goods was not an offer. It was an invitation to treat and therefore the shopkeeper was not guilty of an offence.

In *Pharmaceutical Society of Great Britain v Boots Cash Chemists (Southern) [1953] EWCA Civ 6*, the display of goods in a supermarket was held to be an invitation to treat, not an offer. The customer made the offer at the checkout.

Advertisements in newspapers, magazines, journals, circulars

These may also be mere invitations to treat. This depends on the nature of the offer in that, if there are only a limited number of the items for sale, the seller must be able to limit the number of the contracts entered into. This is called the 'limited stock' argument.

For example, if you advertise your car your car as being for sale at £1,000 it is obvious that there is only one item. If the advert was an offer, then every time a person answered the advert agreeing the price you would have a contract with them. Only one person can have the car, so you would be liable in breach of contract to all the others who responded.

In *Partridge v Crittenden [1968] 2 All ER 421*, an advert for the sale of certain wild birds was held to be an invitation to treat, not an offer. Therefore the advertiser was not in breach of the Protection of Wild Birds Act 1954, which made the sale of such birds illegal. It was obvious that the number of birds the advertiser had for sale was limited.

In *Grainger v Gough [1896] AC 325*, it was held that a wine merchant sending a price list for the wine he sold was merely an invitation to treat, not an offer. It was clear that the merchant had only limited stock.

However, if the advert is placed, for example, by the manufacturer of a *product*, this could be an offer. The manufacturer could make as many of the products as necessary to keep pace with demand. A lot depends on the way the advert appears.

In *Carlill v Carbolic Smoke Ball Co [1893] 1 QB 256*, a smoke ball was advertised by the manufacturers as being, in effect, guaranteed to prevent 'flu in anyone who used it. They offered a £100 reward to anyone who caught the 'flu after using the ball. Mrs Carlill bought and used a smoke ball, caught the 'flu and claimed the reward. The company refused to pay, putting forward a number of defences, all of which failed. Mrs Carlill was entitled to the £100.

The advert was held to be an offer to the world, accepted by anyone who took the smoke ball. This is known as a **unilateral offer** which can be accepted by anyone who satisfies the requirements specified in the offer (in the *Carlill* case, by buying and taking the smoke ball).

However, such an offer can be accepted only if the person 'accepting' actually knows that the offer exists.

In *Inland Revenue v Fry [2001] STC 1715*, Mrs Fry owed the Inland Revenue £113,000 but had no assets with which to pay the debt. Acting on her behalf, her husband tried unsuccessfully to negotiate a settlement. He then sent a cheque for

£10,000, together with a letter stating that this was in 'full and final settlement' of his wife's debt and that, if the cheque was presented for payment, this would show that the Revenue had accepted the offer.

Following Inland Revenue procedure, when the cheque was received it was sent immediately for banking and Mr Fry's letter passed to the relevant case-worker who, upon reading it, phoned Mr Fry to say that the £10,000 could be put against Mrs Fry's debt or the money could be returned. Mr Fry argued, however, that by banking the cheque, the Revenue had accepted his offer. The Revenue sued.

The court held that an offeree could accept a unilateral offer by acting in accordance with its terms only if the offeree actually knew of the terms of that offer. Here, the cheque was cashed without such knowledge so there was no meeting of the minds, no agreement and therefore no contract between Mr Fry and the Revenue.

Adverts inviting tenders

These are normally invitations to treat, so there is no obligation to accept the offer of the person submitting the best tender. Each tender is an offer which can either be accepted or rejected unless the wording of the advert indicates that the highest or lowest tender will be accepted. If there is no undertaking to contract with the highest or lowest bidder and the advert states a clear procedure, it may constitute an offer to consider all tenders which conform to the requirements as to time, date, form etc. Failure to do so could make the person requesting tenders liable in damages to a firm whose tender was not considered.

In *Blackpool and Fylde Aero Club Ltd v Blackpool BC [1990] 1 WLR 1195*, a tender in the correct form was submitted before the deadline but was not considered because the local authority's staff failed to clear a letter box into which the tender had been put. The authority was held liable to the tenderer in breach of the contract to consider all properly submitted tenders.

A tender by referential bid is invalid. In *Harvela Investments Ltd v Royal Trust of Canada Ltd [1986] 1 AC 207*, Harvela and a second defendant were rival offerors responding to a tender request by the first defendant (Royal Trust) to buy a parcel of shares.

Royal Trust invited the parties to submit sealed offers and agreed to accept the highest offer. Harvela tendered a bid of $2,175,000. The second defendant tendered a bid of $2,100,000 ($101,000 above any other offer). Royal Trust accepted the second defendant's offer and sold them the shares for $2,276,000.

The House of Lords held that Harvela's was the only valid bid and had to be accepted. Referential bids are invalid as they require the improper disclosure of confidential information to other bidders and thus defeat the idea of a confidential competitive tender. Harvela's was the highest legitimate bid.

In deciding the effect of a successful tender bid, you must look at the wording of the tender. In *GNR v Witham (1873) LR 9 CP 16*, a company invited tenders for the supply of goods as and when required. The defendant submitted a successful tender to supply these goods for 12 months 'as [GNR] may order from time to time'. A number of orders were placed and fulfilled, but later the defendants stopped further supplies.

The court held that the defendant was in breach of contract. This type of tender created a 'standing offer': every time GNR placed an order, this standing offer was converted into a contract.

If the tender is for a major contract for public works, supplies or services, the freedom to accept one of the tenders is limited by the controls required under EU regulations. These regulations, which have been incorporated into UK law, require that public authorities (being bodies 'governed by public law') must not discriminate against nationals or products of other EU states in awarding major contracts. So, public authorities must advertise across the Community and adopt standard tendering procedures. They must use non-discriminatory specifications and standards and must accept the lowest price or the 'most economically advantageous' tender.

If a tender is accepted in breach of these requirements it will still be valid. However, the tenderer of any valid failed bid can sue the authority for damages provided the action is brought within three months.

The offeror can prescribe the **method of acceptance** that must be used by the offeror. The offeree must use this method for the acceptance to be valid. For example, if I make an offer and say that the reply must be in writing, a telephone acceptance will not suffice.

In *Holwell Securities v Hughes [1974] 1 WLR 155*, H gave HS an option to buy land, acceptance to be 'exercisable by notice in writing' within six months. H posted a letter taking up the option but the letter never arrived. HS claimed that there was a contract and brought an action to enforce it.

It was held that there was no contract. The offeror's requirement for receipt of a written notice had not been met and this had prejudiced the offeror.

The courts, however, adopt a pragmatic view looking at the effect on the offeror if a different method of acceptance to that prescribed is used. It is a question of fact in each case but, as a general rule, if using this different method would not adversely affect the offeror, the acceptance will be valid.

In *Yates Building Co v R J Pulleyn & Sons (York) (1975) 237 EG 183*, the seller of property gave the potential purchaser an option to buy, saying that acceptance had to be by 'notice in writing ... to be sent registered or recorded delivery'. The purchaser sent the acceptance by ordinary post.

The court held that this acceptance was valid. The requirement that registered or recorded delivery should be used was to protect the offeree against the letter being lost. It did not speed up delivery nor did it have any other benefit for the offeror.

When the parties are **negotiating** it is important to identify the point at which the offer is accepted and the contract comes into existence. This depends, to some extent, on the effect of the wording used in the parties' negotiations.

Supply of information

If one party requests further information, the supply of this information is not an offer.

In *Harvey v Facey [1893] AC 552*, the appellants asked the respondents what was the lowest price they would accept to sell their property. The respondent said that the lowest price they would accept was £900. The appellants then sent a telegram saying 'we agree to buy [the property] for £900 asked by you'.

The court held that the statement as to the lower price was merely a giving of information in response to the appellant's request. It was not an offer and therefore could not be accepted. In fact, the appellant's telegram was an offer, which the respondents could either accept or reject. There was no contract.

In *Clifton v Palumbo [1944] 2 All ER 497*, the statement 'I am prepared to sell you my estate for £6,000' was held to be merely a preliminary statement to start negotiations between the parties. It was not an offer, so was not capable of being accepted and used as the basis of a contract.

Letter of comfort

A letter of comfort is not an offer.

In *Kleinwort Benson Ltd v Malaysian Mining Corporation [1989] 1 All ER 785*, the corporation gave a letter of comfort to Kleinwort, saying that it would always make sure that a subsidiary of the corporation, which had borrowed £10 million from Kleinwort, would always have enough funds to repay the debt. The subsidiary went into liquidation, but when Kleinwort asked the corporation to repay the loan, it refused. Kleinwort sued. It was held that Kleinwort should fail in its action. The letter of comfort was not intended to create a legally binding contract.

Subject to contract

When the negotiating parties reach agreement but say that the acceptance is 'subject to contract' the parties will not be bound until a formal contract is made.

A contract to sell property was made 'subject to contract' in *Eccles v Bryant and Pollock [1948] Ch 93*. When the formal contract was drawn up, the purchaser signed but the seller refused. The purchaser sued, but failed in his action. The phrase 'subject to contract' stopped the agreement from being a legally binding contract.

Letter of intent

A letter of intent following negotiations is not legally binding.

Problems can arise when there is a letter of intent or an agreement 'subject to contract' and one of the parties start to perform their side of the bargain before a formal contract is drawn up. This matter was considered in *RTS Flexible Systems Ltd v Molkerei Alois Muller GmbH & Co KG (UK Production) [2010] UKSC 14*.

There were negotiations for the installation of equipment by the claimant (RTS) into one of the defendant's (Molkerei) factories. They reached an agreement, made subject to a detailed written contract being drawn up (i.e. subject to contract). In February, the defendant sent a letter of intent containing the draft contract. This draft included a set of standard terms which, amongst other things, limited the claimant's liability in the event of breach. In March, the claimant wrote to the defendant to say that it had started work on the project. It raised two points in relation to the draft agreement and the claimant accepted these.

In July, a final contract was drawn up. It was stated to come into effect when both parties had signed it and had exchanged the signed copies. This did not happen but the claimant continued working. There were some variations to the draft agreement made in August and the claimant received 70% of the agreed price. However, when the work was finished, the defendant refused to make any further payments, claiming that some of the equipment installed by the claimants was faulty.

The issue before the court was whether, and if so when, a contract had come into existence. Had the contract continued on the basis of the draft in the letter of intent and the subsequent amendments or, as the defendant argued, had the failure to sign the formal contract meant that the terms of the draft should be ignored and that the parties were bound by a simple contract created by conduct in which there was no limitation of liability clause?

Looking at the parties' conduct, the Supreme Court held that, by August, the parties had, in effect, made a binding contract regardless of the 'subject to contract' provision in the agreement. By their conduct, they had impliedly set aside the requirement that the agreement would not be an effective contract until the formal contract was signed and had proceeded on the terms already agreed. These included the limitation of liability clause and therefore the claimant was entitled to its protection and could claim the balance of their fee.

Whether negotiations have resulted in a contract is a matter to be decided objectively, looking both at the parties' communications and at their conduct and seeing whether these show an intention to create legal relations and whether, objectively, it could be said that they had agreed on the terms governing their contract. In other words, it is not what the parties believe to be the position but rather what, objectively, the circumstances surrounding the negotiations show the position to be.

When performance has started before a formal agreement has been drawn up, the court has to decide objectively whether there is a binding contract and, if there is, its terms. In *RTS*, the terms were those in the letter of intent and subsequent correspondence which showed that the parties had reached agreement. These terms applied to the binding contract created by conduct.

It is a question of fact in each case whether a contract has been created. The fact that one of the parties has started work before a formal contract is signed is no guarantee that the court will decide that there is a binding contract. Such a situation fell for consideration in *British Steel Corporation v Cleveland Bridge and*

Engineering Co Ltd [1984] 1 All ER 504, where the court held that, despite the work having been started, not all the essential terms had been agreed and therefore there was no binding contract between the parties.

In *RTS*, Lord Clarke stated that 'the moral of [the cases on this point] is to "agree first and to start work later"'. In other words, never start to perform your side of the agreement until a binding contract has been made.

Provisional agreement

If an agreement is described as a 'provisional agreement' this could constitute a valid, binding contract until a formal contract is signed, as was held in *Branca v Cobarro [1947] 2 All ER 101.*

When does an offer end?

An offer does not remain open indefinitely. It can end by:

Acceptance

Once the offer has been accepted it becomes part of the contract and so cannot be changed.

Rejection

When an offer has been rejected it cannot be later accepted. Rejection ends the offer. Rejection can be a straightforward refusal. For example:

Q. I will sell you my car for £8,000.

A. No, that is too expensive.

The effect of this is that the offer has ended and cannot be revived.

A negotiation often involves an offer being rejected by the offeree who then puts forward a competing offer. This, in effect, is a rejection of the original offer, replacing this with another offer which the original offeror can either accept or reject. This is known as a counter-offer.

In *Hyde v Wrench [1840] 3 Bea 334*, Wrench (the offeror) offered to sell his house for £1,000. Hyde (the offeree) offered to buy it for £950. Wrench rejected this offer, so Hyde said that he would pay the original asking price of £1,000. Wrench refused and Hyde sued in breach of contract.

The court held that Hyde's counter-offer was a rejection of the original offer. This was replaced by Hyde's own offer, which Wrench could accept or reject as he chose. Hyde lost the case.

This negotiating process of offer and counter-offer can lead to what is known as the 'Battle of the Forms' which is dealt with in Part 2, p. 164.

If the offeree's communication is merely a request for information it will not constitute a counter-offer.

In *Stevenson, Jaques & Co v McLean [1880] 5 QBD 346,* McLean offered to sell iron to Stevenson at 40 shillings per tonne. Stevenson sent a telegram to McLean asking 'Would you accept 40 shillings for delivery over two months?'. Later that same day, not having received a reply, Stevenson sent another telegram accepting the original offer. In the meantime, however, McLean had sold the iron to someone else. Stevenson sued. McLean argued that the first telegram was a counter-offer which had destroyed the original offer, but the court held that it was merely a request for information. It did not attempt to add new terms into the contract. Stevenson won his case.

The court is conscious of the need to avoid a party escaping liability by claiming a counter-offer where none actually exists.

In *Pars Technology Ltd v City Link Transport Holdings Ltd [1999] EWCA Civ 1822,* the parties settled a dispute by agreeing that City Link would pay Pars £13,500 plus the £7.50 costs of carriage plus VAT. Pars accepted this offer in a letter, which also said that VAT was payable on the whole amount. City Link claimed that this reference to VAT on the whole amount was a counter-offer and so they were not bound. This argument was rejected by the court which held that the settlement contract remained intact. From the correspondence between the parties it was clear that City Link had made an offer which Pars had accepted. City Link could not avoid liability merely because Pars had restated its obligations in a slightly different way.

Revocation

The offeror can withdraw the offer at any time before it is accepted.

In *Routledge v Grant (1828) 4 Bing 653,* Grant offered to lease Routledge's house, saying that the offer would remain open for six weeks. Before the end of the six-week period, however, he withdrew his offer. Routledge sued Grant in breach of contract but it was held that he should fail as Grant had the right to withdraw the offer.

The only way Routledge could have held Grant to his promise would have been if he had bought an option; in other words, if he had paid Grant to keep the offer open. In these circumstances, if Grant had revoked the offer within the six-month period, he would have been liable in breach of the option contract.

To be effective, the revocation must be communicated to the offeree, either by the offeror or by a reliable third party. In *Dickinson v Dodds* (1876) 2 Ch D 463, Dickinson took an option to buy Dodd's house, the option to remain open until Friday at 9am. On the Thursday, Dodds sold the house to another person. On the Thursday evening, Dickinson heard of this from a reliable third person. Nevertheless, at 9am on the Friday, Dickinson purported to accept Dodd's offer and then sued Dodds for breach of contract. The court held that the action should fail. The revocation of the offer had been communicated to Dickinson by a reliable third party.

In other words, if you take an option on a contract, you should give some consideration (i.e. payment) for that option. However, if you make an offer which you want to withdraw (i.e. revoke) you should make sure that the offeree is informed of the revocation directly. It is not safe to rely on that information being communicated by a third party.

In *Errington v Errington [1952] 1 KB 290*, a man bought a house in his own name but allowed his son and daughter-in-law to live there, provided they paid the mortgage. He told them that the house would be theirs once the mortgage was paid off. Although they were not obliged to, the children paid the mortgage but, after the father died, his widow claimed possession of the house. The court held that the agreement amounted to a contract which could not be revoked provided the children kept paying the mortgage.

To a large extent, the position in relation to revocation of offers which require some action on the part of the offeree depends on the facts of the case. This can be seen in the case of *Luxor (Eastbourne) Ltd v Cooper [1941] AC 108*. Cooper instructed estate agents to find a purchaser for his cinemas. Commission was to be payable 'on completion of sale'. The agents found a purchaser who was ready, willing and able to buy the properties but Cooper refused to go through with the sale. The estate agents, having spent time and money trying to make the sale, sued Cooper in breach of an implied term that Cooper would not refuse to sell other than in exceptional circumstances. The House of Lords held that Cooper could revoke the offer at any time up to the exchange of contracts between Cooper and the purchaser. The estate agent's action failed. The court refused to imply a term into this arrangement.

The court said that it reached its decision 'in the circumstances of the case' and had been taken in view of the fact that the reward (i.e. the commission) was very substantial for comparatively little effort on the part of the agents. They should therefore have assumed that it was possible that the offeror would wish to withdraw from the agreement.

Lapse of time

An offer does not remain open indefinitely. It will end automatically after a reasonable time. What is a reasonable time depends on the facts of the case. So an offer to sell 1 tonne of fresh fish will lapse sooner than an offer to sell 1 tonne of steel.

In *Ramsgate Victoria Hotel Co Ltd v Montefiore (1866) LR 1 Ex 109*, M offered, in June, to buy shares in the hotel company. The shares were not issued until the following November. M refused to take them and the company sued him in breach of contract. It was held that the company's action should fail. The offer had lapsed. Given the fact that shares can fluctuate in value, five months was too long a time to keep the offer open.

Failure of a condition

If an offer was made subject to a condition, whether express or implied, it will end if that condition is broken.

In *Financings Ltd v Stimson [1962] 3 All ER 386*, Stimson saw a car in a dealer's garage on 16 March and offered to take it on hire purchase from Financings. At the dealers he completed and signed Financings' hire-purchase proposal form (in effect this was Stimson's offer to take the car) and the dealers sent it to Financings. A statement on the form said that the agreement would become binding only after Financings had signed their part of the form. There was also a statement that the customer had examined the car and had found it satisfactory. On 18 March, Stimson paid the first instalment and was allowed to take the car away. On 20 March, however, he returned it to the dealers as he was dissatisfied with the vehicle. Financings were not told of this. On 24 March, the car was stolen from the dealers and was recovered badly damaged. On 25 March, Financings signed their part of the agreement, thus accepting Stimson's offer to take the car on hire purchase. Stimson refused to pay any instalments so Financings sued him in breach of contract. The court held that the hire purchase agreement was not binding on Stimson because he had revoked his offer by returning the car to the dealers who were acting as Financings' agent. Also there was breach of the implied condition that the goods would remain in substantially the same condition between the making of the offer and the acceptance.

Death of one of the parties

If the offeror dies:

- if the contract is for personal services, the offer ends; and
- if the contract does not depend on the offeror personally, the offer remains open until the offeree hears of the death.

In *Bradbury v Morgan [1862] 1 H&C 249*, Morgan was the executor of the estate of Leigh. Leigh had guaranteed his brother's account for credit up to £100 with Bradbury. Not knowing of Leigh's death, Bradbury continued to supply goods on credit to Leigh's brother but when Bradbury claimed payment, Leigh's executors refused to pay. The court held that Bradbury should succeed. Leigh's offer to guarantee his brother's debts remained open until Bradbury actually knew of Leigh's death. This guarantee was, in effect, a standing offer to be accepted as and when Leigh's brother raised credit with Bradbury. If, however, the guarantee is not of this type it seems that it cannot be revoked.

In *Lloyds v Harper* (1880) *16 ChD 290*, a father guaranteed his son's dealings as an underwriter with Lloyds in return for Lloyds admitting the son. The father later died. The court held that given that as Lloyds had admitted the son because of this guarantee, the father's executors were liable under it. It was irrevocable and was not affected by the father's death. The estate remained liable to cover the son's defaults.

If the offeree dies, the offer ends, whether or not it involves personal services.

2 – Acceptance

Acceptance is the agreement to all the terms of the offer. It must correspond exactly to the terms of the offer – the so-called 'mirror-image' rule. As we have seen, if the offeree amends the terms of the offer in his 'acceptance', this will be a counter-offer and the onus is then on the original offeror to accept or reject this offer. In *Butler Machine Tools Co Ltd v Ex-Cell-O Corporation Ltd [1979] 1 All ER 965 CA*, the acceptance was made on the terms of the offeree, which contradicted the offeror's terms. This, therefore, constituted a counter-offer which the original offeror unwittingly accepted by returning the tear-off slip at the bottom of the offeree's letter.

If, however, the acceptance contains additional or different terms which do not materially affect the terms of the offer and this discrepancy is not promptly objected to by the offeror, the terms on which the contract is based will be those of the original offer, subject to the modifications in the acceptance. Whether or not the new terms in the acceptance materially affect the basis of the original offer is a question of fact. This will be decided objectively, not on what the parties individually believe, but on how the court views the various terms.

Forms of acceptance

The offeror may specifically state the form an acceptance must take. If this is the case, the acceptance will be valid only if it takes this form.

In *Western Electric Ltd v Welsh Development Agency [1983] 2 All ER 629*, the defendants offered to grant the claimants a licence to occupy factory premises. The offer letter said: 'if you accept ... please complete the acknowledgement and acceptance at the foot of the enclosed copy and return it to us at your earliest convenience'. The claimants did not return the acknowledgement but nevertheless took up occupation of the factory. It was held that this occupation did not constitute acceptance. The offer had expressly stated how it was to be accepted and any other means was invalid.

If the offeror does not specify how acceptance is to be communicated, however, it can take any form, whether in writing, orally or even by conduct. For example, in *Carlill v Carbolic Smoke Ball Co [1893] 1 QB 256*, because of the nature of the offer, by buying and using the smoke ball in accordance with its instructions, Mrs

Carlill was accepting the offer to be paid the reward if she subsequently caught the 'flu. In other words, her conduct showed that she was accepting. She did not have to communicate this fact to the company.

Again, in *Brogden v Metropolitan Railway Co (1877) 2 App Cas 666*, acceptance by conduct was held to be valid. In this case, for several years, Brogden had been supplying coal to the company. The parties then decided to formalise their relationship by drawing up a contract. A draft of this agreement was written by the company and sent to Brogden for approval. He made some slight alterations and returned the document to the company marked 'approved'. No further action was taken and for the next two years, following the terms of the draft agreement, Brogden supplied coal to the company and the company paid for it. B then refused to supply any more coal claiming that there was no binding long-term contract which required him to do so. The House of Lords held that, although mere mental assent by the company to the terms of the amended draft was not enough to constitute acceptance, the parties acting on the terms of the draft did create a valid contract. Acceptance had been shown by conduct.

Communication of acceptance

As a general rule, however, to be valid, acceptance must be actually communicated to the offeror. In *Entores v Miles Far Eastern Corporation [1955] 2 QB 327*, the claimant in London made an offer by telex to the defendants, a company based in Amsterdam which acted as agents for a US corporation. Again using telex, the defendants accepted on behalf of their US principals. A dispute later arose between the parties and the claimant applied to the court for leave to serve a writ on the US corporation. Whether or not they could, depended on whether the UK courts had jurisdiction over the deal. This, in turn, depended on where the contract was made. If it was made when the defendant sent their acceptance by telex, it would have been made in Amsterdam and subject to Dutch law. If, however, it was made when the telex was received on the claimant's machine it would have been made in London and subject to UK law. It was held that the contract was made when the acceptance was received by the claimants in London so the UK court had jurisdiction. This was, therefore, a proper case for the claimant to be granted leave to serve their writ out of jurisdiction.

This decision was confirmed in *Brinkibon Ltd v Stahag Stahl GmbH [1983] AC 34*. An English company, using telex, accepted an offer made in Vienna by an Austrian company. It was held that the contract was made when the telexed acceptance was received. It was therefore subject to Austrian law.

A problem in relation to virtually instantaneous communication arises when, although the acceptance is received, it is not actually seen or heard by the recipient until some time later. This could occur, for example, if a fax stating acceptance is sent one evening but is not read until the business opens the next day or if an acceptance message is left on a telephone answering machine and the message is not picked up until later. This issue was raised in *Mondial Shipping and Chartering BV v Astarte Shipping Ltd [1995] CLC 1011*. In this case, the owners of a ship which was chartered out sent a telex at 23:41 hours on Friday 2 December saying that they were withdrawing the ship from charter because the charterers had not paid the hire charges. Although the telex was received at the charterers' office, it was not read until the business opened again on Monday 5 December. The charterers were entitled to tender payment at any time before midnight on Friday 2 December. The issue before the court was whether the notice was effective as soon as it was received by the charterers (in which case it would have constituted a breach of contract by the owners as, at that time, the charterers were not in default) or whether it was effective only when read by the charterers at the start of business on the Monday (in which case the charterers would have been in breach and the owners would have had the right to withdraw the vessel).

It was held that the notice was effectively communicated on the next working day after receipt (i.e. on the Monday). By then, the owner was entitled to withdraw the ship. It was held that the crucial point was not when the notice was sent, but rather when 'its content reaches the mind' of the other party. This is particularly relevant when the notice is sent outside business hours. It could be argued however, that if notice is sent during business hours it is valid as soon as it is received.

It is a requirement that, as a general rule, acceptance must be communicated. The offeror cannot impose silence by saying, for example, 'if I do not hear from you I will take it that you accept the offer'. This was established in *Felthouse v Bindley (1863) 1 New Rep 401*. In this case, the claimant and his nephew were negotiating for the sale of the nephew's horse to his uncle. They had not finally agreed on a price but then the uncle wrote to the nephew saying: '*If I hear no more about him I will consider the horse is mine for £3:15 shillings*.' The nephew, who decided to accept the offer but did not reply to his uncle, was in the process of selling some of his stock through an auctioneer, the defendant. The nephew told the auctioneer not to put the horse into the sale but, by mistake, the auctioneer sold the animal. The uncle sued the auctioneer in conversion for wrongfully dealing with the horse which, the uncle claimed, now belonged to him. It was held that the auctioneer was not liable because, at the time of the auction, no contract had been concluded between the claimant and his nephew, as silence cannot constitute acceptance. Therefore ownership of the horse had not passed to the uncle, so the auctioneer had not committed any wrong.

This principle applies equally to inertia selling where the seller delivers unsolicited goods and states that, if he does not hear from the recipient, he will take it that the implied offer to sell has been accepted and that the recipient will pay for them. This situation is now covered by *Regulation 24* of the *Consumer Protection (Distance Selling) Regulations 2000 (SI 2000/2334)*. This states that, where unsolicited goods are sent to a person with a view to that person acquiring them, the recipient may use, deal with or dispose of them as if they were an unconditional gift and the seller's rights in the goods are lost. The seller is criminally liable if he makes a demand for payment for the unsolicited goods.

However, the recipient must not have reasonable cause to believe that the goods were sent with a view to them being acquired for business purposes, nor must the buyer have agreed to acquire the goods or have agreed to return them to the seller.

Exceptions

There are exceptions to the rule that acceptance must be communicated. These are:

- where acceptance is by conduct as in *Brogden v Metropolitan Railway* which we dealt with earlier;
- where the offeror waives (i.e. does not require) the need for communication as in *Carlill v Carbolic Smoke Ball Co*; and
- where the **postal rule** applies.

Under the postal rule, where post is the proper method of communication, acceptance takes effect from the moment the letter is posted. This means that, even if the letter never arrives, there is a valid contract. In *Adams v Lindsell (1818) 106 ER 250*, the claimant was offered a quantity of wool by the defendant who asked for acceptance to be sent to him by post. On the day he received the offer, the claimant posted his letter of acceptance. This letter was substantially delayed in the post and by the time it arrived, the defendant had sold the wool to someone else. The claimant sued the defendant in breach of contract. It was held that the claimant succeeded. If post is the correct means of communication, acceptance occurs when a properly stamped and addressed envelope containing the acceptance is put in the post.

In *Household Fire and Carriage Insurance Co v Grant (1879) 4 ExD 216*, the defendant wrote a letter to apply for an allotment of shares in the claimant company (in effect, making an offer to invest). The company sent him a letter of allotment by post but the letter never arrived. As the shares were only partly paid, shareholders had to pay the balance on their holding if and when required. The company went into liquidation and the defendant was called on to pay the balance owing on the shares he had been allotted in order to pay off the company's creditors. The defendant refused to pay claiming that, as he had not received the letter of allotment, he was not a shareholder. It was held that the contract between the parties had been made as soon as the letter of allotment had been posted so the defendant was a shareholder and was therefore liable to pay the amount owing on his shares.

For acceptance by post to be valid on posting the proper postal method must be used. In *Re London and Northern Bank [1900] 1 Ch 220*, it was held that, for the rule to apply, the letter must be properly addressed and stamped. If it is not, communication is only effective upon receipt. Further, the letter must actually be posted, not merely given to a postman whose job is to deliver letters. The acceptance is only valid once it enters the postal system. Also, it must be reasonable to use the post and for the offeror to expect acceptance by post. This could arise, for example, if the original offer was made by post.

In *Henthorn v Fraser [1892] 2 Ch 27*, an offer was made by post but, the day after the letter was posted, the offeror changed his mind and sent a further letter withdrawing the offer. The same day, however, the offeree posted a letter of acceptance: this crossed in the post with the revocation. It was held that, as the offer had been made by post, post was the correct method of communication and so the offer had been accepted as soon as the offeree posted his letter. The revocation would be valid only upon receipt and was therefore too late. A contract had already been formed.

As seen in *Henthorn*, the postal rule applies only to letters of acceptance. Any other part of the contract negotiation is valid only upon receipt. In *Byrne v van Tienhoven (1880) 49 LJQB 316*, on 1 October the defendants in Cardiff posted a letter containing an offer to the claimants in New York. The offer was received by the claimants on 11 October. They immediately accepted by telegram and confirmed acceptance by post on 15 October. On 8 October, however, the defendants had posted a letter withdrawing their offer. This letter was received on 20 October. It was held that the contract had come into existence before the letter of revocation had been received. As a letter of revocation is effective only upon receipt, it was too late to avoid entering a contract.

The postal rule of acceptance will not apply if the offeror specifies that a particular method of communication must be used. In *Holwell Securities Ltd v Hughes [1974] 1 WLR 155*, the defendant granted the claimants a six-month option to purchase certain property. The option could be exercised 'by notice in writing' to the defendant. Solicitors acting for the claimants sent a letter accepting the option but this was never delivered. The claimants brought an action asking the court to make an order of specific performance requiring the defendant to perform the contract.

It was held that the requirement that the option be exercised 'by notice in writing' to the defendant showed that it was never intended that a mere posting of the letter should constitute acceptance. It meant that the defendant actually had to receive the letter. The postal rule had been set aside by the express terms of the offer so no contract had come into existence and no order of specific performance would be granted.

In *Miss Sam (Sales) Ltd v River Island Clothing Co Ltd [1994] NLJR 419*, it was held that a cheque sent through the post will not constitute payment until it is received unless there is an express agreement to the contrary.

Whether or not the postal rule of acceptance applies is very much a question of fact based on the circumstances of the offer. In *Quenerduaine v Cole (1883) 32 WR 185*, an offer by telegram was held to indicate that an equally speedy method of acceptance was required. Therefore, an acceptance by post was not valid. The form of the offer was taken as showing the form the acceptance should take.

In *Tinn v Hoffman (1873) 29 LT 271*, however, it was said that, if an offer required acceptance 'by return of post', an equally quick method would be valid. The quicker method, however, would have to be in writing as this can also be implied from the terminology of the offer.

It must be noted that the postal rule will not be applied where it would cause significant injustice or inconvenience.

Given the uncertainties surrounding the postal rule of acceptance, at the very least if an offer is being accepted by post and post is the valid method of communication, the letter should be sent in a way which proves the time and date of posting. It should also be remembered that any other form of communication of acceptance or communication of the offer or of its revocation is effective only once it is received by the other party. Registered post would give proof of receipt and should be used to ensure that the information has actually been received.

3 – Consideration

There are two types of contract in English law:

- Contracts created by deed – these rely on the form of the agreement.
- Simple contracts – these rely on the substance of the agreement.

A **deed** is a formal contract. For some time, to be valid, a deed had to be signed, sealed and delivered. The sealing requirement became a mere formality and was abolished under the Law of Property (Miscellaneous Provisions) Act 1989.

A simple contract is the most common form of contract. It is based on the element of bargain, on the principle that you cannot get something for nothing; that each party must give something to the other for there to be a valid binding contract. This is called **consideration**. For example, 'I promise to give you my car but if you do not make any corresponding promise to pay or to do some other act in return, you cannot sue me if I change my mind and do not give you the car as promised. You have not given any consideration.'

In other words, consideration is the 'price' paid for the benefit received. When you go to a newsagents and buy a newspaper, your consideration is the money you pay; the newsagents' is the newspaper.

Consideration can be:

- an act – paying the price, handing over the goods, performing a service;
- a promise to perform an act – I promise to buy your car next week in return for you promising to sell it to me. Your promise to sell is good consideration for my promise to buy and my promise to buy is good consideration for your promise to sell. If either of us fails to proceed with the transaction, the other can sue in breach of contract; or
- a promise not to do something, to forego a right – I trespass on your land but you agree not to sue in return for me paying you compensation. This is an enforceable contract.

In *Alliance Bank Ltd v Brown (1864) 2 Dr & Sm 289*, when Messrs Brown were asked to provide security for money they owed the bank they promised to assign to the bank documents of title to certain goods. They failed to do so and the bank sued, claiming specific performance (i.e. that Brown should carry out their promise).

It was held that the bank was entitled to this remedy as, although the bank had not actually undertaken not to sue for the debt, the effect of Brown's promise to assign the documents of title was that the bank gave – and Brown received – the benefit of some forbearance. Following Brown's promise, the bank did not exercise their right to sue.

For forbearance to sue to be good consideration, however, there must be an existing liability or the parties must reasonably suppose that such liability exists. In other words, there must be a genuine claim that is being waived and the claim must be one that the promisor genuinely intends to pursue.

In *Horton v Horton [1961] 1 QB 215*, a husband and wife made a separation agreement in 1954 in which the husband agreed to pay the wife £30 per month. Under a proper interpretation of the agreement the husband should have deducted tax and paid £30 net. He did not do so. In 1955, the husband signed a document stating that, instead of paying £30 per month he would pay *'such sum as after deduction of income tax should amount to a clear sum of £30'*. The husband paid this money for some years but then stopped. When the wife sued, the husband claimed that the 1955 agreement was not supported by consideration and was invalid and that the wife, therefore, was bound by the 1954 agreement.

It was held that the original agreement clearly did not express the parties' intentions so the wife could have sued to have the document rectified. By forbearing to do so, she was providing consideration for the 1955 promise and was therefore entitled to be paid according to this agreement.

Types of consideration

Consideration is sometimes divided into three types:

- executory consideration;
- executed consideration; and
- past consideration.

Executory consideration

This arises where the act is to be performed in the future (e.g. I promise to sell you my car for £500 in return for your promise to pay this money for it). As we saw earlier, this is a binding contract which is to be performed in the future.

Executed consideration

This arises where the promise is made in return for the completion of an act (e.g. I promise to pay £100 to anyone who finds and returns my lost dog). I am only obliged to pay when the act of finding and returning the dog has been completed (i.e. when the other party's consideration has been completed or executed).

Although the distinction between executory and executed consideration is generally recognised, it is not suitable for every contractual situation. When you buy a newspaper at the newsagents, both parties' consideration is effectively given simultaneously.

Past consideration

This occurs when the promise is given after an act has been performed. For a contract to be binding the promise and the act must be part of the same bargain; each must be given in return for the other. In English law, past consideration is not good consideration. For example, I see you waiting at a bus stop and stop to give you a lift. If when we arrive at your destination you promise to pay me £10 towards the petrol but later fail to do so I cannot sue you. My consideration is past – I had performed the act before any promise was made by you. As we shall see later, however, if I was operating a taxi service and you flag me down at the bus stop, your later promise to pay would be enforceable as, from the very beginning, we both knew and expected that there would be payment even though no mention of this was made at the start of the journey.

The general rule, therefore, is that, if consideration is past and is not part of the bargain, it cannot form the basis of the contract.

In *Re McArdle [1951] Ch 669 CA*, a woman who was living with her mother-in-law spent her own money having the mother-in-law's house improved and redecorated. When the work was completed the claimant's in-laws, who were to inherit the house on their mother's death, promised to reimburse their sister-in-law for all her work. However, when the mother died, her children refused to pay anything and the sister-in-law sued. The court held that she should fail in the action. She had performed the act before any mention of payment had been made so her consideration was past and therefore was not recognised by law.

However, as we have seen, what would otherwise be unenforceable past consideration will be accepted by the courts if:

- the act was done at the request of the person who later makes the promise;
- it was understood throughout by both parties that payment would be made; and
- the payment would have been recoverable had the promise been made in advance.

In *Re Casey's Patents, Stewart v Casey [1892] 1 Ch 104 CA*, after Casey had undertaken work on some patents, the patents' joint owners wrote to him saying that, in consideration of this work, they would give him a one-third share in the patents. They broke this promise and, when Casey sued them for breach of contract, argued that his consideration was past consideration and was therefore insufficient to support his claim. It was held that Casey should succeed. He undertook the work in the course of business and there was a clear understanding the he would be paid for his efforts. The fact of this understanding was also shown in the letter the co-owners had written to Casey.

By *s 27* of the *Bills of Exchange Act 1882*, past consideration will also support a bill of exchange, such as a cheque. In *Re McCardle* (above), if instead of merely promising to pay their sister-in-law the cost of the refurbishment of the house, the children had written her a cheque for the money, she could have enforced this payment.

Amount

The courts do not question the value the parties put on the consideration as long as it has some value in the eyes of the law (i.e. something that the law recognises as being capable of being regarded as consideration).

In *Thomas v Thomas [1842] 2 QB 851*, a man said that, after his death, he wanted his wife to continue living in his house. Although this was not mentioned in his will, the man's executors allowed the wife to stay on in the house subject to her paying a nominal rent of £1 p.a.

The executor later tried to have the wife evicted but the court held that this action should fail. The wife had provided good consideration by paying the nominal £1 p.a.

The point about the adequacy of consideration was again raised in *Chappell & Co Ltd v Nestlé Co Ltd [1960] AC 87 HL*. In this case, Nestlé had a promotion offering to sell a record for 1/6d plus three Nestlé chocolate bar wrappers. When the wrappers were received, Nestlé destroyed them. Chappell owned the copyright in the music on the record. Under s. 8 Copyright Act 1956, there was no need to obtain the copyright owner's permission to sell a work, provided the owner was paid 6.25% of the retail price.

The court held that, although the wrappers were destroyed by Nestlé, they were nevertheless part of the retail price for the record. Lord Somerville said: '*A contracting party can stipulate for what consideration he chooses*.'

Nestlé offering 6.25% of every 1/6d they received would not be enough to bring s.8 into operation. The retail price of the records was 1/6d plus the chocolate wrappers.

Value in the eyes of the law

No economic value

If the consideration is too vague it will not be recognised by the courts. In *White v Bluett (1853) 23 LJ Ex 36*, a father agreed to let his son off a debt provided the son stopped grumbling and boring his father about being disinherited. When the father died, his executors sued to recover the debt from the son. The son argued that he had had a contract with his father releasing him from liability. It was held that this argument failed. The son had to pay. His promise to stop grumbling and boring his father had no economic value in the eyes of the law. It was too vague.

In *Midland Bank Trust Co Ltd v Green [1981] AC 513*, a man owned a farm worth £40,000. His son had an option on the property but the father, wanting to prevent the son being able to exercise this option, sold the farm to the father's wife for £500. It was held that this was a valid sale. The court was not concerned with the adequacy of consideration provided it was real, as it was in this case.

Duty

Performing a duty which by law you are obliged to perform is also not good consideration as you are doing nothing more than you are obliged to do. For example, in the case of *Collins v Godefroy (1831) 1 B & Ad 950*, Collins was subpoenaed to be a witness in a case involving the defendant. Although Collins was required by law to attend court, the defendant offered to pay him if he turned up and gave evidence. The court held that Collins could not enforce this promise as he was doing nothing more than the law obliged him to do.

However, if someone exceeds their public duty this can constitute consideration. This was shown in *Glasbrook Bros Ltd v Glamorgan County Council [1925] AC 270 HL.* During a general strike, miners picketed collieries. The police provided a mobile force to prevent strikers damaging mine property but Glasbrook wanted a permanent police presence on their premises. It was agreed to provide this if Glasbrook paid for the service. When the strike ended, however, Glasbrook refused to pay, arguing that the police were doing no more than their existing public duty to protect property. The court held that the police's duty was to provide protection in the way they thought fit. By doing more than this they had provided valid consideration for Glasbrook's promise to pay the charge.

The same principle applies to a promise to pay for the performance of an existing contractual duty (i.e. when there is an attempt to vary a contract). In *Stilk v Myrick (1809) 2 Camp 317*, two sailors deserted their ship. The captain promised the rest of the crew that he would share the deserters' wages amongst them if they agreed to sail the ship back to England. The sailors agreed but, when the ship docked, the captain refused to make the extra payment. The crew sued. It was held that their action failed. They were doing nothing more than their contract required so they had not provided any consideration for the captain's promise to pay.

It can, however, be good consideration for a promise by a third party to pay if you carry out an existing duty owed under a contact with someone else. In *Pao On v Lau Yiu Long [1980] AC 614*, the claimants agreed to sell Fu Chip some shares in return for 4.2 million shares in the company. Were all these shares to be put on the market at once, the value of Fu Chip's shareholding would have fallen, so the claimants contracted that, for one year, they would neither sell nor transfer 60% of the allotted shares. Later, the claimants refused to complete the agreement unless the defendants, who were majority shareholders in Fu Chip, promised to indemnify them against any fall in the value of the shares during this period. The defendants, believing that there was little risk of this happening, agreed to give that indemnity and the deal went ahead. During the year, however, the value of the shares fell substantially and the claimants asked for the indemnity. The defendants refused, claiming that they had received no consideration for their promise. It was held that the consideration for the indemnity was the promise by the claimants to perform their existing contractual obligations to Fu Chip. The promise not to sell 60% of the shares was given at the promisors' request; both parties understood that this promise would be paid for by giving the undertaking to indemnify; this undertaking would have been legally enforceable had it been made in advance. Lord Scarman said that '... *a promise to perform or the performance of, a pre-existing contractual obligation to a third party can be a valid consideration'*.

Also, if someone does more than their contractual duty, this can provide consideration for a promise to pay. In *Hartley v Ponsonby (1857) 7 E & B 872*, so many sailors deserted that it became positively dangerous for the remaining crew to continue sailing the ship. The captain's promise to pay the crew extra if they did continue was held to be enforceable. The remaining crew were doing more than their contract required.

Greater flexibility

Recently, the courts seem to be adopting a more flexible approach to the finding of consideration when a contract is varied. The case most clearly showing this relaxation was *Williams v Roffey Bros & Nicholls (Contractors) Ltd [1990] 1 All ER 512*. Under a contract to refurbish some flats, the defendants, a firm of builders, agreed a substantial liquidated damages provision if the work was not completed on time. The claimants, to whom the carpentry work was sub-contracted for £20,000, started working but were soon in financial difficulties, having underestimated the costs involved. The defendants, realising that this was holding up the refurbishment and that the penalty clause might come into operation, promised the claimants an extra £10,300 if the work was finished on time. In return, the claimants agreed to a change in their working pattern. The claimants completed on time but the defendants refused to pay the extra, arguing the authority of *Stilk v Myrick*. The claimants sued.

The court held that the claimants were entitled to the extra £10,300. It said that:

- If A contracts with B to do work for B
- but at some stage B realises that A may not complete his side of the bargain and therefore promises A extra payment to perform the contract on time
- as a result, B obtains a benefit or avoids a disbenefit (in this case, avoids paying the penalty)
- then, provided A has not been fraudulent or exercised economic duress
- the benefit to B is capable of being consideration to support the existence of a binding obligation to pay the extra money.

In the *Williams* case, the court identified a number of benefits to the defendant:

- Williams continued working on the contract so Roffey did not have to undergo the trouble and expense of employing another carpenter to finish the work.
- Roffey avoided having to pay the penalty.
- Williams agreed to replace his original disorganised system of working with a more formalised scheme (payment on completion of each flat). This enabled Roffey to organise the rest of the refurbishment more efficiently.

This agreement was the consideration for the promise to pay the extra money even though, in fact, the claimant did not do any work in addition to that in the original contract.

In this way, the court was able to show that it was not overruling the *Stilk v Myrick* principle. It therefore follows that if there is no 'practical' benefit to the promisor, the promise will be unsupported and unenforceable.

Nevertheless, *Williams v Roffey* marks a move towards recognising that promises made in a commercial context and without fraud or duress could give rise to an enforceable contractual obligation. Indeed, Russell L J stated: '*... the courts nowadays should be more ready to find [the existence of consideration] so as to reflect the intention of the parties to the contract where the bargaining powers are not unequal and where the finding of consideration reflects the true intention of the parties'*.

In other words, where the parties to a commercial contract have more-or-less equal bargaining power, the court has become more inclined to allow freedom of contract and to enforce contracts which are re-negotiated, provided the variation is entered into freely without fraud or duress and has the potential to benefit both parties. This shows that the courts are moving away from a strict application of *Stilk v Myrick*, which would have enabled a person to renege on a promise freely given and which had operated to give him some advantage.

The decision in *Williams v Roffey* has been followed in later cases such as:

- *Simon Container Machinery v EMBA Machinery [1998] 2 Lloyd's Rep 429* where a promise not to withdraw from a contract was held to be good consideration for a promise to pay extra money in that it kept the promisor performing their side of the existing contract.
- In *Lee v GEC Plessey Telecommunications [1993] 1 RLR 383* again it was held that, by continuing to work under their contract, employees were providing good consideration for the employers' promise to give a pay rise or better redundancy terms. The employer obtained a benefit and the employees stopping arguing about their level of pay and unfavourable terms.

Economic duress

If there is any economic duress, such as an unjustified threat to stop performing the original contract, any attempt at renegotiation will fail. In *South Caribbean Trading Ltd v Trafigura Beheer BV [2005] 1 Lloyd's Rep 128*, the judge expressed strong reservations about the validity of the *Williams v Roffey* principle and said that, if he had had to apply it to the facts of the present case, he would have been able to refuse to enforce a re-negotiated agreement on the grounds that the promisee had put pressure, amounting to economic duress, on the promisor to change the terms of the contract.

Williams v Roffey is, nevertheless, an important decision in the context of the re-negotiation of contracts. In a commercial contract, provided the promisee does not put improper pressure on the promisor to re-negotiate and if it can be shown that the promisee relied on the promise made, the re-negotiated contract could be enforceable. The law relating to economic duress (which we will deal with later) provides a safeguard against improper pressure and ensures that the re-negotiation is genuine and therefore may be valid and enforceable.

Obligation to pay money

A later decision of the court, however, held that the *Williams v Roffey* principle would not apply where the obligation was to pay money. This was decided in *Re Selectmove Ltd [1994] BCC 379*. Selectmove was in arrears in paying its tax and national insurance. In July, Selectmove suggested to the (then) Inland Revenue that, henceforward, it would pay its tax and NI as they fell due and would pay off the arrears owing in instalments. Nothing was heard back from the Revenue until, in October, it demanded payment in full of all arrears and threatened to have Selectmove wound up should they not comply. Selectmove, having assumed the Revenue's agreement to the proposal argued that, under *Williams v Roffey*, a promise to perform an existing obligation can be good consideration provided there were practical benefits to the promise (in this case, the benefit would be that eventually the Revenue would recover all arrears whereas, if Selectmove went into liquidation, this would not be possible).

The court held that the *Williams v Roffey* principle would not be extended to cases where there was an obligation to pay money. The payment of arrears in instalments did not provide consideration for the Revenue's deferral of its demand and therefore there could be a petition for Selectmove's liquidation.

In reaching this decision, the court followed the case of *Foakes v Beer (1884) 9 App Cas 605*. In this case, Beer, who was owed money by Foakes, obtained a judgment against him but agreed to give him time to pay. Foakes paid off all the capital owing but Beer then demanded interest on the judgment debt. The court held that Beer was entitled to claim this interest as she had not agreed to forego the interest which all judgment debts automatically attract. In other words, Foakes had paid less than he owed and could not claim discharge from his debt.

This case brought into law a principle first stated in *Pinnel's Case (1602) 77 ER 237*. This principle is that payment of a smaller sum in satisfaction of a larger debt will not discharge this larger debt unless there is accord (agreement) and satisfaction (fresh consideration). So, even if a creditor agrees to take a smaller sum than the debtor owes and even though he declares it to be accepted in full settlement of the debt, the creditor can still claim the balance owing unless the debtor has provided fresh consideration. This fresh consideration can take the form of:

- early payment at the creditor's request. The debtor's consideration is paying earlier than he has to; the creditor's is releasing the debtor from the balance of the debt;
- payment at the creditor's request at a different place than that specified in the contract;
- payment of a smaller sum together with something different in kind to which the creditor agrees;
- payment of a smaller sum by a third party with the agreement of the creditor. In *Hirachand Punamchand v Temple [1911] 2 KB 330*, the father of a man who owed money to a money lender offered the money lender partial payment of the debt, provided the money lender took the money 'in full settlement' of the son's debt. The money lender agreed, but then sued the son for the balance. It was held that money lender failed. It would have been fraud on the father to allow this action; and
- a composition agreed with creditors to pay a smaller sum to each in discharge of the debts. In *Wood v Robarts (1818) 1 Stark 417*, a debtor agreed with his creditors to pay them a certain amount in full and final settlement of all his debts. The court held that this was binding on all the creditors. To allow one of them to sue for the balance owing to him would be fraud against all the others.

However, for there to be acceptable accord and satisfaction, there must be genuine agreement between the parties. It will not be accepted where one of the parties uses improper means to obtain it.

In *D & C Builders Ltd v Rees [1965] 3 All ER 837*, the defendant owed the claimants £482 for work they had done for her. Knowing the builders had financial problems, the defendant offered them £300 'in full and final settlement', making it clear that, if they did not accept, they would get nothing. The builders reluctantly agreed, received a cheque for £300 from the defendant and gave her a receipt stating 'in completion of the account'. They then sued for the balance owing. The defendant argued, amongst other things, that the cheque should be regarded as 'something different in kind' from cash and therefore there had been accord and satisfaction. The court held that the builders should succeed in their action. A cheque is the same as cash and the defendant, by taking unfair advantage of the builders' financial problems, had behaved improperly and could not be allowed to benefit from this.

Release from liability

There are, however, two ways in which a debtor can be released from liability without providing fresh consideration. These are:

- obtaining release by deed, for which no consideration is required; and
- obtaining release by virtue of the doctrine of **equitable promissory estoppel**.

'Equitable' means that the doctrine applies only in equity; 'promissory' that it is based on a promise unsupported by consideration; and 'estoppel' is a rule of evidence preventing a person going back on their promise.

The doctrine is based on equitable principles that if a person (the promisor) has promised not to insist on their full rights, with the intention that this promise will be relied on by the other party (the promisee) and the promise is relied on, it would be unfair to allow the promissor to ignore what was said and be able to claim their full rights under the contract.

The modern principle of equitable promissory estoppel was stated by Denning J in *Central London Property Trust Ltd v High Trees House Ltd [1947] KB 130.* The claimants, Central London Property Trust, owned a block of flats in London which, in 1937, they let to the defendants on a 99-year lease. The defendants intended to sub-let these flats to individual tenants. With the outbreak of World War II and the air raids on London, the defendants found it difficult to find tenants for the flats as many people were leaving the city. The claimants therefore agreed to reduce the rent by 50% until the flats were again occupied. At the end of the war the flats again started to be in demand so the claimants sued to recover the full rent from the end of the war onwards. It was held that they should succeed. The conditions under which the promise was given had changed and so they were entitled to the full rent. However, Denning J said that if the claimants tried to sue for the full rent for the war years they would fail. They had made a promise which was intended to be binding and to be acted upon and which was, in fact, acted upon. It was therefore binding while the conditions under which it was made (i.e. the war) were still in existence.

This statement was made *obiter* (i.e. it was not part of the judgment on which the decision in the case was made) but it became binding law in *Tool Metal Manufacturing Co Ltd v Tungsten Electric Co Ltd [1955] 1 WLR 761.* In this case, the owners of a patent agreed that, during World War II, licensees of the patent would not have to make the periodic payments to use it. The court held that this promise was binding during the period of suspension (i.e. during the war) but the owners could, on giving reasonable notice to the other parties, start demanding payments again.

In other words, a person's contractual duty to make periodic payments and the other party's right to receive them, may be permanently extinguished during the period of suspension but the full contractual duty may be revived:

- either on the owner giving reasonable notice; or
- when the circumstances which gave rise to the promise have changed (as in *High Trees*).

For such a promise to suspend rights to be effective, however, a number of requirements must be satisfied:

- the promise to forego the rights must be clear and unambiguous and be intended to be acted upon;

- there must be an existing contractual relationship between the parties or at least one that is similar to a contract such as a maintenance agreement between a divorced husband and wife;
- the promisee must have acted in reliance on the promise. This is to show that it would be inequitable to allow the promisor to go back on his word;
- the promisee must have acted equitably. In *D & C Builders v Rees,* Mrs Rees had acted inequitably by using improper pressure on the builder and so the builder could go back on his word and sue for the balance owing on the building work;
- equitable promissory estoppel can only be used as a defence, not as a cause of action – it is a 'shield, not a sword'. In *Combe v Combe [1951] 1 All ER 767*, a wife started divorce proceedings and obtained a decree nisi. Her husband agreed to pay her £100 p.a. free of tax as permanent maintenance. Because of this, the wife voluntarily chose not to apply to the divorce court for maintenance. The husband never made any payments and the wife sued him on his promise, claiming that he was estopped from going back on his word. It was held that the wife's action failed as she had not given any consideration for the husband's promise. She could not use promissory estoppel as a cause of action.

To sue on a contract you must have given consideration

In *Tweddle v Atkinson (1861) 1 B & S 393*, T's father and prospective father-in-law agreed with each other to pay £100 and £200 respectively to T when he married. T duly married but his father-in-law refused to pay. T sued him.

It was held that T failed. Even though the contract was for his benefit, as he had not given any consideration for his father-in-law's promise he could not enforce the agreement. There are, however, a number of exceptions to this rule. For example, the payee of a cheque can enforce payment even though he has not given consideration for it and the assignee of a legal right can, in certain circumstances, enforce that right despite his lack of consideration.

The Contracts (Rights of Third Parties) Act 1999 also gives third parties certain rights to enforce a contract even though they have not provided consideration. To be able to do this, however, the non-contracting party must show that the contract expressly allows him to enforce a contract term in his own right or that the term purports to confer a benefit on him unless the contract shows that the parties intended otherwise. For the right to be exercised:

- the third party must be identified in the contract by name; or
- as a member of a class; or
- as answering a particular description.

However, the third party need not be in existence when the contract is made. For example, the third party could be a pre-formation company.

A third party who has rights under this act takes subject to any defence or right of set-off that would have been available to the promisor had the promisor been sued by the promisee. Also, if relevant, the promisor has a right of counterclaim against the third party and is protected from double jeopardy in that, if the promisee has already recovered damages from the promisor in relation to the third party's loss, this recovery will be taken into account to reduce the amount awarded to the third party.

The act was applied in the case of *Laemthong Inter Lines Co Ltd v Artis (The Laemthong Glory No 2) [2005] EWCA Civ 519*. In this case, the buyer of sugar (the defendants) contracted with a firm of charterers to charter a ship. The charterers obtained the ship from Laemthong. In the contract, the defendants promised to indemnify the charterers and their servants and agents for any loss caused by, amongst other things, the arrest of the ship in connection with the delivery of the cargo. The ship was arrested by a bank for non-payment in relation to the cargo.

The issue before the court was whether the owner of the ship (Laemthong) a third party to the defendant–charterer contract, could enforce the indemnity even if they were not in a direct contractual relationship with the defendants.

It was held that the 1999 Act applied, so the ship owners could claim indemnity from the defendants for the loss of their ship. The contract conferred this benefit on them. They were agents of the charterers, as chartering the ship from them was the only way in which the charterers could perform their contract with the defendants. The ship owners fell within the definition of 'agent' for the purpose of the indemnity clause in the contract.

4 – Intention to create legal relations

Mutual promises do not, of themselves, necessarily mean that there is an enforceable contract. It must also be shown that the parties made the agreement with the intention of creating legal relations.

The parties' intentions are judged objectively by their words and conduct rather than by their subjective thoughts. In the context of intention, contracts can be divided into:

- social and domestic arrangements, where there is a rebuttable presumption that the parties do not intend to create legal relations;
- commercial agreements, where the presumption is that there is an intention to make the agreement legally binding. This, again, is a rebuttable presumption in that it can be set aside by evidence to the contrary; and
- collective bargaining agreements, where there is a presumption of lack of intention to create a legally binding agreement.

Social and domestic agreements

The presumption is that there is no intention to create a legal relationship. In the case of *Balfour v Balfour [1919] 2 KB 571*, a husband went abroad leaving his wife, who was ill, in the UK. He promised to pay her £30 a month if she agreed to support herself and not to ask for any further maintenance. When the husband failed to pay, his wife sued him for this money.

It was held that her action failed. The promise was unenforceable as it was a purely domestic arrangement and was not intended to *'be attended by legal consequences'*.

The same principle applies to other family relationships such as mother and daughter, but if the agreement is made when the parties are in dispute with one another, the presumption of lack of intention may be rebutted (i.e. set aside).

In *Merritt v Merritt [1970] 1 WLR 121*, for example, after a husband deserted his wife, he wrote to her saying: *'In consideration of the fact that you will pay all charges in connection with the house ... when the mortgage has been completed I will agree to transfer the property in to your sole ownership'*. The wife paid off the mortgage but the husband refused to transfer his share in the house into her name. The wife sued him.

It was held that the wife succeeded in her action. There was a clear intention on the husband's part that the agreement should be legally binding. *Balfour's* case was distinguished on the fact that, in *Merritt*, the parties were '*not living in amity but are separated or about to separate … they then bargain keenly. They do not rely on honourable understandings*'.

Furthermore, in domestic situations involving other than close family members, the presumption of a lack of intention can be fairly easily rebutted.

In *Simpkins v Pays [1953] 3 All ER 10*, a grandmother, her granddaughter and a lodger entered a weekly Sunday newspaper competition, each paying their share of the entrance fee. The entries were submitted in the grandmother's name and, when one week they won, the winnings were paid to her. She refused to share this money and the lodger sued.

The lodger won the case. There was an intention here to create legal relations.

Commercial agreements

In relation to commercial or business agreements, there is a strong presumption that there is an intention to create legal relations. There has to be clear contradictory evidence to rebut this presumption. In *Edwards v Skyways Ltd [1964] 1 All ER 494*, the claimant, a pilot employed by the defendants, was made redundant. As part of his redundancy package, he was promised a substantial *ex gratia* payment in return for him agreeing not to claim his full pension rights. The defendants failed to make the payment to him arguing that, as it had been described as *ex gratia*, it showed that there was no intention to create a legal relationship. The claimant sued. The court held that this was a commercial contract, so there was a strong presumption of intention to create legal relations. Megaw J stated: '*In a case of this nature the onus is on the party who asserts that no legal effect was intended, and the onus is a heavy one.*' The defendants had not discharged this burden of proof. The term *ex gratia* merely showed that the defendants would make the payment without admitting any liability.

'Subject to contract'

When, in negotiations, the term 'subject to contract' is used, this is generally taken to show that the parties do not intend to be bound until a formal contract is drawn up, especially if the contract is still unexecuted (i.e. has not yet been performed).

However, if, despite the phrase 'subject to contract', one of the parties has, with the assent of the other, started to perform their duties under the contract, the court may find that there was intention and that a contract has come into existence.

In *Confetti Records v Warner Music UK Ltd [2003] EWHC 1274*, the defendants were going to release a compilation album and wanted to include a track of music whose copyright was owned by the claimants. After a discussion between the parties to establish the terms of the contract, the defendants sent the claimants a fax listing the terms which had been agreed, but marking the fax 'subject to contract'. The claimants signed this document and faxed it back. A little later, the claimants sent the defendants a copy of the track and an invoice stating it was licensed for 'three years non-exclusive'. The defendants started to use it in their compilation. The claimants brought an action to have the track withdrawn from the compilation.

It was held that at the time of the exchange of faxes there was no contract in existence. However, when the claimants sent the copy of the track this was an offer, which was accepted when the defendants started to use it. At that point there was a binding contract so the claimants could not withdraw the track.

The problem which could arise in these cases is in deciding which terms apply to the contract. This was addressed in *RTS Flexible Systems Ltd v Molkerei Alois Muller Gmbh and Company KG (UK Production) [2010] UKSC 14.* RTS were negotiating to make and deliver an automated packing system for Muller. The negotiations, which took some time, included several different quotations from RTS, the final one being 'Quotation J' which was for a fixed price of £1,682,000 and which outlined the scope of the work to be carried out by September. To comply with this date, RTS agreed to start work in February. This agreement was based on a letter of intent or understanding in which Muller said they wanted to 'proceed with the project as set out in [Quotation J]' with a long-form contract to be agreed and signed within four weeks. The letter of intent also stated that that this long-form contract would be based on a model long-form contract published by the Institute of Electrical Engineers (known as MF/1). Clause 48 of the draft long-form contract expressly stated that it would not take effect until it was executed (i.e. a 'subject to contract' clause). It also included a liquidated damages clause.

The letter of intent expired in the May but RTS continued with the work, delivered the machines and were paid 70% of the agreed price. Most of the terms of the long-form contract were agreed, but the contract was never signed as the parties disagreed as to whether some of the machines which had been delivered complied with specifications

RTS brought this action claiming the rest of the money due under the agreement or, alternatively, damages. The case eventually reached the Supreme Court which had to decide whether there was a binding contract between the parties and, if there was, its terms. If the MF/1 terms were included, the liquidated damages clause would apply.

Lord Clarke stated:

> *Whether there is a binding contract between the parties and, if so, upon what terms ... depends not on their subjective state of mind, but upon a consideration of what was communicated between them by words or conduct, and whether that leads objectively to a conclusion that they intended to create legal relations and had agreed upon all the terms which they regarded or the law requires, as essential for the formation of legally binding relations.*

The court has to decide whether the parties have reached a basic agreement and intend to be legally bound by what they have already agreed. A finding that they have done so is more likely where the agreement in question was already being performed on both sides. The test is whether an 'honest and sensible businessman', looking at the parties' conduct objectively, would consider that they intended to be bound by contract. If essential terms are still left to be agreed, the courts would be reluctant to impose a contract which the parties had not yet reached. This would be the case where an agreement is made 'subject to contract' unless it could be shown by the parties' words and conduct that they had waived this provision.

In *RTS*, it was held that a contract had been created after the expiration of the letter of intent. To decide that there was no intention to create a legal relationship would be unrealistic given that performance of the contract had already started and all the major terms such as the price had already been agreed and acted upon. Only a few minor matters in the long-form agreement remained to be agreed.

The Supreme Court held that the contract under which the parties were operating incorporated the MF/1 conditions, including the 'subject to contract' term in clause 48. From the parties' conduct, it was clear that they had decided to waive the effect of this clause and not to allow the clause '... to get in the way of the project'. This was shown by the delivery of the machines and the part payment of the sum agreed in the letter of intent.

In effect, what the court was doing was to adopt a commercial approach to the issue of whether there was an intention to create legal relations and on what terms. The decision was reached not by adopting a legalistic approach, but rather one that the 'reasonable businessman' would believe to be the case.

In other words, when an agreement is made 'subject to contract' the court will generally, but not automatically, apply the parties' intentions not to create a legally binding contract until a formal contract is signed unless the circumstances suggest that the parties have waived this restriction. It is very much a question of fact in each case. To be safe in these circumstances, work on a project should not start until the full-form contract has been both agreed and concluded by the parties. To start work before this could lead to a finding that the parties have committed themselves to unintended contractual duties and liabilities.

Honour clause

If the parties to a commercial agreement do not wish it to be legally binding they can do this by inserting an '**honour clause**'. In *Rose and Frank Co v J R Crompton Bros Ltd [1925] AC 445*, the parties had been dealing with each other for some time and, in 1913, signed an agreement that this arrangement should continue for a specified period, with prices set for six months at a time. The agreement contained what was called an 'honourable pledge' clause. This stated that:

> *This arrangement is not entered into ... as a formal or legal agreement, and shall not be subject to legal jurisdiction in the law courts ... [and] the ... parties ... honourably pledge themselves.*

Later the claimant sued the defendant for general breach of contract and also for non-delivery of an order.

It was held that the general breach of contract action failed as the intention to create legal relations had been expressly excluded. However, once a specific order had been given and accepted, a full, legally binding contract came into existence for that order so the defendant was liable for this breach.

No intent to create legal relations

In *Jones v Vernon's Pools Ltd [1938] 2 All ER 626*, when the claimant sued on a football pools coupon he failed because the coupon stated that 'any agreement or transaction entered into or any payment made by or under it shall not be attended by or give rise to any legal relations, rights, duties or consequences whatsoever or be legally enforceable'. By this clause it was shown that there was no intention to create legal relations.

Collective bargaining agreements

By the Trade Union and Labour Relations (Consolidation) Act 1992, collective agreements negotiated between employers and their workforce, usually represented by a trade union, are conclusively presumed not to be intended to be legally binding unless there is an express written statement to the contrary.

The term of a collective agreement becomes legally binding if it is expressly incorporated into a contract of employment.

5 – Certainty

Unless the terms of an agreement are clear and unambiguous, the courts will not be able to tell what the parties have actually agreed or even whether they have even reached an agreement. In other words, if a major term in an agreement is uncertain, the contract the parties thought they had will fail.

In *Scammell (G) & Nephew Ltd v Ouston (HC & JG) [1941] AC 251,* Ouston agreed to acquire a new van for use in his business from Scammell '... on hire-purchase terms over a period of two years'. Part of the agreement was for Scammell to take Ouston's existing van in part-exchange, but they later decided that this van was not in satisfactory condition and asked Ouston to sell it locally. Ouston refused and, after a lot of correspondence between the parties, issued a writ against Scammell claiming damages for non-delivery of the new van. Scammell argued that there was no contract.

It was held that Ouston's action failed for uncertainty. The phrase 'on hire-purchase terms' was too vague to show any true agreement and it could not be made certain. There were no 'usual' hire-purchase terms and, as the parties had had no previous dealings, the court could not discover the meaning of the term that way. No term as to hire-purchase was implied by statute and the agreement did not contain any machinery to make the term certain.

The courts work on the principle that, wherever possible, they will make a superficially vague or incomplete agreement certain. They will not, however, rewrite an agreement. If an agreement is found to be irredeemably uncertain it will fail.

'Irredeemably uncertain'

In *Baird Textile Holdings Ltd v Marks and Spencer plc [2001] EWCA 274,* the claimant had been a major supplier of clothes to M&S for 30 years although there had never been a formal written contract between them. In 1999, without warning, M&S stopped all supply agreements with the claimant from the end of the current production season, costing the claimant around £50 million.

The claimant sued, arguing that M&S should have given reasonable notice of the termination on the basis of an implied contract that they would acquire garments *'in quantities and at prices which ... were reasonable'*. M&S had deliberately chosen not to enter an express contract with the claimants so that they would not be obliged to place orders in the future or to have to give reasonable notice of the termination of the agreement.

It was held that, given that M&S had deliberately avoided entering into a contract, it would be unusual for the court to imply one. In any event, the obligation on the firm to acquire goods *'in quantities and at prices which … were reasonable'* was too uncertain. The court had no criteria on which to judge reasonableness in this context. The lack of certainty showed that the parties had no intention to create legal relations between them. In fact, the conduct of the parties showed the absence of a contract.

The claimant lost the action. There was a long-term business relationship between the parties, but this could not be extended into a contractual relationship. The whole relationship was based on individual orders and sales, nothing more. Each of these was, in effect, a separate contract but there was no evidence of a wider, long-term relationship.

The claimant had also argued that M&S had induced them to assume that they did have a long-term relationship which could only be ended by reasonable notice. During their time supplying M&S the claimant had invested money to ensure that they satisfied M&S's requirements and had, in effect, allowed M&S to influence their business. Furthermore they had not developed a relationship with other buyers. The claimants argued that, in equity, M&S should be estopped (prevented) from changing this position without reasonable notice. This claim also failed because, as we have seen, the claim of equitable promissory estoppel can be used only as a defence – not as a cause of action.

Negotiating

If the parties are in the process of negotiation, a contract will not come into existence as the terms have not yet been finalised. In *Whittle Movers Ltd v Hollywood Express Ltd [2009] EWCA 1189*, Hollywood Express invited tenders' 'subject to contract' for a distribution service, asking for indicative pricing for one- , three- and five-year contracts. Whittle submitted a successful tender and, while further negotiations were taking place, Hollywood Express issued a letter of intent which was signed by Whittle. Before the long-term contract was finalised, Whittle began to perform the distribution services and invoiced for them on the basis that the actual contract would be for over five years. The price they charged, therefore, was lower than it otherwise would have been. The parties finally agreed all the terms of the contract but, before it could be signed, Hollywood Express was sold and the contract remained unsigned. Hollywood Express gave Whittle six months' notice of termination of what was described as the 'interim contract' (i.e. the arrangement which occurred between the agreement being made and the formal contract being completed).

Whittle argued that no contract had come into existence and that they were entitled to a restitutionary remedy (payment to cover the fact that, had they known that the contract was for such a short time, they would have had the right to charge extra for their services). The argument was based on the claim that H had been unjustly enriched by paying prices on a long-term contract basis.

It was held that there was no contract between the parties. Such a contract would not occur while the parties were still in the process of negotiation. As there was no contract and as the distribution was short-term, Hollywood Express had been unjustly enriched and had to pay Whittle. All the negotiations were 'subject to contract'. No contract could come into existence until it had been formally signed by both parties.

Where possible, however, the court will make terms certain if this can be done without rewriting the contract. This will be done where:

(a) The contract itself provides a means of clarifying the parties' intentions (e.g. by agreeing that any dispute be referred to an arbitrator).

In *Foley v Classique Coaches Ltd [1934] 2 KB 1*, a contract was made whereby the defendant agreed to buy all its petrol from the claimant 'at a price to be agreed by the parties in writing and from time to time'. Under the contract, any dispute was to be referred to arbitration. The agreement operated for three years but then the defendant repudiated it.

It was held that there was a valid contract. Even though the parties had not actually agreed a price for the petrol, there was provision for any dispute to be settled, not by the parties themselves, but rather by an independent third party, the arbitrator.

If there had merely been a statement that the parties would agree a price in the future this would have meant that they had agreed to agree and the contract would fail for uncertainty.

In *Sudbrook Trading Estate Ltd v Eggleton [1983] 1 AC 444*, there was an agreement whereby a tenant could buy the rented premises from the landlord 'at such price ... as may be agreed on by two valuers'. The landlord and tenant were each to appoint a valuer for this purpose. When the tenant decided to buy, he appointed a valuer according to the agreement. The landlord refused to make an appointment and claimed that the agreement was not binding because there was no way in which the price could be fixed. It was held that, under the agreement, there was a provision to sell the property at a fair and reasonable price to be assessed by the valuers. As the landlord had, by his conduct, made this valuation impossible, the court itself would assess a price by using expert opinion as to what might be fair and reasonable. The important point was that the price was to be set by professional valuers who would apply both professional and reasonable standards. The condition that both parties should appoint a valuer was a 'subsidiary and inessential' part of the contract. The tenant succeeded in his claim for the property.

(b) There is standard trade practice which can be implied into the contract to make it certain.

(c) There has been a previous course of dealings between the parties.

In *Hillas & Co Ltd v Arcos Ltd [1932] All ER 494*, the defendant contracted to sell wood to the claimant 'over the season 1930'. The contract gave an option to the claimant to buy more wood the following year but did not specify matters such as the kind or size of the wood nor did it give it give details of, say, how the wood was to be shipped. The 1930 contract, although lacking some specific details, was nevertheless performed without any major problems. However, when the claimants tried to exercise their option in 1931, the defendants refused to supply the wood claiming that, as so many details had been left to be settled, the contract should fail on the grounds of uncertainty. The claimant won the case .It was held that the option to buy wood in 1931 was valid and enforceable. The course of dealings between the parties in 1930 could be used to resolve any uncertainties in the 1931 contract as could normal practice in the timber trade.

(d) A term is implied by statute. Under the Sale of Goods Act, 1979, as soon as the parties have agreed to buy and sell goods, a contract comes into existence, even though the details of the contract, such as the price, have not been fixed. Under s. 8(2) of the Act, where the parties have not agreed a price, there is an implied term that the buyer will pay a 'reasonable' price that will, in effect, be fixed by the court. This applies only to a contract covered by the Sale of Goods Act. Again, in contracts for the supply of a service, where the Supply of Goods and Services Act 1982 applies, under s. 15(1), if the parties have not fixed a price, a term is implied that the party obtaining the service will pay a reasonable price.

'The usual conditions of acceptance'

If a term is completely meaningless and the contract can exist without it, the court will enforce the agreement without this term.

In *Nicolene Ltd v Simmonds [1953] 1 All ER 882*, a contract was made on *'the usual conditions of acceptance'*. There were no such 'usual conditions' either in the trade or in previous dealings between the parties. All the terms of the contract had been agreed therefore this phrase was meaningless and irrelevant. The contract stood without it and was enforced.

Note that this phrase had no relevance to the contract as opposed to the phrase *'on hire-purchase terms'* in *Scammel v Ouston*. In that case, the phrase was an essential part of the contract in that it determined how the contract was to be performed. As the words lacked certainty, they caused the whole contract to fail.

6 – Terms

Terms and representations

The terms of the contract contain the parties' rights duties and liabilities. A term is a part of the contract and, if it is broken, the innocent party will be entitled to sue in breach of contract and treat the contract as if it has been repudiated (ended by the other party's breach) and/or claim damages.

When a contract is being negotiated, therefore, it is important to decide which of the statements made are terms forming part of the contract and which are mere representations which, if wrong, give rise to an action in misrepresentation (especially if the contract is purely oral rather than being put in writing).

The distinction between terms and representations is based on the intention of the parties but to help discover this intention, the courts have developed a number of guidelines:

(a) If the person making the statement has special knowledge not possessed by the other, the statement will generally be regarded as a term; if the contrary is true it will be a mere representation. In *Dick Bentley (Productions) Ltd v Harold Smith (Motors) Ltd [1965] 1 WLR 623*, the defendant car dealers sold a car to the claimant who knew nothing about cars. The defendant wrongly, but innocently, claimed that the car's engine and gearbox had been fitted only 20,000 miles earlier. In fact, since this work had been undertaken, the car had driven 100,000 miles. It was held that, given the defendant's specialist knowledge, his statement was a term of the contract and the buyer could succeed in his action for breach.

    On the other hand, in *Oscar Chess Ltd v Williams [1957] 1 WLR 370*, a private person, in selling his car to a garage, described the car as a 1949 model. He made this claim in good faith relying on the car's log book which, unknown to him, had been forged. The car was, in fact, a 1939 model. It was held that, given that the seller had less expertise than the buyer, the statement made was a mere representation. The garage's only action was in innocent misrepresentation but, as there had been too long a time between the contract and the action they had lost their right to rescind (set the contract aside).

(b) If the maker of the statement suggests that the other party checks on the accuracy of the statement, it will probably be regarded as a mere representation. If, however, he dissuades the other from checking, the statement will be regarded as a term. In *Schawel v Reade [1913] 46 ILT 281*, the seller of a horse told the buyer he '... *need not look for anything. The horse is perfectly sound. If there was anything the matter I should tell you*'. Relying on this statement, the buyer bought the horse without any further examination. The horse was not sound. It was held that the seller's statement had dissuaded the buyer from checking the horse's condition. He had bought it on the strength of the seller's statement. This statement, therefore, was a term of the contract and the buyer could succeed in his action for breach.

(c) If the accuracy of the statement is vital to the contract, the statement will probably be treated as a term. In *Bannerman v White (1861) 10 CB(NS) 844*, the potential buyer of a crop of hops asked the seller if sulphur had been used in their cultivation, saying that 'if it has. I'll not bother asking the price'. The seller wrongly assured him that sulphur had not been used and, on the strength of this, the buyer bought the crop. It was held that, as the contract would not have been made but for the seller's assurance, the statement that sulphur had not been used was a term of the contract.

(d) The greater the lapse of time between the making of the statement and the conclusion of the contract, the more likely it is that the statement will be regarded as a mere representation.

(e) If an agreement is converted into a written contract, statements made in the negotiations which are not included in the written contract are generally assumed to be mere representations. In *Routledge v McKay [1954] 1 All ER 855*, the parties, both private individuals, were discussing the sale of the defendant's motorbike. On 23 October, the defendant, taking his information from the bike's log book, said that the vehicle was a 1942 model. No mention of the bike's age was made in the written contract which was drawn up on 30 October. When it was discovered that the bike was, in fact, a 1930 model, the buyer sued for damages in breach of contract.

It was held that the buyer should fail in his action. The statement not having been included in the written contract was treated as a mere representation. Furthermore, the gap between the time the statement was made and the drawing up of the contract showed that the matter was not in the parties' minds when the contract was finally made.

(f) A pre-contractual statement may also be regarded as a collateral warranty or as part of a collateral contract. This occurs when a person gives an undertaking on the basis of which the person to whom the undertaking is given enters a contract with someone else. The person who gave the undertaking may be liable in breach of collateral contract if it proves to be false. It is an implied secondary contract running alongside the principal contract. How this occurs is shown in the case of *Shanklin Pier Ltd v Detel Products Ltd [1951] 2 KB 229*. The claimants, who wanted their pier repainted, consulted the defendant paint suppliers. The defendants recommended its paint as being suitable for the work. Relying on this recommendation, the claimants instructed their contractors to use the defendants' paint, which they did. The paint proved totally unsuitable and the claimants sued the defendants in breach of collateral warranty.

It was held that the claimants were entitled to damages. But for the defendants' promise, Shanklin would not have instructed the contractors to buy the defendants' paint and the defendants would not have made a sale.

In *Andrews v Hopkinson [1957] 1 QB 229*, the claimant was thinking of obtaining a car on hire-purchase. The defendant, a car dealer, recommended a particular car saying: *'It's a good little bus. I'd stake my life on it. You'll have no trouble.'* On the basis of this recommendation, the claimant agreed to take the car on hire-purchase from a finance company under a contract which excluded the finance company's liability for breach of contract (such a clause would not be possible now). The garage sold the car to the finance company which, in turn, hired it to the claimant. The car turned out to be defective.

The claimant could not sue the finance company because of the exclusion clause so he sued the garage proprietor in breach of collateral contract. The action succeeded. But for the garage's statement, the claimant would not have taken the car on hire-purchase, which meant that the garage would not have sold the car to the finance company. In other words, in return for the undertaking, the claimant took the car from the third party; this, in turn, meant that the garage obtained a benefit by selling the vehicle.

(g) Since the passing of the Misrepresentation Act 1967, the distinction between terms and representations is not as important as before. Before 1967 if a statement was a mere representation, the innocent party's only right to damages would be if the statement was made fraudulently. If the wrong statement was made innocently the only remedy would be rescission, a discretionary remedy which could be lost through no fault of the representee. In the 1967 Act, however, as we shall see later, the concept of negligent misrepresentation was introduced, giving the representee a right to damages unless the maker of the statement could show that he both believed and had reasonable grounds for believing, the truth of what he was saying.

Types of terms

Terms may be divided into three types:

- conditions;
- warranties; and
- innominate terms.

To a large extent, the category into which a term falls depends on the intention of the parties, but ultimately it is for the court to decide the nature of a term. The distinction is important in that the remedy for breach of a term depends on whether it is a condition, warranty or an innominate term.

Conditions

A condition is a term which goes to the very basis of the contract. It is fundamental: any breach will entitle the innocent party to treat the contract as being repudiated and to claim damages for any loss suffered as a result of the breach. Alternatively, the innocent party can choose to let the contract continue and merely claim damages for breach. The choice is his.

In *Poussard v Spiers and Pond (1876) 1 QBD 410*, the defendants dismissed a performer who, in breach of contract, did not turn up for the first night of a performance in which she was contracted to play a leading part. She sued the defendants but lost the action. The opening night was of great importance so the breach was of major importance. The defendants were therefore entitled to treat the contract as repudiated.

What the parties call a term is of strong evidential value as to whether it is a condition or a warranty, but this is not necessarily conclusive – some contracts describe all their terms as conditions. It is ultimately for the court to decide how the term should be regarded and dealt with. In *L Schuler AG v Wickham Machine Tool Sales Ltd [1973] 2 WLR 683*, the claimants contracted with the defendants to give them the exclusive right to sell the claimants' tools in England. Under the agreement, there was a term – described as a condition – that the defendants' sales representatives had to visit and canvass orders for the claimant's tools from six firms each week. Occasionally, however, the representatives failed to keep to this schedule. The claimants argued that, as this was a breach of a condition in the contract, they were entitled to treat the contract as repudiated.

It was held that, although the term was described as a condition in the contract, the defendants' breaches were too minor to entitle the claimants to treat the contract as at an end. It was unreasonable to treat the term as a condition even though this was what it was called in the contract.

Warranties

A warranty is a term which is not vital to the main purpose of the contract. It is a lesser term than a condition and if it is broken, the injured party's only remedy is in damages. The contract itself remains in force.

In *Bettini v Gye (1876) 1 QB 18*, a performer turned up for rehearsals three, rather than the contractual six, days before the first performance. It was held that this was a breach of warranty which did not entitle the producers to end the contract. The term as to rehearsals was ancillary to the main point of the contract. The producers' only remedy would be to sue the performer for damages.

Innominate terms

For many years terms were categorised as either conditions or warranties, the effects of a breach being regarded as almost irrelevant. So, as a general rule, if there was a breach of a term accepted as a condition, the innocent party would have a right to treat the contract as being repudiated, however minor the effects of the breach.

The advantage of this approach was that it gave certainty to commercial contracts. The parties would know that if the term was broken the innocent party would be entitled to treat the contract as at an end (if the term was a condition) or be able merely to claim damages (if the term was a warranty).

More recently, however, the courts have developed a third approach to the way terms are classified. This is to treat a term as 'innominate' (or 'intermediate') being neither a condition nor a warranty at the time of the contract. In these cases, the court adopts a 'wait and see' approach and looks at the effects of the breach in deciding the remedy to be granted. If the effects of the breach are serious, the innocent party can treat the contract as being repudiated. If they are not, the only remedy will be in damages. This type of term was considered by the court in *Hong Kong Fir Shipping Co Ltd v Kawasaki Kisen Kaisha Ltd [1962] 1 All ER 474*. H chartered a ship to K for 24 months. One of the terms of the charter was that the ship was 'in every way fitted for ordinary cargo service' (i.e. that it was seaworthy). As the ship was old it needed to be maintained by an experienced, competent and adequate engine-room team. H did not provide this and, as a result, there were many breakdowns. For five out of the first seven months of the charter the ship was unusable while repairs were carried out to make it seaworthy but eventually it was fit for purpose. K, however, refused to continue with the charter, arguing that the term as to seaworthiness was a condition which had been broken.

It was held that the term was not a condition. The undertaking as to seaworthiness was an innominate term, so the court looked at the effect of the breach. On the facts, the delays which had already occurred and those which were likely to occur in the future as a result of the ship's condition, together with the conduct of H in taking steps to remedy the defects, did not deprive K of 'substantially the whole benefit' of the contract. The ship could still be used for the bulk of the period of the charter. K could be awarded damages for the loss suffered while the ship was out of action, but could not treat the contract as being repudiated.

In *Cehave NV v Bremer Handelgesellschaft GmbH (The Hansa Nord) [1975] 3 WLR 447*, the court again held that an express term was innominate. In this case, the contract was for the sale of citrus pulp pellets which were shipped from the USA to Holland, the buyers paying in advance. In the contract there was a term that the pellets would be 'shipped in good condition'. When the ship arrived in Holland, it was discovered that some of the pellets had deteriorated and the buyers rejected the cargo for breach of the 'in good condition' term. They demanded return of the price paid. The seller refused. While the dispute was ongoing, the court ordered a sale of the pellets by a court-appointed official, the proceeds to be paid into court pending the outcome of the case. The pellets were sold by this official to a third party at a substantially lower price than under the original contract. The third party then re-sold them to the original buyers at this lower price and the buyers used them, at slightly lower concentrations, for their original purpose (i.e. as cattle feed).

It was held that the term 'shipped in good condition' could not obviously be categorised as a condition or warranty. It was an innominate term, so the remedy depended on the effects of the breach. By buying the pellets from the third party and using them for their original purpose, the buyers showed that the defects were not very serious. Their only remedy was damages. The original contract remained valid and enforceable.

To discover whether or not a term is innominate, the court will consider the following points:

(a) does the contract provide that a breach of a specific term would entitle the innocent party to treat the contract as repudiated or merely to claim damages? If it does, then the court will follow this; if it does not, then
(b) does the contract imply such a right by describing terms as conditions or warranties in the legal meaning of these words? As a general rule the court will follow this categorisation, but as we have seen in *Schuler v Wickman*, it does not have to do so; if the contract does not give this categorisation or does not use the terms in their strict sense, then
(c) does the law categorise the term as a condition or warranty, either by statute, such as the Sale of Goods Act 1979 or by judicial precedent established in a previous case or by custom? If it does, the court will follow this categorisation; if it does not, then
(d) the term is innominate and the court will look at the effect of the breach and award a remedy accordingly. If the effects are serious and substantially deprive the innocent party of the benefits of the contract, he will be entitled to treat the contract as having been repudiated. If the effects are not so serious, the only remedy will be in damages and the contract will continue to be operative.

The problem with innominate terms is that they may deprive commercial contracts of certainty in that the parties will not know in advance the remedies for any breach but will have to wait and see its effects. As a result, some judges are reluctant to use this method of categorisation. For example, in *The Chikuma [1981] 1 All ER 652*, Lord Bridges said that, where parties are of equal bargaining power and make contacts using 'common form' clauses, it is important that the meaning and legal effect of these clauses is certain. In dealing with such clauses, the court should aim to produce a result that means that both parties know the consequences of the breach rather than being 'tempted to embark on long and expensive litigation in the belief that victory depends on winning the sympathy of the court'.

In *Bunge Corp v Tradax Export SA [1981] 1 WLR 711*, the sellers were require to load goods on board a ship at a Gulf port to be nominated by them. The loading was required to be undertaken by 30 June. The buyers had to give the sellers 'at least 15 consecutive days' notice' of the probable readiness of the ship and of the approximate quantity to be loaded. The buyers did not give the notice until 17 June, so less than 15 days of the loading period remained. The sellers claimed that the buyers were in default and claimed damages for repudiation of the contract on the grounds that the term as to notice was a condition.

The House of Lords held that this term, although not expressly stated in the contract to be a condition, was a condition by implication. The sellers were entitled to treat the contract as having been repudiated by the buyers. In general, the court said that as time is of the essence in mercantile contracts and this term will be treated as such (i.e. such terms will be treated as conditions).

Express or implied terms

Express terms

These are terms which the parties include in the contract; the terms containing their agreed obligations. Express terms state the basis of the contract.

If the contract is oral, the terms will be identified by oral evidence and the interpretation put on those terms by the court.

If the contract has been put in writing, the terms are as set out in that writing although, if the contract refers to another document, the provisions in that second document are incorporated in the contract as far as is relevant. For example, a car parking ticket may refer to the contract being subject to terms displayed on the premises. It is also sometimes possible that a document will be taken to be included in the contract even though the contract does not refer to it. For example, in the case of *Edwards v Aberayron Mutual Ship Insurance Society Ltd (1876) 1 QBD 563*, although an insurance policy made no express reference to the rules of the Insurance Society, it was held that these rules were incorporated in the policy.

As a general rule, however, the court will not allow oral or other extrinsic evidence 'to add to, vary or contradict' the terms of the written contract. The parties' rights and duties are limited to the wording of the agreement. This is known as the 'Parol Evidence' rule. A rigid application of this rule, however, could cause injustice in some cases so the courts will allow extrinsic evidence where:

(a) it is necessary to prove a local custom or trade usage. In *Smith v Wilson (1832) 3 B & Ad 728*, there was a written agreement for the lease of a rabbit warren. Oral evidence was allowed to show that, by a local custom, '1,000 rabbits' meant '1,200 rabbits'. In *Grant v Maddox (1846) 15 M & W 737*, evidence was allowed to show that a reference to 'three years' in a theatrical contract meant three theatrical seasons;

(b) it is necessary to show that the contract was not intended to take effect immediately. In *Pym v Campbell (1856) 6 E & B 370*, a contract for the sale of an invention was set out in a written memorandum. Although it was not stated in the memorandum it had been agreed that the contract would not become operative until a named third party approved the sale. This approval was not given. Pym sued Campbell in breach of contract but his action failed. The court allowed oral evidence to prove the parties' agreement that the contract would not take effect until there was approval by the third party;

(c) it is necessary to show that the contract does not contain all the agreed terms. The courts are willing to allow extrinsic evidence to prove these terms. In *Allen v Pink (1838) 4 M & W 140*, the defendant sold the claimant a horse, signing a receipt naming the parties, the horse and the price. Oral evidence was allowed to show that the seller had verbally promised that the horse 'would go quietly into harness'. When it turned out that it would not, the buyer sued. It was held that the note was intended as nothing more than a mere '*memorandum of the transaction or as an informal receipt for the money, not as containing the terms of the contract itself*'. The buyer succeeded in his action.

In *Birch v Paramount Estates (1956) 16 EG 396*, a promise that a new house would be 'as good as the show house' was not included in the written agreement. The court held that, given the importance of this promise, oral evidence would be permitted to show that this was a term of the contract.

Extrinsic evidence will be allowed where the writing does not contain all that has been agreed. In *Malpas v L&SW Railway Co (1866) LR 1 CP 336*, the claimant made an oral contract with the defendant railway company to carry cattle to Nine Elms then on to King's Cross. The consignment note, however, gave Nine Elms as the destination. The claimant signed the note without reading it and the cattle were delayed at Nine Elms where some were injured. It was held that the claimant was allowed to give oral evidence to show that the intended destination was King's Cross.

The issue of oral evidence to prove what was agreed was discussed in the case of *J Evans & Son (Portsmouth) Ltd v Andrea Merzario Ltd [1976] 2 All ER 930*. For many years, the claimant had shipped goods on trailers with the defendant company subject to the defendants' standard conditions. These gave the defendants absolute discretion as to where to store the trailers on board the ship. However, the defendant had given the claimant an oral assurance that storage of his cargo would be below deck. When the defendant wanted to change from carrying goods on trailers to carrying them in containers, the claimant agreed as long as the containers were stored below deck. On one occasion, a container was stored on deck and was lost overboard in a storm.

It was held that the claimant could recover damages for breach of contract. Evidence of the oral promise to store the containers below deck was permitted to show that it was part of the contract and was therefore enforceable.

Roskill LJ said that the parol evidence rule forbidding extrinsic evidence would not apply where the contract was '*partly oral, partly in writing and partly by conduct*'. In these circumstances '*the court is entitled to look at and should look at, all the evidence from start to finish in order to see what the bargain was that was struck between the parties*'.

In these circumstances, therefore, oral evidence will be permitted to contradict the actual terms in the written contract. In *Harling v Eddy [1931] 2 KB 739*, the defendant was selling a heifer at a market. The printed conditions of sale said that '*no animal ... is sold with a warranty unless specially mentioned at the time of offering and no warranty so given shall have any legal force or effect unless the terms thereof appear on the purchaser's account*'.

When there were no bids for the heifer, the defendant gave an assurance that there was nothing wrong with the animal and that he would take it back if anything was found to be wrong with it. The claimant then bought the heifer which, in fact, turned out to be suffering from tuberculosis.

When the claimant sued for damages, the defendant argued that his statement had been a warranty and so was covered by the terms of sale. As it had not appeared on the claimant's account, he was not bound by his promise.

It was held that the promise to take the heifer back if it proved to be defective was a condition and, even if it had been a warranty, the court would have admitted evidence to show that it was clear that both parties intended that it should apply to the exclusion of the printed conditions;

(d) the written agreement has been varied by an oral representation.

In *Curtis v Chemical Cleaning and Dyeing Co Ltd [1951] KB 805*, when the claimant took her wedding dress in for cleaning she was asked to sign a document, one of the clauses of which stated that the company was not liable for any damage '*howsoever arising*' to articles left for cleaning. The claimant asked the sales assistant what this notice meant and was told that it excluded liability for damage to beads and sequins. The claimant signed the document which was, in fact, intended to cover all and any loss to garments. The dress was ruined because of the cleaners' negligence. The cleaners tried to rely on the exclusion. It was held that the assistant's oral representation overrode the exemption.

In *City and Westminster Properties (1934) Ltd v Mudd [1959] Ch 129*, the defendant was a sitting tenant in a room in the claimant's property. The claimants wanted to convert the property to business use but, to do this they needed the defendant's permission. When he was assured that, after the conversion, he could carry on living on the premises, the defendant signed the agreement. No mention of his right to remain was contained in the document. After the claimants had obtained the licence to convert the property they tried to evict him.

The court held that the claimants would not be allowed to evict him. Oral evidence was permitted to prove the promise made to the defendant. This oral evidence varied the contract between the parties;

(e) an interpretation based on the ordinary use of language '*makes no commercial sense*', the courts will allow extrinsic evidence to help it construe the words. In *Chartbrook Ltd v Persimmon Homes Ltd [2009] UKHL 38*, under an agreement for the development of land, P, a property developer, contracted to develop C's land. P was to obtain planning permission and then build and sell properties on the land. P would then pay C for the land, the price to be paid including an 'Additional Residential Payment' (ARP). Later, the parties disputed with each other as to how the ARP should be calculated, with P contending that the payment should be just over £897,000 and C claiming that it came to almost £4.5 million.

The House of Lords held that the wording of the ARP provision, if construed literally, made no commercial sense so the Lords held that it would exercise its power to give an interpretation which corrected what had to be a mistake. It was decided that, under the ARP, C was entitled to the amount given by P.

The court will only take this step, however, if there is a clear mistake on the face of the contract and if the correction which should be made to deal with the mistake is obvious. In other words, the court will interpret the agreement to achieve, as far as possible, the parties' intended meaning.

The Lords affirmed the general rule that pre-contractual negotiations are inadmissible in evidence. If an ordinary interpretation of the words of a contract would make sense without leading to an absurd meaning the courts will not imply a term or alter the interpretation even though the natural interpretation appears unfairly favourable to one of the parties.

However, pre-contractual negotiations may be looked at as part of the background to show what was meant by the language used in the contract (e.g. if that language is ambiguous or if a literal interpretation would not make commercial sense). In *Chartbrook*, Lord Hoffmann said that evidence of previous communications may give *'potentially relevant background'*, not to give an interpretation to the contract as a whole, but to enable the court to deal with the difficulties that were raised in *Chartbrook*.

Sometimes, preliminary negotiations are described as being 'without prejudice'. The use of such a phrase is encouraged on the grounds of public policy in that they encourage parties to resolve problems themselves without having recourse to litigation. Although, since *Chartbrook*, such negotiations may give the court guidance as to the meaning of ambiguous terms or those that make no sense, the general rule is that they are inadmissible in evidence unless:

- they are necessary to show whether they have resulted in a concluded settlement, or
- they are relevant in showing whether the agreement should be avoided on the grounds of misrepresentation, fraud, duress or undue influence, or
- they are necessary to show a clear statement by one of the parties which could mean that that party should be estopped.

In *Oceanbulk Shipping and Trading v TMT Asia [2010] UKSC 44*, a more flexible approach to the use of such negotiations seemed to be applied when evidence of preliminary negotiations undertaken *'without prejudice'* was ruled permissible as an aid to discover the true meaning of the resulting agreement.

Implied terms

These are terms which are not agreed by the parties but which are automatically brought into the contract by:

- custom or trade usage;
- statute; or
- the courts at Common Law.

Terms implied by custom or trade usage

A custom will be implied into a contract if it can be shown that the custom is generally accepted by those in that particular trade.

In *Hutton v Warren (1836) 150 ER 517*, H, a tenant on W's farm, gave six months' notice that he was quitting the property. W insisted that, during the notice period, H should keep cultivating the land. H did so, but left the farm before harvest so he gained no benefit from his work. He brought this action asking for a fair allowance for the seeds he had used and the labour he had undertaken in farming the land.

It was held that, by custom, a tenant was bound to farm for the whole of the tenancy, including any notice period, but on quitting, he was entitled to a fair allowance for seeds and labour.

In contracts between clients and solicitors there is an implied term that there should be no conflict of interest either between the solicitor and the client or between two clients. If there is a conflict of interest, the solicitor should advise one of them to obtain independent legal advice. Failure to do so could render the solicitor liable to the client in damages. In *Hilton v Barker Booth and Eastwood [2005] 1 All ER 651*, H, a property developer, acquired a piece of land on which he was going to build flats. Interest in buying some of these flats was expressed by B, who, like H, was a client of the defendant solicitors. The defendants were aware that B was an undischarged bankrupt and had been convicted for, amongst other things, fraudulent trading. The defendants did not inform H of this and, in fact, lent B money to enable him to pay H a deposit on the flats, again not informing H of this. B intended to sell the flats to a third party but when the flats were built, B failed to complete his contract with H. At this stage, the defendants advised H to go to another firm of solicitors. H sued the defendants.

The House of Lords held that the solicitors were liable for breach of duty. There was a clear conflict between their duties to H and B in breach of the implied duties that solicitors owe their clients.

Terms implied by statute

Some Acts of Parliament imply terms into certain contracts. For example, the Sale of Goods Act 1979 implies into contracts for the sale of goods terms that the seller has or will have the right to sell the goods (s. 12); that if the goods are bought by description they will correspond with that description (s. 13); that the goods will be of satisfactory quality, that is, fit for their normal purpose (s. 14(2)); and that, if the buyer makes his purpose known, whether expressly or, if the buyer wants them for their normal purpose, impliedly by asking for them, the goods will be fit for the buyer's specific purpose (s. 14(3)). All these terms are implied conditions.

In *Wilson v Rickett Cockerell & Co Ltd [1954] 1 QB 598*, the claimant bought Coalite – a smokeless fuel – from the defendant coal merchants. Unknown to the parties, the consignment contained a detonator which exploded when the claimant put it on her fire. It was held that the defendants were liable in breach of the implied conditions in the Sale of Goods Act. The Coalite was not of satisfactory quality nor was it fit for purpose.

Another statute which implies terms into contracts is the Supply of Goods and Services Act 1982. One of these terms is contained in s. 13 which implies that where services are performed in the course of business, those services will be carried out with reasonable care and skill (e.g. this term would apply to the work of a person supplying a service, from a garage repairing a car to a lawyer or accountant advising clients).

Terms implied by the courts

Terms implied by the courts may be separated into two types. These are terms implied as:

- a matter of fact; and
- a matter of law.

Terms implied as a matter of fact

These terms are implied to give the contract 'business efficacy'.

In *The Moorcock (1889) 14 PD 64*, a contract was made for the claimant's ship to be berthed and unloaded at the defendant's riverside wharf. Both parties knew that the ship would ground at low tide as the river bed was not level. The ship was duly damaged. There was nothing in the contract saying that the moorage would be safe, but the court implied such a term into the contract. The claimant, therefore, was entitled to damages. This term was necessary to give the contract business efficacy and to give effect to the parties' presumed intentions. In the court's opinion, leaving the term out was an obvious oversight – the parties had intended to have this provision but had not bothered to state it.

This test became known as the 'officious bystander test' in the case of *Shirlaw v Southern Foundries (1926) Ltd [1939] 2 All ER 113*. In 1933, the claimant was appointed managing director of the defendant company for ten years. However, in 1936, when the defendant company was taken over, the new owners changed the articles of association to remove the claimant as director so that he could not continue in his role as managing director. The original articles did not allow for the claimant's removal in this way. The court held that it would imply a term that such removal would not occur during the ten years.

MacKinnon L J explained the circumstances in which a term would be implied into a contract. He said:

> *Prima facie that which in any contract is left to be implied and need not be expressed is something so obvious that it goes without saying; so that, if while the parties were making the bargain an officious bystander were to suggest some express provision for it in their agreement, they would testily suppress him with a common 'Oh, of course.'*

The court again implied a term into a contract in the case of *Associated Japanese (International) Ltd v Credit du Nord SA [1989] 1 WLR 255*. Under a sale-and-leaseback transaction, the claimant bank bought four specified machines from B and then leased them back to him, B receiving over £1 million under the deal. As a condition of the contract, B's obligations under the leaseback were guaranteed by the defendant bank, both the claimant and the defendant believing the machines existed and were in B's possession. When B defaulted in making payments under the leaseback it was discovered that, in fact, the machines had never existed. B was declared bankrupt and the claimant sought to enforce the guarantee against the defendant.

The question before the court was whether there was an implied condition that the machines existed. It was held that a term could be implied if a reasonable person would, when this term was suggested, 'without hesitation' say that it is such an obvious term that its inclusion goes without saying. In light of the lease contract and of the fact that both parties were told the machine existed and given the terms of the guarantee, it was held that there was an implied condition that the lease related to existing machines.

The non-existence of the subject matter of the lease was of fundamental importance to the guarantee and the court therefore implied a condition that the machines existed. As this term was broken, the claimant bank lost and therefore could not claim under the guarantee.

The issue as to when the court will imply a term into a contract was discussed again in the case of *Attorney-General of Belize v Belize Telecom Ltd [2001] 2 All ER 1127*.

A company's articles of association gave certain 'special shareholders' the power to appoint directors and to remove the directors they had appointed. The matter came before the court when it was realised that the percentage of 'special shareholders' had fallen below that necessary for them to exercise this power. The Privy Council implied a provision into the articles giving them the power to continue being able to remove the relevant directors.

Lord Hoffman said that the court's power to imply a term is based on construction of the contract to find out what a reasonable person, having the knowledge possessed by the parties, would think the contract meant. As a general rule, if the contract does not make provision for what will happen on the occurrence of an event, the court will not intervene. The loss will lie where it falls.

However, the court will imply a term, not to add to the contractual instrument, but rather to deal with a point that was not mentioned in that instrument but which the contract must have meant to happen on the occurrence of a particular event. Such a term will be implied if, on construction of the contract, it is consistent with the rest of the instrument and which, in the light of the relevant background, the contract must have meant. This appears to be a move away from the subjective approach of the business efficacy and officious bystander tests to the more objective one of implying a term as a matter of fact, based on the court's construction of the contract.

The courts will not add terms in order to fill gaps in the contract. They will imply terms only as part of their construction of the contract as a whole in the light of what they consider a reasonable person would understand the contract to mean.

So the courts will not imply a term:

- When one of the parties could not have known of the term and could not reasonably be expected to have knowledge of it. In *Spring v National Amalgamated Stevedores and Dockers Society [1956] 2 All ER 221*, in 1939 the defendants and the Transport and General Workers Union made what was known as the Bridlington Agreement, laying down rules for the transfer of members from one union to another. In 1955, in breach of this agreement, the defendants admitted the claimant to their society. The claimant had never heard of the Bridlington Agreement nor was it incorporated into the defendant's rules. The breach of the agreement was referred to the Disputes Committee of the Trades Union Council which ordered the defendants to expel the claimant. When the defendants tried to do this, the claimant sued in breach of contract, arguing that the expulsion was *ultra vires* (i.e. beyond their powers). He asked for an injunction to stop his expulsion.

  The defendant argued that a term should be implied into their contract with the defendant that they should comply with the Bridlington Agreement and take any necessary steps to ensure compliance. It was held that no such term would be implied. The claimant was entitled to an injunction. The judge said that, *'if the MacKinnon test was applied to the facts of the case and the bystander had asked the [claimant] at the time he paid his subscription and signed the acceptance form "Won't you put into it some reference to the Bridlington Agreement?" I think (indeed I have no doubt) that the [claimant] would answer "What's that?"'* In other words, the court asked, what would the reasonable man in the claimant's position have known? As he was unaware of the Bridlington Agreement, it could not be said that its inclusion was necessary to give effect to the parties' reasonable expectations.
- When it is not clear that both parties would have agreed to the inclusion of the

term. In *Luxor (Eastbourne) Ltd v Cooper [1941] AC 108*, the claimant estate agents were instructed to sell the defendant's cinemas. Commission of £10,000 was to be payable 'on completion of sale'. They found a purchaser who was ready willing and able to purchase but the defendant refused to go through with the sale and refused to pay the claimants the commission. They sued the defendant, asking the court to imply a term that the client would not behave unreasonably and withdraw his promise to pay once they had started working on the sale.

It was held by the House of Lords that, in the circumstances, no such term would be implied. It was usual for a seller of property to employ more than one estate agent and he would not expect to pay commission to each of these if one of them sold the property. If estate agents wanted to protect themselves they should do so in their contract with the client.

In *Shell (UK) Ltd v Lostock Garages Ltd [1976] 1 WLR 1187* L operated a garage tied to Shell. Shell introduced a subsidised support scheme for two of L's competitors but not for L, so L started obtaining petrol from another supplier in breach of its agreement with Shell. When Shell sued for an injunction and for damages for breach of contract, L argued that there should be an implied condition in the contract that Shell should not discriminate against L in favour of L's competitors.

It was held that such a term would not be implied. It was not clear that Shell would have agreed to it in making the contract. Such a term would also be too vague and uncertain. Furthermore, Lord Hoffman said in *Belize Telecom* that the decision in *Shell* was an example of the court saying that, on a construction of the contract, the suggested implied term was not one which the reasonable man would have understood the contract to mean.

- When the parties have excluded such terms or their agreement shows a contrary intention.
- When it is requested merely to make the contract more workable. In *Trollope and Colls Ltd v Metropolitan Regional Hospital Board [1937] 1 WLR 601* a contract provided that building work should be completed in phases. The completion dates for each phase was given, but no provision was made as to what would happen if the first phase ran over deadline.

  The court refused to imply a term to deal with this eventuality even though this would have made the contract more workable. The terms of the contract were clear and unambiguous so the court applied these. The court would not re-write the contract.

Terms implied as a matter of law

These are terms which the court thinks should be included in all contracts of a certain sort regardless of the parties' wishes. Such terms are based on the court's objective assessment that such provision is necessarily incidental to contracts of this particular type. They occur when the courts feel there is a 'gap' that needs filling and, as a matter of public policy, they fill this gap by implying the relevant term.

Once a term has been implied as a matter of law it will automatically be included in all contracts of that type.

In *Liverpool City Council v Irwin [1977] AC 239*, the council was the landlord of a block of flats. The defendants were tenants who lived on the ninth floor. A list of the tenants' obligations was prepared by the council and signed by the tenants but the landlord gave no express undertakings of any kind.

The common areas of the flats were in poor condition. The stairs were unlit, the rubbish chutes were blocked and the lifts were frequently out of order caused by vandalism, non-cooperation by the tenants and neglect by the Council.

The defendants refused payment of the rent, claiming that the council was in breach of an implied term in the tenancy agreement that common parts of their property should be kept in good repair. The council sought repossession of the flats from these tenants.

It was held by the House of Lords that because of the nature of this type of contract it contained an implied obligation on the part of the landlord to keep the common parts of the property in a state of reasonable repair and there was a corresponding duty on the tenants to behave reasonably. It was held that, in this case, the landlord was not in breach of this implied term. However, the term that landlords must keep the common parts of their property in good repair is now automatically implied in all contracts of this type.

7 – Exclusion and limitation clauses

Exclusion and limitation clauses are express terms in a contract which operate in the event of a breach and which attempt to:

- completely exclude the liability of one of the parties to a contract in the event of that party's breach;
- exclude or limit remedies in the event of breach;
- impose time limits on claims;
- subject a person to any prejudice in the event of his pursuing a claim by, for example, giving less favourable credit terms; or
- restrict liability arising out of negligence.

The use of exclusion and limitation clauses is controlled by both case law and statute. For a person to rely on such a clause it has to be shown that:

(a) the clause has been incorporated into the contract as a term of that contract;
(b) on a construction of the contract, the clause covers the breach that has occurred; and
(c) the clause satisfies the requirements of the Unfair Contract Terms Act 1977, the Unfair Terms in Consumer Contract Regulations 1999 (SI 1999/2083) and other pieces of legislation designed to control the use of exclusion and limitation clauses.

We will deal with each of these in turn.

Has the term been incorporated?

A person seeking to rely on this type of clause has to show that it is an integral part of the contract, having been incorporated into it either before or at the time the contract was made. There are three ways in which this can be done.

Incorporation by signature

If the term is included in a contract which is signed by the other party, that party is taken to be aware of the term, whether or not they have read and/or understood it.

In *L'Estrange v Graucob [1934] 2 KB 394*, the claimant, the owner of a café, bought a cigarette vending machine, signing, without reading, a sales agreement, one of the terms of which stated that '... any express or implied condition, statement or warranty ... is hereby excluded'. The machine proved faulty, but when the claimant sued in breach of contract she lost her action. By signing the contract, she had agreed to all the terms even though she had not read them, thinking the document was merely an order form and despite the fact that the seller had not drawn her attention to the clause.

Scrutton L J stated:

> *Where a document containing contractual terms is signed then, in the absence of fraud or ... misrepresentation, the party signing it is bound and it is wholly immaterial whether he had read the document or not.*

This point applies even if the party signing cannot understand the document (e.g. where he is illiterate or does not understand the language) unless the other party knows that he does not understand. So, if a company operates in or with a country where English is not the first language, terms should be translated to ensure that they can be relied upon.

For a signatory to be bound, however, the document signed must be contractual. In *Grogan v Robin Meredith Plant Hire (1996) 15 TLR 371*, it was held that, if the document signed is not contractual (e.g. a time sheet) the clause will not be incorporated into the contract by signature.

If, however, the document signed is contractual, the signatory will be bound by its terms unless the signature was induced by misrepresentation, the document was signed under a non-negligent mistake as to its nature or there is a misrepresentation of the terms in the contract. As we saw earlier, this is what occurred in the case of *Curtis v Chemical Cleaning and Dyeing Co Ltd [1951] 1 KB 805*.

Incorporation into an unsigned document

For a clause to be incorporated in these circumstances, it has to be shown that the document was intended to be a contractual document which could be expected to contain terms.

In *Chapleton v Barry Urban District Council [1940] 1 KB 532*, the claimant wanted to hire a deck chair from the defendants. He went to heap of deck chairs behind which was a notice stating *'Hire of chairs 2d per session of three hours'*. When the claimant took and paid for two chairs he was given tickets on the back of which was a statement that: *'The council will not be liable for any accident or damage arising from hire of chairs.'* One of the chairs collapsed and the claimant was injured. He sued the council which relied on the exclusion clause on the ticket. It was held that the clause did not apply as it was contained in a mere receipt and not in a contractual document. The contract had been made by the heap of chairs and the notice there made no mention of any exclusion. The ticket had been given after the contract had been made. However, under the Unfair

Contract Terms Act 1977, any attempt to exclude liability for personal injury caused by negligence is now void.

It must also be shown that reasonable notice of the exclusion was given before the contract was made. In *Thompson v LMS Railway [1930] 1 KB 41*, the claimant had a railway ticket on the front of which was printed *'For conditions see back'*. On the back of the ticket was a notice that the ticket was issued subject to conditions stated in the company's timetables. One of these conditions excluded liability for injury howsoever caused. The claimant, who was illiterate and therefore could not read the notice, was injured because of the negligence of one of the company's employees. She sued the company. It was held that her action failed. She had constructive notice of the conditions which would have been properly communicated to a reasonable person. *'Illiteracy is a misfortune not a privilege'* said the court. (Although, under s. 2 of the Unfair Contract Terms Act 1977 such an exclusion would not be valid, the principle that there must be reasonable notice remains.)

In *Sugar v LMS Railway Co* [1941] 1 All ER 172 on the front of a railway ticket there were the words *'For conditions see back'*. These conditions included an exclusion clause. These words had been obscured by the date stamp put on the ticket by the booking clerk. The claimant was injured and sued the company. The company relied on the exclusion clause. It was held that there was not sufficient notice to incorporate the conditions into the contract. The claimant therefore was not bound by the exclusion and succeeded in her action.

As the above cases show, the clause must be brought to the claimant's attention either before or at the time of the contract. If it is not, the clause will not be incorporated into the contract and so will not be a term on which the other party can rely.

In *Olley v Marlborough Court Hotel Ltd [1949] 1 All ER 127*, the claimant booked into the defendant hotel at the reception desk and then went up to the bedroom where there was a notice stating: *'The proprietors will not hold themselves responsible for articles lost or stolen unless handed to the manageress for safe custody.'* Some of the claimant's property was stolen from the room because of the hotel's negligence. When the claimant sued, the hotel relied on the exclusion clause but this defence failed. The contract had been made when the claimant checked in at reception. The notice in the bedroom was not a part of that contract so the exclusion did not apply.

In *Thornton v Shoe Lane Parking Ltd [1971] 1 All ER 930*, the claimant entered the defendant's car park, taking a ticket from a machine as he passed through an automatic barrier. On the ticket there was a statement that parking was subject to conditions displayed on the premises. These conditions excluded liability for damage to property and personal injury. When he returned to collect his car, the claimant was involved in an accident in which he was injured and his car was damaged. When he sued, the defendant relied on the exclusions stated in the notice.

It was held that the exclusion did not apply. The contract was made when the motorist was committed irrevocably to enter the car park. The machine was a standing offer which the customer accepted by putting his money in the slot. The terms were communicated after this had happened.

It follows that the party wanting to rely on the clause must show that they took reasonable steps to bring the clause to the attention of the other party. What is 'reasonable' is a question of fact in each case. In *O'Brien v MGN Ltd [2002] CLC 33*, the *Daily Mirror* had a scratchcard game, including cards in each copy of the paper. On the card was printed a statement that for the rules and how to claim a prize '*see the Daily Mirror*'. One of the rules stated that, if more than one person won a prize, '*a simple draw will take place for the prize*'.

The claimant's scratchcard showed that he had won £50,000 but, because of an error by the person responsible for deciding the winning combination of numbers, 1,472 people also had the £50,000 winning cards. The newspaper held a special draw for one £50,000 prize and shared another £50,000 amongst the other winning cardholders. The claimant received £4 as his share of this second amount and he sued for the full £50,000.

The claimant lost his action as it was held that the rules as referred to on the card and stated in the newspaper had been incorporated into the contract. He had had sufficient opportunity to obtain and read the terms of the contract. Even though these terms were contained in a separate source they could be incorporated into the contract provided there was sufficient reference to the other document.

What is meant by 'sufficient notice' depends on the nature of the term. The more unusual or onerous the clause, the greater the degree of notice that must be given for it to apply.

In *Interfoto Picture Library Ltd v Stiletto Visual Programmes Ltd [1989] QB 433*, the defendants borrowed some transparencies from the claimants. The transparencies were sent with a contractual delivery note which stated that they must be returned within 14 days and giving details of the daily penalty fees payable for late return. The defendants were three weeks late in returning the transparencies and were presented with a bill for £3,783.50, which they refused to pay. The claimants sued.

It was held that this sum could not be recovered as the clause was so unreasonable that it should have specifically been drawn to the attention of the defendant by, for example, being written in bold or red type or by having a special notice included referring to it. As it was not, the court would not apply it and awarded damages of £3.50 per transparency per week.

Although this case did not involve an exclusion clause, it establishes the general principle that, the more unusual or punitive the clause, the greater the steps that must be taken to bring it to the attention of the party affected by it. In *AEG (UK) Ltd v Logic Resource Ltd [1996] CLC 265*, a clause requiring customers to return defective goods at their own expense was not a common term and was so onerous and unusual that it should have been brought to the customer's attention. As it had not been, the court held, it was not part of the contract and so did not bind the customer.

Incorporation by a previous course of dealings

A party to a contract may be deemed to be aware of a clause because there has been a previous course of dealings, despite the fact that no notice was given on the particular occasion in question.

In *Spurling (J) Ltd v Bradshaw [1956] 2 All ER 121*, a grocer regularly put his surplus stock into store in a warehouse. It was a regular practice of the warehouse that, a few days after delivery, it would send the grocer a receipt of delivery. This receipt referred to a clause exempting the warehouse from '*any liability for any loss or damage to the goods resulting from any negligence, wrongful act or default on its part*'. The grocer deposited some barrels of orange juice with the warehouse. When he later came to collect these barrels, he found that they were empty. He refused to pay the warehouse's charges. When the warehouse sued him he counter-claimed in negligence. The warehouse pleaded the exemption clause but the grocer argued that this could not apply as it had been contained in a receipt and so was not a part of the contract. It was held that, because there had been regular, consistent activity, the exemption clause was incorporated in the contract and the grocer was bound by it.

For a clause to be incorporated into the contract by a course of dealings between the parties, this course of dealings must be *consistent*. In *McCutcheon v David MacBrayne Ltd [1964] 1 WLR 125,* the respondents operated a ferry service between the Scottish mainland and the islands. The appellant regularly used this service to transport his car. On this occasion, the appellant asked a relative, McSporran, to arrange for the respondent's car to be transported. McSporran paid the freight charge and received a receipt which referred to the respondents' conditions, one of which excluded their liability for loss or damage to goods being transported. These terms were displayed in the respondents' offices and were also contained in a risk note which the appellant was sometimes asked to sign. On this occasion, McSporran was not asked to sign such a note even though one had been prepared. The ship carrying the car sank because of the respondents' negligence and the appellant's car was a total write-off but, when he sued, the respondents relied on the exclusion clause.

It was held that the exclusion had not been incorporated in the oral contract made between the parties. The conditions on the receipt came after the contract had been made. The respondents had not done what was reasonably necessary to draw the attention of the appellant or McSporran to the notices in the office and the previous course of dealings had not been sufficiently consistent to allow the conditions to be implied into the contract.

Furthermore, for a term to be implied into a contract from a course of dealings, these dealings must have been *frequent*.

In *Hollier v Rambler Motors (AMC) Ltd [1972] QB 71,* the claimant had had his car repaired by the defendants three or four times in the previous five years. Each time he had signed a note which contained a clause excluding the defendants' liability for damage *'caused by fire to the customer's cars on the premises'*. On this particular occasion, the claimant was not asked to sign a form. His car was damaged by a fire caused by the defendant's negligence. When the claimant sued, the defendants pleaded the exclusion clause.

It was held that the claimant succeeded in his action. The clause did not apply because, as a matter of construction, it did not cover negligence and the fact that the claimant had dealt with the defendant only three or four times in five years meant that there had not been a sufficiently frequent course of dealings for the court to hold that the term had become part of the contract.

However, if both parties are aware of a term which is common in their trade or industry, this term may be implied into their dealings even though it is not mentioned in the contract. For example, in *British Crane Hire Ltd v Ipswich Plant Hire Ltd [1975] QB 303*, the defendants hired a crane from the claimants. The agreement was made orally with a printed form being sent out later setting out the claimants' terms and conditions. One of these conditions was that the hirer was liable to indemnify the owner against all expenses in connection with the use of the crane. Before the defendants signed the form, the crane sank into marshy ground. There was no blame attached to the defendants for this. The claimants incurred expense in having the crane repaired and they brought this action claiming an indemnity under the contract. The defendants argued that the indemnity had not been incorporated into the oral contract of hire.

The claimants' action for an indemnity was successful. It was held that as the parties were dealing at arm's length, being of equal bargaining power and, as the defendants knew that terms similar to those of the claimants were in common use in the industry, the condition had been incorporated into the oral contract. It was a common term and both parties were aware of it.

Construction (interpretation) of the exclusion clause

In interpreting an exclusion clause and deciding whether it applies to the event that has occurred, the courts will interpret any ambiguity against the party seeking to rely on the exclusion. This is known as the *contra proferentem* rule.

The *contra proferentem* rule

In *Houghton v Trafalgar Insurance Co [1954] 1 QB 247*, the insurance policy for a five-seater car excluded the insurers' liability if the car was involved in an accident whilst carrying 'a load' in excess of that for which it was constructed. The car was involved in an accident whilst carrying six passengers and the insurers, relying on the exclusion, refused to pay.

It was held that the words 'a load' meant goods not people so the exclusion did not apply and the insurers were liable.

Again, in *Andrews Bros (Bournemouth) Ltd v Singer & Co [1934] 1 KB 17* in a contract to buy 'a new Singer car' there was a clause excluding *'all conditions, warranties and liabilities implied by statute, common law or otherwise'*. One of the cars sold was a used vehicle but when the buyer sued in breach of contract, the seller denied liability by quoting the exclusion clause.

It was held that the term 'a new Singer car' was an express term and, as the wording of the clause only related to implied terms, it could not apply to this contract. The garage was liable in breach of contract.

The *contra proferentem* rule is applied strictly if there is an attempt to exclude liability for loss caused by negligence. Clauses attempting to exclude or limit this type of liability must expressly refer to negligence or be written in the widest terms possible so that it could be taken to cover negligence. In *Hollier v Rambler Motors* (see above) it was held that a clause which excluded liability for *'damage caused by fire to customers' cars on the premises'* was not sufficiently clear to cover loss suffered by the claimant.

If the clause specifically covers negligence, effect will be given to it by the courts. If the clause does not expressly refer to negligence but is worded widely enough to cover it and liability could not have arisen in any way other than by negligence, the clause will be construed as covering negligence. However, if liability could have arisen in some way other than by negligence, the courts will assume that it did so even where the words used are wide enough to cover negligence and the clause will be construed as applying to that other cause. In the case of *Alderslade v Hendon Laundry Ltd [1945] KB 189*, clothing sent by the claimant to the laundry was lost. When sued, the laundry pleaded a clause in the contract with the customer exempting it from liability for *'lost or damaged'* articles. It was held that such a clause exempted them from liability in negligence, as there was no other way in which the wording could be interpreted.

If the clause attempts to *limit*, rather than exclude, liability the courts are less strict in their application of the *contra proferentem* rule as it is felt that such clauses are more likely to reflect the intentions of the parties and to be a genuine part of the bargain as they will take account of the likely loss suffered.

In the case of *Ailsa Craig Fishing Co Ltd v Malvern Fishing Co Ltd and Securicor (Scotland) Ltd [1983] 1 All ER 101* the appellants' ship, which was moored in Aberdeen harbour, sank and in doing so fouled Malvern's ship which was moored next to it and which also sank. Securicor had a contract to protect the ships. In the Securicor contract there was a clause limiting Securicor's liability *'for any loss or damage of whatever nature arising out of or connected with the provision of or failure in provision of the services covered by this contract ... to a sum ... not exceeding £1,000 [for] one claim ... and ... £10,000 for the consequences of any incident involving fire, theft or any other cause'*. The accident happened because of a rising tide and, at the time, Securicor's employee had left his post to celebrate the New Year.

When the appellant sued it was claimed that the limitation clause was ambiguous and should therefore be interpreted in the appellant's favour. It was held, however, that on their natural and plain meaning, the words covered what had happened and therefore Securicor's liability was limited to the amount in the clause. In dealing with limitation clauses, the court said, it would be more flexible in its interpretation than if the clause attempted to exclude liability altogether.

Oral representations may override the exemption

As we saw in *Curtis v Chemical Cleaning and Dyeing Co*, the assistant's interpretation of the exclusion clause limited the effect of this clause to the beads and sequins on the dress. Her oral statement overrode the effect of the exclusion clause.

Fundamental breach of contract

A fundamental breach of contract is so serious that that the whole underlying basis of the contract is destroyed. For some years there was judicial dispute as to whether an exclusion clause could actually cover such a breach but it has now been established that it can.

In *Photo Productions Ltd v Securicor Transport Ltd [1980] AC 827*, the claimants had a factory in which it developed film. It employed Securicor to protect these premises under a contract which provided that Securicor would not accept liability *'for any injurious act or default by any employee of the company'*. One night, an employee of Securicor lit a small fire inside the factory. The fire got out of control and completely destroyed the claimants' premises at a cost of £615,000.

It was held by the House of Lords that the exclusion clause clearly covered negligence, so the defendants were entitled to rely on it and were not liable in damages. The reasoning behind this decision was that the parties were of equal bargaining power and the claimants could cover their risk by insurance. In fact, in this case, the issue before the court was which of the parties' insurance companies should bear the loss. Photo Production's insurance had to pay for the loss suffered.

Nowadays, to be enforceable, such a clause would have to be shown to be reasonable under the Unfair Contract Terms Act 1977.

Statutory control of exclusion and limitation clauses

If the exclusion or limitation clause has been incorporated in the contract and has been found to cover the breach that has occurred, the next step is to see how, if at all, it is affected by the legislation that controls the application of such clauses. The most important act dealing with this area is the Unfair Contract Terms Act 1977. Certain clauses are also covered by the Unfair Terms in Consumer Contract Regulations 1999.

Unfair Contract Terms Act 1977

The Unfair Contract Terms At 1977 (UCTA) covers exemption clauses, terms and notices. It applies to clauses which attempt to:

- exclude all liability;
- prevent liability arising in the first place;
- limit or restrict liability;
- restrict one of the parties' remedies;
- restrict the time in which a remedy may be claimed; and
- make the enforcement of a remedy subject to restrictive conditions or penalties.

The Act does not apply to:

- contracts of insurance;
- the transfer or termination of interests in land;
- the transfer or termination of interests in intellectual property;
- the formation or dissolution of companies;
- the transfer of securities;
- contracts for the international supply of goods;
- contracts for the carriage of goods by sea or charter parties; and
- contracts not involving business liability (other than in relation to the sale or supply of goods).

Despite its name, the Act does not actually deal with all unfair terms but rather controls clauses which either attempt to exclude or in some way limit, liability caused by one of the parties' negligence or by their breach of contract, especially where one of the parties is dealing as a consumer.

Under s. 12 UCTA 1977, a party will '*deal as a consumer*':

- when they neither act nor hold themselves out as acting in the course of business;
- the other party does act in the course of a business; and
- in the case of sale or supply of goods and hire-purchase contracts, if the buyer is not an individual, the goods passing under the contract are of a type ordinarily supplied for private use or consumption.

Applying this definition, the courts have held that, in certain circumstances, a business may be regarded as 'dealing as a consumer'. For example, in *R & B Customs Brokers Co Ltd v United Dominions Trust Ltd [1988] 1 WLR 321*, the claimant shipping company owned and controlled by Mr and Mrs B, bought a car in the company's name from the defendants for both business and personal use. The company had made two or three similar purchases in the past. The car was defective and the claimants sued for breach of s. 14 of the Sale of Goods Act 1979. The contract of sale included an exclusion clause and the defendants relied on this in responding to the action. Under UCTA 1977, any exclusion of ss. 12–15 of the

Sale of Goods Act is void in consumer dealings. The issue before the court, therefore, was whether this contract could be classed as a consumer dealing.

It was held that, in making this purchase, for the purposes of UCTA the company was acting as a consumer so the exclusion was void. The claimant's action succeeded. The court said that to be acting in the course of a business either:

- the contract was integral to the business (here, the business was shipping so the purchase of the car was not integral to it); or
- if not integral, the business had undertaken contracts of this type on a regular basis (here, it had only made similar contracts on two or three occasions).

This case was criticised but was applied by the Court of Appeal in *Feldaroll Foundry plc v Hermes Lessing (London) Ltd [2004] EWCA Civ 747*. Here, the foundry company contracted with the defendants to acquire a Lamborghini for its director on hire-purchase. The contract excluded the defendants' liability for breach of all express and implied terms as to description, quality and fitness for purpose (i.e. the implied conditions in the Sale of Goods Act). The contract also included a declaration by the director that the car was to be used for business purposes. The vehicle was defective and the claimant tried to reject it for breach of the implied conditions in the Sale of Goods Act 1979.

Applying *R & B Customs Brokers*, the court held that the company was dealing as a consumer and therefore the exclusion was void. The issue as to whether the car would be used for business purposes was relevant only in relation to the uses to which the car would be put and not to the capacity in which the company was dealing when it bought the car.

UCTA 1977 covers liability in contract and tort but, other than in relation to ss. 6 and 7, is only concerned with 'business liability'. Under s. 1(3) 'business liability' covers liability for breach of obligations or duties arising from:

- things done or to be done by a person in the course of business (whether his own or another's); or
- the occupation of premises used for business purposes of the occupier.

Clauses made void by UCTA

- Under s. 2(1), liability for death or personal injury caused by negligence can never be excluded or restricted by any contractual term or non-contractual notice.
- Under s. 5, a manufacturer's guarantee cannot exclude or restrict the manufacturer's liability for loss or damage arising from defects in goods when used by a consumer if such loss etc results from negligence in manufacture or distribution. In fact, a consumer guarantee is binding on the person giving it as a contractual obligation.
- Under ss. 6 and 7, exclusion of liability in a *consumer dealing* for breach of the

implied terms in the Sale of Goods Act 1979, the Supply of Goods and Services Act 1982 and the Supply of Goods (Implied Terms) Act 1973 is void. This covers exclusions of the implied terms in contracts for the sale and supply of goods, in hire-purchase contracts and in contracts for the hire of goods.

Clauses which can be enforced but only if they can be justified as reasonable

- Under s. 2(2), liability for loss or damage, other than death or personal injury, resulting from negligence can be excluded or restricted only if the term or notice can be shown to be reasonable.
- Under s. 3, where one party to the contract is a consumer or where both parties are businesses but one of them deals on the other's written standard from contract or standard terms, then that party cannot exclude or restrict:
  - liability for breach of contract,
  - liability for a substantially different contractual performance, or
  - liability for no performance at all,

  unless the clause satisfies the test of reasonableness.
- Under ss. 6 and 7, in a *non-consumer dealing*, any clause by which one party tries to exclude or restrict liability for breach of the implied terms in the Sale of Goods Act 1979, the Supply of Goods and Services Act 1982 or the Supply of Goods (Implied Terms) Act 1973 will be enforceable only if it can be justified as reasonable.
- Under s. 8, any attempt to exclude liability for misrepresentation will be enforced only if the clause can be justified as reasonable. This section applies whether or not the dealing is a consumer dealing.

The reasonableness test

Under s. 11, it is up to the party claiming that the exclusion is reasonable to prove that it was so at the time the contract was made.

Schedule 2 of UCTA 1977 provides guidelines to help the court to decide whether a clause is reasonable in relation to ss. 6 and 7. In practice, the courts also apply them when considering the issue in relation to other parts of the Act. The guidelines, which are not binding on the courts, suggest that account should be taken of:

- The relative bargaining strength of the parties, looking at alternative means of meeting the customer's requirements or whether the customer received an inducement to agree to the clause.

  In *Woodman v Photo Trade Processing Ltd (1981) (unreported)*, the claimant took a roll of film containing pictures of a friend's wedding into the defendants' store for processing. These pictures were the only ones of the wedding and were to be given to the bride and groom as a wedding present from the claimant. In the contract with the defendants there was a clause which limited the defendants' liability for any loss or damage to films taken in developing to the replacement cost of the film. This was a standard clause throughout the trade.

The claimant's film was lost and he was offered the replacement cost of the film. When he sued, the defendants relied on the limitation clause in the contract.

The court held that the customer had had no real alternative but to have his film developed by a company which had such an exclusion clause in its contract. The defendants could foresee that some films might be irreplaceable and it was unreasonable for them to apply such a limitation clause to all persons. The claimant was awarded compensation of £75. The court did say, however, that a similar clause may be reasonable if the processor offered a premium scheme, at a higher cost to the customer, which offered greater protection.

In the *Woodman* case, the parties were not of equal bargaining power. Woodman could not go to another developer to obtain better terms, as all processors imposed the same type of limitation on their liability. If, however, the parties are of equal bargaining power, the court is more inclined to allow such a clause.

In *Watford Electronics Ltd v Sanderson CFL Ltd [2001] EWCA Civ 317*, a contract to supply computer software was made on the defendants' standard terms, one of which limited their liability for breach to the price paid for the software, which was £104,600. The software was faulty and the claimants sued for the losses this caused, amounting to £5.5 million.

The Court of Appeal held that the clause could be considered to be reasonable and therefore enforceable as the contract had been negotiated between experienced businesses which were, in effect, equal in bargaining power and skill. When a contract is negotiated between two such undertakings the court would be reluctant to interfere with it unless one of the parties had taken unfair advantage of the other or the terms were so unreasonable that its effect could not have been properly understood or considered. In this case, these factors did not apply so the limitation clause was upheld.

- Whether the customer knew or ought reasonably to have known of the existence and extent of the term.

In *Stag Line Ltd v Tyne Ship Repair Group Ltd [1984] 2 Lloyd's Rep 211*, a clause in the repairers' contract provided that, if the ship repairs proved defective, the repairers would not be liable unless the ship was returned to the repairers' yard for the defect to be remedied. This was held to be unreasonable as there could be no saying where the ship might be when the defect arose and whether it would be either practicable or economical to return it to the yard.

It was also said that a clause written in small print or using complex legal terminology could be considered unreasonable as it would be less certain that the other party ought to have known of its existence and extent. The court also stated that a clause which attempts to limit, rather than totally exclude, liability is more likely to be considered reasonable.

- The reasonableness of the conditions imposed on claims. So, in *Stag Line*, the requirement that the ship should be returned to the yard was an unreasonable condition.
- Whether the goods were manufactured, processed or adapted to the customer's special order.
- What resources were available to the defendant to meet any claim and what was the availability of insurance to meet these claims?

In *St Albans City and District Council v International Computers Ltd [1996[4 All ER 481*, the claimant bought a computer program from the defendants to deal with the collection of the community charge. In the standard-form contract, which the claimants signed, the defendants limited their liability for breach to £100,000. The program was defective and, as a result, the claimants lost over £1.3 million. When they sued for this amount, the defendants pleaded their limitation clause.

It was held that this clause was unreasonable and unenforceable. The defendants could not justify the £100,000 limit by any attempt to pre-assess possible loss. This sum was small compared to the potential and actual risk and to the practical consequences of the breach. Furthermore, the defendants were insured for an aggregate sum of £50 million worldwide. The defendants were better able to bear the loss of the size in question as it could insure itself and pass on the costs to its customers. It was pointed out that it was reasonable that the firm which made the profit should bear the risk.

In other words, if an arbitrary sum is stated as the limit on liability, this could be fatal to the limitation clause. There has to be some attempt to assess the possible loss that may arise in the event of a breach of contract. Further, the court will take account of the question of insurance and who, realistically, should insure against loss, given the nature of the contract.

The court in *St Albans* was applying the judgment of Lord Griffiths in the case of *Smith v Eric S. Bush (a firm) and Harris v Wyre Forest District Council [1990] 1 AC 831.*

In both these cases, surveyors carried out their work negligently with the result that the people who purchased the properties on the strength of the surveys suffered substantial loss. When the claimants sued, the surveyors relied on exclusion clauses in the contracts which stated that they did not warrant the accuracy of the report and accepted no responsibility for any inaccuracy therein.

It was held in both cases that this attempt to exclude liability for negligence fell within s. 2(2) of UCTA 1977 and therefore had to be justified as reasonable. In both cases, it was held that the clauses failed the reasonableness test and so the claimants succeeded in their actions.

Lord Griffiths detailed four factors to be taken into account in determining the reasonableness of such clauses:

- Were the parties of equal bargaining power?
- How reasonably practicable was it for independent advice to be taken in view of the costs and time that obtaining such advice would take (e.g. first-time property buyers would have limited resources)?
- How difficult was the task being undertaken for which liability is being excluded? The surveyors were only required to exercise the normal skill and care such professional people should show.
- What would be the practical consequences of the decision on the question of reasonableness? In these cases, the purchasers of the property were subjected to very substantial losses which they would be unlikely to insure against. The surveyors, however, could easily guard against loss by means of professional indemnity insurance.

Being aware of the fact that businesses deal at arm's length and are more capable of taking out insurance policies to cover potential loss, the courts are reluctant to interfere in freely negotiated contracts which contain exclusion or (especially) limitation clauses. They will, however, interpret the words of the clauses strictly and not allow a party in breach to escape full liability if their actions are not covered by the clause or if there is no justification for the party in breach to argue the protection of the clause.

In *Overseas Medical Supplies Ltd v Orient Transport Services Ltd [1999] CLC 1243*, the defendants agreed to transport equipment for the claimant under a contract which limited the defendants' liability to £600 if there was a breach of contract and the equipment was lost. The contract also required the defendants to arrange insurance for the equipment. They failed to do this. When the defendants lost the equipment, valued at £8,590, the court had to decide whether or not the limitation clause applied.

It was held that the limitation clause relating to the loss of equipment satisfied the test of reasonableness so it would be applied. However, the clause was not reasonable in respect of liability for failure to insure the cargo, as the effect of this was that the claimant was deprived both of the opportunity to recover its losses from the defendant and the chance to claim under an insurance policy.

Finally, in *Bovis Construction (Scotland) Ltd v Whatlings Construction Ltd [1995] NPC 153* the claimants, who were the main contractors in the construction of a concert hall, contracted with the defendant sub-contractors. One of the terms of the contract limited the defendants' liability for *'time-related costs'* to £100,000. After a time, the claimants realised that the defendants' work was not being carried out with due diligence and they dismissed them, later bringing this action against them for breach of contract, claiming damages of £2,714,000. The defendants relied on the limitation clause.

It was held by the House of Lords that a limitation clause must be clear and unambiguous in its coverage of the event which has occurred. In this case, *'time-related costs'* could only refer to a loss from delays in the time the defendants took to perform the contract. It did not cover the defendants' breach of contract which, in effect, meant that they had repudiated the contract. They could not rely on the limitation clause for their non-performance therefore the claimants were entitled to recover the full amount of damages for their losses.

Unfair Terms in Consumer Contract Regulations 1999

The Regulations apply to unfair terms generally, not just to exemption or limitation clauses They may, at times, overlap with UCTA 1977.

The Regulations apply only to *consumer contracts*, defined by reg. 3 as *'contracts for the sale or supply of goods or services where the seller or supplier is acting for purposes related to his business and the recipient is a natural person not acting in the course of business'*. The Regulations, therefore, will not provide protection where the recipient is a company (not a natural person) or where he is a sole trader or partnership acting within the course of their business.

Furthermore, the Regulations apply only to such consumer contracts where the terms are not individually negotiated (i.e. where the parties deal on the basis of a standard-term or standard-form contract). In other words, they will apply where the consumer deals on the basis of a contract which he has not been able to negotiate. The fact that the consumer negotiates some parts of the contract will not enable the other party to escape the control of the Regulations if the overall agreement has been pre-formulated by the supplier. The burden of proof is on the supplier to prove that the contract was individually negotiated.

If a term is held to be unfair it is not binding on the consumer. The rest of the contract remains valid and enforceable provided it can continue without the unfair term.

A term is unfair if, contrary to the requirement of good faith, it creates a significant imbalance in the parties' rights and obligations under the contract to the detriment of the consumer (reg. 5(1)). The assessment of fairness is made by taking account of the goods and services for which the contract was made and by looking, as at the time of the making of the contract, at all the circumstances relating to the contract and to all the other terms of both the contract and of any other contract on which it is dependent. However, the test of fairness will not apply to the CORE terms of the contract. These are terms relating to the price or remuneration for the goods or services or which identify the goods or services to be supplied, provided these terms are expressed in plain intelligible language.

If there is any ambiguity the interpretation most favourable to the consumer will be given to the relevant words. The issue as to whether a term was a core term was considered in the case of *Abbey National plc & others v Office of Fair Trading [2009] EWCA Civ 116*.

In this case, the court had to determine whether bank charges for unauthorised overdrafts could be examined under the Regulations or whether they were core terms and thus outside the Regulation's scope. In other words, the court had to decide whether the OFT could challenge the charges as excessive in relation to the services provided for them.

It was held that the charges for unauthorised overdrafts were part of the 'package of services' provided by the bank; part of the price paid by the customer for their banking service. They were therefore core terms and could not be looked at to decide whether or not they were fair.

Lord Walker accepted that the *'free if in credit'* system meant that customers who regularly incurred charges for unauthorised overdrafts heavily subsidised those who did not and that this could be regarded as unfair. However, these charges were part of the package offered to current account customers and were therefore part of the consideration provided to the bank. They were core terms and so were exempt from the test of fairness. The fact that charges for unauthorised overdrafts were contingent and were not paid by the majority of customers was therefore irrelevant.

In *Director General of Fair Trading v First National Bank plc [2001] 3 WLR 1297*, the court was asked to consider a term in the bank's standard-form contract which provided that, if a borrower defaulted on his/her loan from the bank and the bank obtained judgment against them for the outstanding money due, interest at the contract rate on the loan would continue to run until the debt was paid in full.

Under the Regulations, the Office of Fair Trading has a duty to consider any complaint made to it about the unfairness of a term in a contract drawn up for general use. Where appropriate, it can apply for an injunction to stop the use of this term in contracts made with consumers. It was under this power that this action was brought.

The court held that this particular term was not a core term and so could be looked at to consider whether or not it satisfied the criterion of fairness. Lord Bingham said that *'significant imbalance is caused'* where a *'term is so weighted in favour of the supplier as to tilt the parties' rights and obligations under the contract significantly'* in favour of the party whose standard-form contract is being used. For a term to be included in good faith meant that it had to *'be expressed fully, clearly and legibly, containing no pitfalls or traps'*. Terms that are disadvantageous to consumers should be given prominence. The supplier should not, either deliberately or unconsciously, take advantage of the *'consumer's necessity, lack of experience, unfamiliarity with the subject matter of the contract [or] weak bargaining position ...'*

In this case it was held that that when a bank lends money to a borrower who agrees to pay it back with interest, neither party would think that the bank would forego any part of the consideration. This clause was not unfair. Without such a term banks would stop lending money. If the term was not included in the contract, the result would be an imbalance in the relationship to the detriment of the lender.

The Regulations give an *'indicative and non-exhaustive'* list of terms which may be regarded as unfair. Many of these terms are similar to those covered by UCTA 1977. In effect, the court decides on the facts of each case.

Finally, it should be noted that although the OFT has the power to bring legal action to challenge terms in standard-form contracts, in practice it tries to resolve the issues without having recourse to court action. However, if this is unsuccessful and there is a breach of the Regulations which harms the collective interests of consumers, Part 8 of the Enterprise Act, 2002 gives the OFT the power to apply for an enforcement order. Such an order will stop the infringement and prevent further breaches.

8 – Misrepresentation

Matters which could affect the validity of a contract

Even though there has been apparent offer, acceptance, consideration and intention shown between the parties, if there has been an error in the making of the contract, whether deliberate or not, this could affect the rights of the parties.

The question to be asked is if there was some flaw in the making of the contract. Such a flaw can arise because the contract:

- was induced by a false statement of fact (i.e. by **misrepresentation**);
- was made under a fundamental **mistake** which destroys the whole basis of the contract;
- was not freely entered into because there was **duress** or **undue influence**; or
- is based on an **illegality**, whether in relation to its substance, purpose or performance.

These are known as vitiating factors and will affect the contract in various ways.

If there has been an actionable misrepresentation, the contract is **voidable**. In other words, the contract can be avoided (set aside) by the innocent party. Until it is avoided, however, the contract is valid and enforceable.

If there has been an operative, fundamental mistake, the contract will be *void ab initio*. In other words, it will be treated as if it had never been made. No rights, duties or liabilities can arise under it.

If the contract was made after one of the parties was subjected to duress or undue influence (i.e. improper pressure) the contract will be **voidable**.

If the contract is illegal then, depending on the nature of the illegality, it may be *void* or merely **unenforceable** by action in the courts. In this context, illegality includes both contracts which are basically criminal and also those which, although not against the criminal law, are not regarded as valid by the courts or by statute.

Chapters 8 to 11 now look at these various vitiating factors in turn.

Misrepresentation

While a contract is being negotiated, many statements will be made by the parties. As we have seen, some of these will become terms of the contract which, if broken, will give the innocent party the right to sue in breach. Other statements, however, will be merely intended to persuade the other party to enter the contract but are not intended to be part of the final deal. Of themselves, mere representations are not actionable. They may, for example, be promotional statements which no-one is expected to take seriously (e.g. a washing powder was advertised by the claim that it '... washes whiter – and it shows'). This is meaningless and is known as a 'puff'. It does not give rise to liability.

However, if the representation is one of fact and it proves to be false, the innocent party may have an action in misrepresentation.

When will a statement be a misrepresentation?

An actionable misrepresentation may be defined as a false statement of fact by the maker of the statement (the representor) which induced the other party (the representee) to enter the contract.

There are four key elements to this definition.

The statement must be false

The statement must be false. This could have been done deliberately, negligently or innocently. The statement may be written, spoken or even by conduct – *'a nod or a wink or a shake of the head or a smile'* could constitute a statement in relevant circumstances (*Walters v Morgan* (1861) 3 De GF & J 718).

In *Spice Girls Ltd v Aprilia World Service BV [2002] EWCA Civ 15*, the Spice Girls, a pop group, took part in a photo shoot for Aprilia, a manufacturer of motor scooters, prior to entering a contract to promote the scooters. Although the group knew that one of them was planning to leave, they did not tell Aprilia. After the contract was signed, one of the members left the group.

It was held that, by taking part in the photo shoot, the group was making a representation that they did not know and had no reasonable grounds to believe that any of their existing members had, at that time, declared an intention to leave. This was untrue. They were therefore liable in misrepresentation.

Whatever form it takes, however, there has to be some form of statement. A misrepresentation will not be implied from silence. In *Hamilton and others v Allied Domecq plc [2007] UKHL 33*, the defendants were negotiating the purchase of a shareholding in the claimant's mineral water business. The purpose of this was to increase sales distribution through further investment. The claimants alleged that, when the parties discussed the various options, the defendant's representative said that his firm would sell 'on trade' (i.e. to hotels, restaurants and public houses). 'Off trade' distribution, to shops and supermarkets would follow from the success of the 'on trade' sales strategy. This was an approach to marketing that the claimants wanted from the agreement. The defendants, however, said that they made it clear that they would initially aim for the 'off market' distribution and claimed that their representative had not made any undertaking about an 'on trade' strategy.

The defendants' initial marketing was to the 'off trade' but was unsuccessful and the claimant's business was eventually put into liquidation. The claimant sued arguing that, had they known that the marketing would not concentrate on the trade market, they would not have entered the contract.

The House of Lords held on the evidence that the alleged misrepresentation by the defendants' representative had not been proved. The court therefore had to decide whether, in the circumstances, the representative's silence could constitute misrepresentation. Lord Rodger said: *'A failure ... to speak might be regarded as morally questionable. But that is different from saying that [the defendant] was under a legal duty to speak.'* The court confirmed that, in negotiations, there is no general duty in law to disclose all material facts. It is up to each party to decide whether or not to enter the contract. Lord Rodger cited *Peak v Gurney (1873) LR 6 HL 377* in which it was said that mere non-disclosure of material facts, although morally censurable, did not give rise to a course of action. Furthermore, in the *Hamilton* case, the final agreement drawn up by lawyers for both sides made no mention of a distribution strategy. The court said that this was a strange omission if the strategy was such a major element in making the contract. The claimants lost their action.

The practical implications of this kind of case are that, in negotiations, it cannot be assumed that the parties will disclose all material facts. There is no obligation in law on them to do so. Any issue that is material to one of the parties should be discussed and, for evidential purposes, agreed in writing and incorporated in the final contract, especially if there is an 'entire agreement' clause in this final contract which precludes reliance on any pre-contract representations.

In certain circumstances, however, silence can constitute misrepresentation. This is when the contract is one of the utmost good faith.

In such contracts there is a duty to disclose all material facts (i.e. everything that is of relevance to the agreement). A contract of insurance is one of the utmost good faith. If a proposer does not disclose a fact which could materially affect the risk against which the insurance policy is being taken out, the insurers can avoid the policy when they discover the true situation.

A contract of guarantee is also of the utmost good faith as is a contract involving family arrangements. For example, in *Gordon v Gordon (1821) 36 ER 910*, two brothers agreed to divide the family estate. The elder brother mistakenly believed that he was illegitimate and so should receive a smaller share. The younger brother knew that this was wrong but said nothing. Nineteen years later, the elder brother discovered the truth and sued for his proper share. He won his case and the agreement was set aside. The younger brother owed a duty to disclose all material facts and had failed to do so.

Silence will also be misrepresentation where there is a fiduciary relationship between the parties. In contracts such as those between principal and agent, solicitor and client or between partners there is a duty to make full disclosure. Failure to do so could amount to misrepresentation.

Furthermore, silence will constitute misrepresentation where the statement made is accurate as far as it goes but it is a half-truth – in other words what is left unsaid alters the validity of the statement actually made. In the case of *Dimmock v Hallett (1866) 2 Ch App 21*, a landlord selling his property said that it was fully let. This was true, but what the landlord did not say was that the tenant had served notice to quit the premises. It was held that the landlord's silence on this point amounted to a misrepresentation as he was giving only part of the position.

In *Nottingham Patent Brick & Tile Co v Butler (1866) 16 QBD 778*, the prospective purchaser of land asked the seller's solicitor whether the property was subject to any restrictive covenants. The solicitor truthfully said that he was not aware of any but what he did not say was that he had not read the documents which would have revealed any such covenants. The claimant bought the land but then discovered that it was subject to a restrictive covenant.

It was held that the solicitor's silence in not disclosing that he had not looked at the relevant documents was a misrepresentation.

Where there has been a change in circumstances between the making of the statement and the conclusion of the contract, this change must be made known to the other party. To keep quiet about it could amount to a misrepresentation. In *With v O'Flanagan [1936] Ch 575*, when negotiating the sale of his medical practice, a doctor truthfully stated that it was worth £2,000. Between the making of this statement and the completion of the sale five months later, the doctor had been ill and the value of the practice had fallen considerably. The doctor did not inform the buyer of this change.

It was held that the silence amounted to a misrepresentation and the contract could be set aside.

A statement of fact

The statement must be a statement of fact. A statement will not be a misrepresentation if it is:

A STATEMENT OF LAW

It is the role of the courts rather than the parties to interpret the law so a misinterpretation of an Act of Parliament, for example, will not amount to a misrepresentation unless it can be shown that there were no reasonable grounds for belief in the accuracy of the interpretation.

In *Pankhania v Hackney London Borough Council [2002] EWHC 2441*, the claimant was bidding for a commercial property from the defendants. Part of the property was occupied by NCP and was used as a car park. On the basis of a statement in the auction brochure that NCP was a contractual licensee whose occupancy was subject to three months' notice to quit, the claimant bought the property. He then discovered that, in fact, NCP was a business tenant and was therefore protected by the Landlord and Tenant Act 1954. He had to pay NCP a substantial sum to obtain their agreement to move out of the property. When the claimant sued the defendants in misrepresentation claiming damages to recover this loss, they argued that any misrepresentations were misrepresentations of law and therefore not actionable.

It was held that the misstatement as to the law could be an actionable misrepresentation as the defendants could not show that they had reasonably believed this statement about NCP's position to be true.

A statement of intention

As long as the statement of intention was sincerely meant when it was made, it will not constitute a misrepresentation even though the intention was not carried out. If, however, there never was an intention to do what was said this can amount to misrepresentation.

In *Edgington v Fitzmaurice (1885) 29 ChD 459*, the directors of a company persuaded the claimant to lend the company money by telling him that they would use the loan to improve the company's premises and to extend its operations. In fact, they only ever intended to use the money to pay off the company's existing creditors.

It was held that the directors were liable in misrepresentation. They had never had the intention they claimed.

If, on the other hand, they had originally intended to use the money as claimed, but had later changed their minds and used it to pay the company's debts there would have been no misrepresentation.

A statement of opinion

In *Bisset v Wilkinson [1927] AC 177*, the defendant, who was selling a farm, said that, in his opinion, it would support 2,000 sheep. The land had never been used for sheep farming and neither party had any experience of such farming on the land. When the claimant bought the land but found that it would not support 2,000 sheep he sued the seller in misrepresentation.

It was held that the statement was a mere statement of opinion, not a misrepresentation.

However, if the opinion contains an element of fact and a representor, who is in the best position to know the facts, does not actually hold the opinion or has no reasonable grounds for claiming to hold it, there will be an action in misrepresentation if the statement is wrong.

In *Smith v Land and House Property Corp (1884) 8 ChD 7*, the sellers of a hotel described it as let to a Mr Flack who they described as *'a most desirable tenant'*. In fact, Mr Flack paid his rent only occasionally and then only under pressure.

It was held that the sellers' statement was more than just a statement of opinion as they were impliedly claiming knowledge of facts which would justify this description of Mr Flack. The claimant, therefore, succeeded in his action for misrepresentation.

An apparent opinion will also be treated as a statement of fact and therefore constitute misrepresentation if the representor has expert knowledge and could be taken to be in a position to base the opinion on accurate facts.

In *Esso Petroleum Co Ltd v Mardon [1976] QB 801*, Esso, which was opening a garage, offered the tenancy of the business to Mardon telling him that, by the third year of its operation, the garage could sell 200,000 gallons of petrol per year. Mardon expressed some doubts about this figure but Esso assured him that the estimate was accurate. Mardon took the tenancy and did everything that was expected of him but he never managed to sell above 60,000 gallons of petrol p.a. When he sued Esso in misrepresentation, Esso argued that the estimate they had given was a mere opinion and not a statement of fact.

It was held that as Esso were experts in this field they could be taken to have based their estimate on accurate facts and were therefore liable in misrepresentation.

Inducement

The statement must have **induced** the representee to enter the contract. A misrepresentation will not have induced the other party to enter the contract if:

(a) *the representee was unaware of the misrepresentation*. In *Horsfall v Thomas (1862) 1 H&C 90* the buyer of a gun did not examine the weapon before he bought it. In fact the gun had a defect which had been concealed. When he discovered the defect, he sued in misrepresentation but it was held that, as he had not made any examination, the concealment had not affected his decision to purchase. There was no misrepresentation.

(b) *the misrepresentation did not influence the representee's decision* to enter the contract. In *Smith v Chadwick (1884) 9 App Cas 187*, the claimant bought shares in a company having read the company's prospectus which stated, falsely, that a person called Grieve was a director. The claimant had never heard of Grieve but when he discovered the false statement he sued in misrepresentation and tried to avoid the contract and claim damages.

    It was held that, given the claimant's lack of knowledge of anyone called Grieve, the statement in the prospectus was completely irrelevant to his decision to buy the shares. He could not have placed any reliance on it and therefore lost his action.

(c) *the representee either checks or authorises checks, on the representation*. In *Attwood v Small (1838) 6 Ch & Fin 232*, the seller of a mine exaggerated the earning capacity of the property. Before purchasing, the buyer had his own experts check this claim and when they confirmed that the seller's statement was accurate be bought the mine. When he discovered the truth, the buyer tried to rescind the contract for misrepresentation. It was held that he failed in his action as he had not relied on the seller's claim but had instead based his decision on his own experts' report.

So, if the representee checks on the validity of the representor's statement there will be no action in misrepresentation as there was no reliance. However, the representee is under no duty to check on the accuracy of a representation.

In *Redgrave v Hurd (1881) 20 ChD 1*, in selling a partnership in his firm, a solicitor made a false claim as to the value of the business. He gave the buyer an opportunity to check the firm's accounts but the buyer did not do so. Had he checked these documents he would have discovered the firm's true value.

It was held that the solicitor was liable in misrepresentation. The fact that the buyer had not taken the opportunity to undertake a check was irrelevant.

The problem with this decision is that it could be said to encourage people not to check on the validity of information before acting on it. Nevertheless, *Redgrave v Hurd* was upheld in *Cherrilow Ltd v Richard Butler-Creagh [2011] EWCA 2525*. In this case the defendant, who had agreed to buy a large property from its owners, then entered into negotiations to sell the property to the claimants. Amongst other things, the defendant told the claimants that the property was valued at over £22.5 million whereas its true market value was only about £10 million. He also said that there were other potential buyers so the claimants had to decide on the deal very quickly. In the light of this, the claimants bought the property without having full checks made on what had been said. They then discovered the defendant's misrepresentations and sued him in fraud.

It was held that the claimants succeeded in their action and were entitled to damages for fraudulent misrepresentation. They had been induced to enter the contract on the basis of the defendant's false estimate of its value. The defendant argued that this was a mere opinion and, on the basis of *Bisset v Wilkinson* could not be a misrepresentation. The court held, however, that a statement of opinion can be treated as a statement of fact if the representor, as here, had no genuine belief in the opinion. There were no grounds for the defendant to argue that he believed in his estimate as there was no evidence of any other purchaser willing to pay £22.5 million or more for the property. The defendant's argument that the claimants should not have relied on his statements but should have carried out their own enquiries was also rejected. The court upheld the reasoning in *Redgrave v Hurd*, the judge, Eady J, saying: '*The justification for this aspect of legal policy is especially evident in a case such as this where the defendant has made representations as to urgency, specifically with view to discouraging independent checks being made on his claims.*'

(d) The representations were mere sales talk and no reasonable person would take what was said as being a statement of fact.

The types of misrepresentation

There are three types of misrepresentation:

- fraudulent
- negligent
- wholly innocent.

Fraudulent misrepresentation

Fraudulent misrepresentation has been defined as a false statement of fact made *'knowingly or without belief in its truth or recklessly, careless whether it be true or false'*.

This definition was given by Lord Herschell in *Derry v Peek (1889) 14 App Cas 337*. In this case, a company was permitted by act of Parliament to operate horse-drawn trams in Plymouth. The act also provided that the company could operate steam-powered trams, subject to Board of Trade approval. The company's directors, genuinely believing that this approval was a mere formality, issued a prospectus stating that the company had the right to operate steam-powered trams and people invested in the company on the strength of this.

The Board of Trade later refused approval and the company was wound up. The investors lost their money and sued the directors in the tort of deceit, claiming fraudulent misrepresentation.

It was held that, as the directors had a genuine belief in the truth of what they said, this was not deceit. Mere inaccuracy could not amount to fraud.

The burden of proof is on the representee to show that the statement was made fraudulently according to Lord Herschell's definition. So, no action in fraud will lie for an honest statement no matter how *'ill-advised, stupid, incredulous or even negligent'* the representor was.

Negligent misrepresentation

Until 1967, if a misrepresentation could not be shown to have been made fraudulently, it was an innocent misrepresentation. There was no 'middle ground' and the only remedy for the representee was to rescind the contract, if the court allowed this. There was no claim in damages available.

In the Misrepresentation Act 1967, however, the concept of negligent misrepresentation was introduced. Under s. 2(1) of the Act, if a representation is not fraudulent it is *presumed* to have been made negligently and the burden of proof is on the representor to show that he did believe and had reasonable grounds to believe in the truth of what he was saying.

If the representor cannot show this, the false statement will be a negligent misrepresentation and the representee will be entitled to rescind the contract and claim damages.

In *Howard Marine & Dredging Co Ltd v A. Ogden & Sons (Excavations) Ltd [1978] QB 574*, in the negotiations for the charter of two sea-going barges, the owners' shipping clerk, relying on his recollection of a statement in Lloyd's register, claimed that the vessels had a payload of 1,600 tonnes. This was wrong. The barges' own shipping documents, which the clerk had seen, gave their true payload weight which was much lower. Because the barges could carry much less than had been claimed, the work for which they had been chartered took much longer than had been anticipated and the charterer refused to pay the agreed charges. The owner recovered the barges and sued for the balance due. The charterer counterclaimed for £600,000 on the grounds of misrepresentation, this amount representing the loss suffered because of the low carrying capacity of the barges.

The Court of Appeal held that the owners were liable under s. 2(1) of the Misrepresentation Act. Lord Bridges said: 'the statute imposes an absolute obligation not to state facts which the *representor cannot prove he had reasonable grounds to believe'*.

The court awarded the charterer £600,000 damages, being the direct loss suffered because of the misrepresentation.

Wholly innocent misrepresentation

If the representor can show that he did believe and had reasonable grounds to believe in the truth of the statement, the misrepresentation will be wholly innocent. The representee's remedy will be rescission or, at the court's discretion, damages in lieu of rescission.

Remedies for misrepresentation

There are three remedies for misrepresentation:

- avoid the contract
- obtain an order or rescission
- damages.

Avoidance of the contract

All misrepresentations make the contract voidable. That means that the contract is valid and enforceable unless and until the representee avoids it. Once it has been avoided it is as if the contract had not been entered into.

A representee has a choice of actions. They can:

- continue with the contract;
- refuse to perform and plead the misrepresentation as a defence if he is sued; or
- avoid the contract by giving notice to the representor in either words or by conduct.

In *Car & Universal Finance Co Ltd v Caldwell [1965] 1 QB 525*, Mr Caldwell owned a Jaguar. Norris bought the car, but paid for the vehicle by means of a fraudulent cheque. Payment by cheque which the issuer knows will be dishonoured is, in effect, a misrepresentation. When Caldwell discovered the fraud he informed the police and the Automobile Association (AA) and asked them to recover the car. Later, Norris sold the car to Car and Universal Finance, who were unaware of the fraud.

It was held that, by telling the police and the AA, the original owner had effectively avoided the contract. Norris therefore had no title to pass to the innocent purchaser who had to return the car to its original owner. The purchaser's only remedy would be to sue Norris, if he could be found.

Had Norris sold the car before the seller avoided the contract, the innocent third party would have obtained good title. It depends on timing, the moral being to act promptly once the misrepresentation has been discovered. Notice of the intention to avoid should be given to the representor. If, however, as in *Car & Universal Finance*, the representor cannot be found, the notice requirement may be waived if all reasonable steps have been taken to end the contract by doing something to show that this is your intention.

Application for an order of rescission

Avoiding the contract as described above is a form of self help. As well as or instead of, giving notice that he is avoiding the contract, however, the representee may apply to the court for an order of rescission. Such an order formally ends the contract but, being an equitable remedy, it is exercised at the court's discretion. The representee will be advised to apply for an order of rescission:

- if it is difficult to recover money or property from the representor;
- to obtain a formal release from the contract; and
- to recover indemnity.

Indemnity is compensation for money necessarily spent under obligations imposed under the contract. In *Whittington v Seale-Hayne (1900) 82 LT 49*, W leased property from the defendant's agent, having been innocently assured that the premises were sanitary and in good repair. W started rearing poultry there but found that the water supply was poisoned and that the premises were insanitary. As a result, W's manager became ill and many of the chickens died. The premises were declared unfit for human habitation and the local authority ordered W, as tenant, to repair the drains. W sought an order of rescission and claimed an indemnity for:

- the value of the stock lost;
- the cost of the manager's medical treatment;
- loss of profits;
- rent paid;
- rates paid; and
- the cost of repairs to the drains.

It was held that W was entitled to be indemnified only for expenses necessarily incurred in performance of the contract. He could only claim for the rent and rates he had paid and for the cost of repairing the drains as these were all the costs he had to pay as tenant. The other expenses did not necessarily result from the contract. He did not have to introduce livestock or a manager onto the premises under his contract with the defendant.

As this case occurred before the Misrepresentation Act 1967, a misrepresentation could only be either fraudulent or wholly innocent. In *Whittington*, the misrepresentation was not fraudulent so the claimant's only action was in innocent misrepresentation and his only remedy was rescission and indemnity which, as we have seen, is limited in scope. Had the action occurred after 1967 the claimant could possibly have succeeded in his other claims as the misrepresentation could have been classed as being negligent.

As rescission is an equitable remedy, it is awarded at the court's discretion. Unlike damages, which is a common law remedy, it is not available *'as of right'*. Neither rescission, nor the right to avoid the contract, will be allowed in the following circumstances.

1 If an innocent third party has already obtained an interest in the subject matter of the contract before the attempted rescission. In *Phillips v Brooks [1919] 2 KB 243* a rogue went into the claimant jeweller's shop and selected some jewellery. He wanted to pay by cheque and take the jewellery away with him before the cheque was cleared. The claimant was reluctant to allow this. The rogue then said that he was Sir George Bullough and gave an address which, when the jeweller checked on it, was accurate. So the jeweller, believing the rogue's lies, accepted a cheque the rogue signed 'Sir G. Bullough' and allowed him to take the jewellery away with him. The rogue pawned the jewellery with the defendant pawn broker and disappeared. The defendant was unaware of the fraud.

   When the claimant discovered the forgery and traced the jewellery, he sued the defendant to recover it. It was held that the jeweller's action failed. The rogue had already transferred the jewellery to the innocent defendant before the claimant tried to avoid the contract. Rescission therefore was not possible. The jeweller's only hope was to argue that the whole of his contract with the rogue was void for mistake but, as we shall see in the next section, this was not possible either.

2 If *restitutio in integrum* is not possible. The effect of rescission, and avoidance of a contract, is to restore the parties to the position they were in before the contract was made. If this is not possible because the subject matter of the contract has changed so substantially that restoration virtually in its entirety (*retitutio in integrum*) cannot occur, rescission will not be possible. In *Vigers v Pike (1842) 8 C I & Fin 582* a company bought the lease of a mine following a misrepresentation by the mine owners as to its earning capacity. The company mined the property before they discovered the misrepresentation so by the time they brought this action for rescission the mine was exhausted. It was held that, as restitution was impossible, rescission could not be granted.

   If the misrepresentation is fraudulent, the representee need only hand back what he received if he himself sues for rescission. But if he does nothing and waits for the representor to sue in breach of contract, the representee can use the fraud as a defence and keep what has been obtained under the contract. For example, if an insurance contract was made after the insured person made a fraudulent misrepresentation and the insurance company waits for him to sue and then pleads the fraud as a defence, the company can keep the premiums already paid. If the company brings the action it may have to return these premiums. The danger of waiting, however, is that if the representee knows of the misrepresentation and does nothing, waiting for the representee to sue, it may be held to have affirmed the contract or be held to have delayed too long.

3 If there is a delay in applying for the remedy. Equity works on the principle that 'delay defeats Equity'. In other words the claim for rescission must be made within a reasonable time of the event complained of.

In *Leaf v International Galleries [1950] 2 KB 86* the claimant bought a painting from the defendants who had wrongly, but innocently, described it as being by Constable. It was therefore worth much less than the claimant paid for it. The misrepresentation was discovered 6 years later and the claimant brought this action to have the contract rescinded.

It was held that the action failed. Too long a time had elapsed between the misrepresentation and the bringing of the action.

4 If the innocent party affirms the contract. In other words, if, knowing of the misrepresentation, the representee carries on with performance of the contract, he will be unable later to change his mind and try to rescind. Affirmation can be shown either by words or by conduct which shows the intention to affirm.

In *Long v Lloyd [1958] 1 WLR 753*, the claimant was induced to buy a lorry by the defendant's representation that it was 'in excellent condition'. On its first journey after the sale, the lorry's dynamo broke and the claimant noticed several other serious defects. He told the claimant of these and offered to pay half the cost of some of the repairs. The claimant carried on using the lorry but when, on the next long journey, the vehicle broke down completely he realised that it was in very bad condition. His attempt to rescind the contract failed. The first journey was not affirmation, being undertaken merely to test the lorry. The second journey, however, did constitute an affirmation. The claimant knew that the representations were untrue when he undertook this journey.

Damages

If the misrepresentation is fraudulent, the representee can claim damages in the tort of deceit. If the misrepresentation is negligent, damages can be claimed under s. 2(1) of the Misrepresentation Act 1967.

Under s. 2(2) of the Act, however, if the misrepresentation is wholly innocent, damages are awarded at the court's discretion and only in lieu of [in place of] rescission. If the right to rescind is lost, so is any possibility of being awarded damages.

Furthermore, under s. 2(2), if the court believes it equitable, having regard to the nature of the misrepresentation and the competing effects on the parties of upholding or rescinding the contract, it may also award damages instead of rescission in a case of negligent misrepresentation. Under s.2(3) if it decides that this course of action would be fair and awards damages instead of rescission, anything awarded under s. 2(1) will have to be taken into account.

In other words, the difference between the remedies for negligent and wholly innocent misrepresentation is that, for negligent misrepresentation, the representee is entitled to damages while for wholly innocent misrepresentation there is no such entitlement. It is purely the court's decision if it feels that rescission would not be fair in all the circumstances of the case. The court also has this power in relation to negligent misrepresentation but here the damages would be awarded as well as those available as of right under s. 2(1).

The issue of the losses for which damages can be recovered has caused some dispute.

If the misrepresentation was fraudulent, the damages will be awarded for the tort of deceit. The tortious measure is that damages will be awarded for the direct consequences of the fraudulent statement. In *Doyle v Olby (Ironmongers) Ltd [1969] 2 QB 158*, the claimant bought a business from the defendant company, following the defendants' fraudulent misrepresentation that the business was 'all over the counter'. In fact, half the business was obtained by a travelling salesman. Because he relied on this misrepresentation in running the business, the claimant made heavy losses.

He successfully sued for damages, claiming the money he had paid to cover his 'out-of-pocket' expenses for the business and the losses he had incurred. These can be called 'reliance' losses. Lord Denning stated that the damages were based on the direct consequences of the fraudulent statement. He said:

> *The defendant is bound to make reparation for all the actual damage directly flowing from the fraudulent inducement … It does not lie in the mouth of the fraudulent person to say they could not have been reasonably foreseen.*

So, damages will cover the amount by which the innocent party is worse off after entering the contract. However, unless the misrepresentation has become a term of the contract, there is no entitlement as there would be on breach of contract, to recover damages to put the representee into the position he would have been in had the representation been true – so-called *'loss of bargain'* damages.

If the misrepresentation was negligent, it is believed that damages will be assessed in the same way as for fraud. There has been some debate as to whether they should be based on the contractual measure but it now seems settled that the tortious measure is applicable. This follows *Royscott Trust Ltd v Rogerson [1991] 3 All ER 294*. In this case, the defendant car dealer negligently misrepresented to the claimant finance company that a prospective hire-purchaser of a car had paid a 20% deposit. As a result, the finance company advanced a greater sum than it otherwise would have done. The hirer later stopped paying the instalments and then dishonestly sold the car. It was held that, under s. 2(1) of the Misrepresentation

Act 1967, the finance company could recover damages to cover the loss of the unpaid instalments, even though these may not have been foreseeable. These were damages directly flowing from the misrepresentation.

Following this case, it would seem that the distinction between fraudulent and negligent misrepresentation has little practical significance in terms of the damages to be awarded, although the matter is still far from clear. In the case of *Smith New Court Securities Ltd v Scrimgeour Vickers (Asset Management) Ltd [1996] 4 All ER 769* although not relevant to the facts of the case, Lord Steyn suggested that it was wrong in measuring damages to treat a person who was '*morally innocent*' as if he has committed fraud. He said that, under s. 2(1), the damages recoverable should not go beyond the consequences of the negligent misrepresentation.

The issue is still to be definitively decided by the courts.

If the misrepresentation was wholly innocent there is no right to damages. The remedy is rescission. However, the court can award damages in lieu of rescission if it considers that this would be the fairest, most equitable, solution. In *Gosling v Anderson (1972) EG 1743*, the claimant, who was negotiating to buy a flat from the defendant, said that she would buy the property only if she could have a garage built. The defendant's agent, honestly believing he was telling the truth, wrongly told her that planning permission for such a building had been granted. It was held that the claimant was entitled to damages in lieu of rescission as this would be the most equitable solution in the circumstances.

Damages awarded in lieu of rescission are based on the difference between what the claimant thought he was getting and the value of what he actually received, calculated at the time of the contract. Consequential loss should not be taken into account. The compensation is for the loss caused by the misrepresentation as a result of the court's refusal to grant rescission, not the loss caused by entering the contract.

It is important to note that damages for wholly innocent misrepresentation are only awarded in lieu of rescission. If the right to rescind is lost, the claimant will have no remedy at all. In *Zanzibar v British Aerospace (Lancaster House) Ltd [2000] CLC 735*, the Zanzibar Government bought a jet from BAE in 1992, following misrepresentations as to the type of jet and its airworthiness. In 2000, they claimed rescission or, alternatively, damages under s. 2(2) of the Misrepresentation Act.

The court held that, because of the lapse of time, the claimant had lost its right to rescind and therefore they had no right to damages in lieu of rescission. There was no remedy available to them.

Negligent misstatement

An action in misrepresentation will lie only if the representee enters into a contract with the representor. It is possible, however, for a false statement to result in a contract between the person to whom the statement was made and a third party. In that case, there is no right of action in misrepresentation against the maker of the statement even though the person to whom it was made has suffered substantial loss. There is, however, a possible right of action in tort for negligent misstatement. This remedy was established in *Hedley Byrne & Co Ltd v Heller & Partners Ltd [1864] AC 465*. In this case, the claimants, advertising agents, were considering taking on a contract which would require them to allow the client a substantial amount of credit. The claimant, therefore, asked their own bank, the defendants, to advise on the potential client's financial standing. The defendants, who were aware of the reason for this request, reported that the client was financially sound and, on that basis, the claimants went ahead with the contract, advancing the client the necessary credit. In fact the clients were in a poor financial state and eventually became insolvent without repaying the claimants. The claimants sued the defendant bank for the loss they had suffered because of the negligent report.

Because the defendants' report contained a disclaimer that the advice given was *'without responsibility'*, the claimants lost their action. However, the House of Lords held that, had it not been for this exclusion, the defendants would have been liable.

The defendant owed a duty of care to take all reasonable steps to make sure that the information given was accurate. They had not met this duty of care and the claimant had suffered loss as a result.

In other words, the Lords established a duty on someone giving advice not to act negligently in giving this advice. This duty, which is independent of any fiduciary or contractual relationship between the parties, arises where there is a *special relationship* between them; that is where there is sufficient proximity between the parties for the action to be brought.

Initially, it was believed that this special relationship arose only when the advice was given by a professional person whose business involved advising clients. It was therefore thought that the duty of care in these circumstances would be owed exclusively by people such as solicitors, barristers, accountants, bankers, surveyors and similar professionals. However, in *Esso Petroleum Co Ltd v Mardon*, it was held that a special relationship can also exist in a purely commercial transaction where the person making the statement has superior knowledge and expertise to the other party and it is reasonable for this other party to rely on the statements. As we saw earlier, Esso made an inaccurate claim as to the amount of petrol Mardon would sell if he took over the lease of the garage. This negligent misstatement meant that Esso did not meet its duty of care.

If a contract is made between the person who made the negligent misstatement and the person to whom it was made, the innocent party can bring an action for misrepresentation under s. 2(1) of the Misrepresentation Act and/or an action in negligent misstatement at common law. If the action is brought at common law, the representee must show:

- the existence of a special relationship;
- the existence of a duty of care;
- breach of that duty of care; and
- resulting and foreseeable loss arising from that breach.

If an action is brought under s. 2(1) of the Misrepresentation Act, the burden of proof is on the representor to show that he did believe, and had reasonable grounds to believe, in the truth of what he was saying. Where possible, therefore, it is better to sue under the Misrepresentation Act. If, however, the negligent misstatement did not lead to a contract between the maker and receiver of the statement, but rather to a contract with someone else if the receiver of the statement can show a special relationship, his only action will be in negligent misstatement at common law.

9 – Mistake

Whereas a contract induced by a misrepresentation is voidable, a contract made under a mistake will be **void**, that is, of no effect at all. It will be as if the contract had not been made. So, as was seen in Chapter 8, if a contract is entered into following a misrepresentation it can be set aside by the representee. Until it is avoided, however, the contract is valid and the representor can pass a good title in the subject matter of the contract to an innocent third party. In these circumstances, the representee's only hope is to show that the misrepresentation has resulted in an operative mistake and thus have the contract declared void. This would mean that the rogue had never obtained any title and so had no title to pass to anyone else. As we shall see, in dealing with mistake, the courts are often required to decide between the claims of two innocent parties.

No 'meeting of the minds'

However, not every mistake will affect a contract. To do this, the mistake must be **operative** in that it is fundamental to the whole basis of the contract. It must be more than just an error of judgement. It must be so important that it means, in effect, that the parties had never actually reached the agreement they thought they had. There is no *consensus ad idem*, no *'meeting of the minds'*.

In *Bell v Lever Bros Ltd [1932] AC 161*, Bell had two contracts with Lever Bros Ltd. One appointed him to Lever Bros board of directors for five years, the other was an agreement by Lever Bros to pay Bell £30,000 compensation if he retired within this service period. Whilst he was employed by Lever Bros, Bell secretly made certain speculative trading contracts on his own account. This activity would have given Lever Bros the right to dismiss him without compensation.

Bell retired within the service period and Lever Bros, not knowing of Bell's breach of contract, paid him the £30,000. Lever Bros later discovered the true position and sued to recover the money. In the trial, it was found as a fact that at the time of his retirement, Bell had not had his breaches of contract in mind. In other words it was found that Bell had not been fraudulent in not declaring his earlier activities. Lever Bros only hope, therefore, was to plead that the money had been paid under a mistake.

The House of Lords held that there was no operative mistake. The compensation contract was valid and binding and Bell did not have to pay back the £30,000. There was a mistake, but it was as to quality not substance. The basic aim of the contract was to release Lever Bros from Bell's contract of service and this is what they had achieved. The mistake, therefore, was not operative. It was said that only in the most extreme circumstances will the court intervene and hold a contract void for mistake. Lord Atkin said that, for a mistake to be operative it must be as to the existence of some quality which makes the thing without that quality essentially different from the thing it was believed to be.

Types of mistake

There are four types of operative mistake:

- Unilateral mistake
- Bilateral common mistake
- Bilateral mutual mistake
- Mistake as to the nature of the contract being signed.

Unilateral mistake

As its name suggests, a unilateral mistake occurs when one of the parties to the contract has made a mistake. This must be more than a mere error of judgement. It must be a mistake as to the nature of the subject matter or as to the terms of the contract or the identity of the other party. To be an operative mistake in these circumstances, the mistaken party must believe that the other party has the same belief as him whereas this other, in fact, knows or ought to know, of the mistake and is not dealing in good faith.

In *Hartog v Colin and Shields [1939] 3 All ER 566*, in negotiations for a contract to buy hare skins it was agreed that the skins would be sold at a certain price per piece, the normal method of pricing in the trade. When the formal contract was drawn up, the defendants mistakenly offered to sell the skins at a price per pound weight. The effect of this would have been that the claimant would have paid about one-third of the normal price. Fully aware of the mistake, the buyer nevertheless accepted the offer. When the sellers refused to perform the contract, he sued them in breach of contract.

It was held that the contract was void for unilateral mistake. The sellers had not been merely negligent in the negotiations. They had made a fundamental mistake as to the terms of the contract and the buyer, knowing how skins were normally priced in the trade, was aware of this mistake.

The situation in which unilateral mistake most often arises is in relation to the mistaken identity of one of the parties. To succeed in this claim, the mistaken party must show that:

- they intended to deal with the person the other party claimed to be, not the person they were actually dealing with. The claimed identity has to be shown to be vital to the contract; and
- they took reasonable steps to check the alleged identity; and
- the other party was aware of the mistake. In practice, in most cases, as this other party is acting fraudulently, this point is not difficult to prove.

Given these requirements, it is easier to prove unilateral mistake when the parties are not dealing face-to-face (i.e. when they are not *inter praesentes* (in each other's presence)).

PARTIES NOT DEALING 'FACE-TO-FACE'

When the parties are not dealing face- to-face, such as when the negotiations are by letter, the innocent party has to show that he intended to deal with someone other than the person with whom he actually contracted.

In *Cundy v Lindsay (1878) 3 App Cas 459*, a man called Blenkarn sent a written order to Lindsay, a linen manufacturer, giving his address as '37, Wood Street, Cheapside, London' and signing the order 'Blenkiron & Co' which was the name of a respectable firm dealing from 123 Wood Street, Cheapside. Lindsay had heard of this firm and so, believing he was dealing with Blenkiron sent the ordered goods on credit, addressed to Messrs Blenkiron, 37, Wood Street, Cheapside, London. The goods were delivered to Blenkarn who sold them to the defendant who bought them without knowing of the fraud.

When Lindsay discovered the whereabouts of his goods he claimed them back from the defendant, arguing that the defendant was liable in conversion (wrongful dealing with the property of another). Blenkarn had obtained the goods by fraudulent misrepresentation but Lindsay had lost the right to rescind when the goods had been sold to the innocent third party. Lindsay's only hope, therefore, was to claim unilateral mistake.

It was held that there was a unilateral mistake and therefore the contract between Lindsay and Blenkarn was void. Lindsay had intended to deal with Blenkiron and Blenkarn was aware of this. Blenkarn had no title to pass to the defendant and that meant that the defendant was liable in conversion to Lindsay. The defendant's only recourse would be to find and sue Blenkarn.

In *Cundy's* case, Lindsay thought he was dealing with one person whereas in fact he was dealing with another and that other was, obviously, aware of this. If there is no such confusion there will be no unilateral mistake. For example, in the case of *Kings Norton Metal Co Ltd v Edridge, Merrett & Co. Ltd (1897) 14 TLR 98*, the claimants, wire suppliers, received an order from a firm called Hallam & Co. The order was on headed notepaper showing a representation of a large factory and a statement that the firm had depots in Belfast, Lille and Ghent. On the strength of this, and believing that Hallam & Co was a reputable firm, the claimants sent it goods on credit.

Hallam & Co did not exist as such. It was merely a name used by Wallis. Wallis did not pay for the goods but sold them to the defendants who were innocent of his fraud. The claimants sued the defendants in conversion.

The claimant lost the action. The mistake was not as to the identity of Hallam & Co. The claimant intended to deal with Hallam and did deal with Hallam. His only mistake was as to the 'firm's' creditworthiness. This mistake was not operative. The claimant's only action would have been in misrepresentation against Wallis to avoid the contract with him, but as he had already sold the goods to an innocent purchaser this was not possible. The defendant, therefore, was entitled to keep the goods. All that the claimant could do would be to find and sue Wallis for damages.

A recent discussion of this area of the law occurred in the case of *Shogun Finance Ltd v Hudson [2003] UKHL 62*, in which a rogue obtained a car on hire-purchase from the claimants. The contract had been arranged through a car dealer where the rogue had seen the car and decided to acquire it. The rogue showed the dealer a genuine but stolen or unlawfully obtained licence which had been issued to a Mr Patel. The rogue filled in the relevant H-P proposal forms at the dealer's garage, forged Mr Patel's signature and paid a deposit on the agreed price of £22,250.

Before signing their part of the agreement the claimants, believing the rogue to be the person named on the licence, checked Mr Patel's creditworthiness and, finding it to be in order, agreed the contract. The rogue, who was allowed to take the car away, sold it to the defendant, an innocent purchaser, for £17,000 and then disappeared. The finance company brought this action to recover the car from the defendant.

The House of Lords held that the contract between the claimants and the rogue was void for unilateral mistake and therefore the defendant had not obtained a good title to the vehicle and had to return it to the claimants. The claimants had intended to deal with the person the rogue claimed to be and not with the rogue himself.

(The decision was based on the finding that the parties had not dealt face-to-face but rather through the car dealer. However, the court did not consider the relevance of s. 56 of the Consumer Credit Act 1974 which states that in preliminary negotiations for a regulated credit agreement, the negotiator, in this case the dealer, is taken to be the agent of the creditor, the finance company. Had this been considered, the decision might have been different as it could have meant that the parties were, in effect, dealing face-to-face.)

Parties dealing 'face-to-face'

Where the parties are dealing face-to-face in each other's presence (*inter praesentes*) it is much more difficult for the innocent parties to show that they intended to deal with someone other than the person in front of them.

In *Lewis v Averay [1972] 1 QB 498*, the claimant advertised his car for sale. In response to the advert, a person offered to buy the vehicle. He told the claimant that he was Richard Green, a famous television actor whom he resembled. He was, in fact, an imposter. The claimant believed him but, when the buyer wanted to pay by cheque and take the car away immediately, the claimant asked for proof of identity. The buyer showed him a pass for Pinewood Studios which contained the buyer's own photograph and the name Richard Green. Satisfied with this proof of identity the claimant accepted a cheque signed 'R. Green' and allowed the imposter to take the car away. The cheque, of course, was dishonoured but, in the meantime, the imposter had sold the car to the defendant, an innocent purchaser. Having discovered the whereabouts of the car, the claimant sued the defendant in conversion, claiming that the contract between the claimant and the imposter was void for unilateral mistake (he could not recover the car by claiming misrepresentation because the vehicle had been sold before the claimant avoided the contract).

It was held that the claimant's action failed. His mistake was as to the creditworthiness of the buyer rather than his identity. He would have sold the car to anyone who paid cash and the fact that he thought that he was selling to Richard Green was relevant only in relation to his allowing the car to be taken before the cheque was cleared.

Application of the same principle can be seen in *Phillips v Brooks [1919] 2 KB 243*, which we looked at in misrepresentation. In this case, again, the rogue's identity was relevant only in relation to his creditworthiness in that he wanted to take the jewellery away before his cheque was cleared. This meant that the contract was not void for unilateral mistake.

In summary, therefore, it can be seen that to succeed in a claim for unilateral mistake in face-to-face negotiations, the claimant must show that he intended to deal with the person the rogue claimed to be and not the person actually in front of him. Such a claim has succeeded only once, in the case of *Ingram v Little [1961] 1 QB 31*, in a decision of the Court of Appeal, but this case was stated to be wrongly decided in the *Shogun Finance* case above. The House of Lords in *Shogun* said that there is a presumption in all contracts made face-to-face (and, possibly, over the telephone) that the contract was being made with the person in the claimant's presence. This presumption can be set aside where the facts show it should not apply.

Bilateral common mistake

As its name suggests, this occurs where both parties to the contract are mistaken. Unlike in cases of unilateral mistake, there is no fraud here. The court has to decide which of two innocent parties has to bear the loss.

This mistake is called 'common' because both parties have made the same mistake but, to be operative, it must be so fundamental that it affects the whole basis of the contract. Earlier, we discussed the case of *Bell v Lever Bros.* This was an example of common mistake in that both parties mistakenly believed that the director's contract could be ended only on payment of £30,000. However, as the main purpose of the agreement was to end the director's employment and, as this had been achieved, the mistake was not operative and so was not void. The mistake was one of quality, not substance.

There are a number of recognised types of common mistake.

Common mistake as to the ownership of property

In *Cooper v Phibbs (1867) 30 TLR 531*, the defendant agreed to lease a fishery to the claimant. Unknown to both parties, however, the claimant already owned the fisheries.

It was held that the contract was void for a common operative mistake that affected the whole basis of the agreement.

Common mistake as to the existence of the subject matter of the contract

This arises where unknown to both parties, the subject matter of the contract has ceased to exist at the time of the agreement. In *Couturier v Hastie (1856) 5 HLC 673*, a cargo of corn, which was being shipped from Greece to the UK, became overheated in transit. The captain put in to an intermediate port and, using his authority as agent, sold the cargo. In the meantime, the bill of lading for the corn was sent overland to London so that it could be sold before the shipment arrived. A bill of lading is a record of the goods loaded on board ship and, amongst other things, is a document of title. This means that it represents the goods, so anyone in possession of it can sell the goods as if they were in his physical possession.

Using the bill of lading, the seller's agent sold the corn in London. Neither the seller, nor his agent, nor the buyer knew that the corn had been sold. For the purpose of the contract, the corn no longer existed.

When the ship arrived in London without its cargo, the buyer naturally refused to pay. The seller's agent was a *del credere* agent meaning that, in return for extra commission, he undertook to his principal that, if the buyer he introduced wrongfully refused to pay for the goods, he, the agent, would pay the price the buyer had agreed.

The seller brought this action against the agent. The issue before the court, therefore, was whether the buyer's refusal was wrongful.

It was held that there was an operative common mistake as to the existence of the subject matter of the contract so the contract was void. The buyer was not wrong in refusing to pay for the goods so the *del credere* agent was not liable to his principal, the seller.

However, if one of the parties has made an unwarranted promise as to the existence of the goods and the contract is based on this promise, there will be no common mistake and the person who made the promise will be liable in breach.

In other words, a person cannot rely on his own wrongdoing to escape liability. In *McRae v Commonwealth Disposals Commission (1951) 84 CLR 377*, the claimants bought a wreck from the defendants, who described it as lying off the Jourmand Reef at a specific map reference. The claimants went to considerable expense fitting up a salvage expedition to recover the wreck but when they arrived at the map reference point they found that neither the wreck nor the reef existed. When they sued the defendants in breach of contract, the defendants pleaded that the contract should be held void for common mistake as to the existence of the subject matter of the contract.

It was held that the whole contract depended on the implied warranty by the defendants that there was a wreck at the reference points given. They could not rely on their own error, which was at best negligent and at worst fraudulent, to escape their liability. The defendants were therefore liable in breach of contract.

Common mistake as to the existence of a state of affairs which is presumed to exist but which does not

Galloway v Galloway (1919) 30 TLR 531, a man and a woman, believing they were married, entered into a deed of separation. In fact the marriage ceremony they had undertaken was invalid, so they were not married.

It was held that the separation deed was void on the basis of common mistake. The deed depended on a state of affairs which, unknown to the parties, did not exist.

In *Great Peace Shipping Ltd v Tsaviris (International) Ltd (Great Peace/Cape Providence [2002] EWCA Civ 1407*, the defendants' ship, the Cape Providence, was so badly damaged while in the South Indian Ocean that it was in danger of sinking with all hands. A rescue tug would have taken five or six days sailing from the nearest port so it was decided to find a merchant ship sailing in the vicinity of the Cape Providence to give assistance. The defendants' agent heard that the claimants' ship, the Great Peace, was within 12 hours sailing of the Cape Providence and contracted with the claimants to divert this ship to help the damaged vessel. The contract was a standard form marine contract which provided for payment of the equivalent of five days' hire in the event of cancellation.

The defendants' agent, however, had made a mistake as to the position of the Cape Providence and in fact the claimants' ship was over 38 hours sailing away. An alternative rescue ship was found and the contract with the claimants was cancelled, whereupon they claimed the compensation, offering to accept two days' hire in full satisfaction. The defendants refused to pay anything, arguing amongst other things, that the contract was void for mistake.

It was held that the contract was based on a critical, but incorrect, assumption of fact as to the Cape Providence's position by the defendants' agent. The defendants therefore had to take responsibility for the mistaken state of affairs and could not argue that the contract was void for common mistake. They had to pay the compensation.

Bilateral mutual mistake

This arises where both parties are mistaken but each makes a different mistake. In these cases the courts will try to find the sense of the promise and enforce the contract on that basis. It is only if no sense of the promise can be found that the contract will be held void. The sense of the promise is what an impartial third person would understand the contract to mean.

In *Raffles v Wichelhaus (1864) 2 H & C 906*, a contract was made for the shipment of cotton on the 'SS Peerless ex Bombay' but no arrival date was given. There were two sailings of an SS Peerless from Bombay, one in October, the other in December. The buyer thought he was contracting for the October sailing, but the seller meant the December sailing. When the buyer refused to accept delivery of the cotton on the December sailing, the seller sued him in breach of contract.

It was held that nothing in the agreement could point to one or other of the vessels as the one intended in the contract and therefore the offer and acceptance did not coincide. As there was no sense of the promise that could be found, the contract was void for mutual mistake and the buyer was not liable.

In *Wood v Scarth (1858) 1 F & F 298*, the defendant made a written offer to the claimant to lease him a public house at a rent of £63 p.a. Negotiations for the lease were conducted through the defendant's clerk. The defendant had instructed this clerk to make it clear that he also required the claimant to pay a £500 premium, but the clerk forgot to do this. The claimant accepted the defendant's offer of the lease but the defendant, on discovering what had happened, refused to go through with the deal unless the claimant also paid the premium. The claimant refused and sued to enforce the contract.

It was held that, although there was a mutual mistake here, all the circumstances would suggest that this was a lease without a premium and this, to an objective outsider, would be the sense of the promise. The contract was therefore valid on the terms as understood by the claimant.

Mistake as to the nature of the document signed

This occurs when a person signs a document believing it to be something substantially different from what it actually is. If the person so signing was not negligent, the contract may be held void. This is known as a plea of *non est factum* (it is not my deed) and would usually only apply to people who are blind, illiterate, senile, of low intelligence or unable to read English.

In *Saunders v Anglia Building Society [1971] AC 1004*, Mrs G, a 78-year-old house owner, who needed spectacles to read, had left her house to her nephew, Wally in her will. Wally and his friend, Lee, persuaded Mrs G to sign a document which, they said, would transfer the house to Wally as a gift and thus enable him to raise money using it as security. Mrs G, who had lost her spectacles and therefore could not read the document, believed what Wally told her and signed. In fact the document transferred ownership of the house to Lee and stated that he had paid her £3,000 for the property. Lee had paid nothing.

Lee then mortgaged the house to the building society, spent the money and defaulted on the mortgage repayments. When Anglia claimed possession, Mrs G pleaded *non est factum,* that is that there was a mistake as to the nature of the document she had signed and that therefore the contract with Lee was void. The case reached the House of Lords but, before it did, Mrs G had died and Saunders, as her executor, represented her estate.

It was held that the plea of *non est factum* failed. The contract Mrs G signed was not substantially different from the contract she thought she was signing. She thought that she was transferring ownership of her house to someone else and she was in fact doing this. The mistake was as to whom the transfer was being made.

Mrs G therefore was bound by her signature and the building society was entitled to the property.

Remedies for mistake

If a contract has been made under an operative mistake it will be void at common law. However, the court's decision must be enforced. To do this, the mistaken party will have to ask for a remedy in the law of equity. Equity will follow the common law in that, if a contract is declared void, equity will also regard it as void. However, equity does have a role to play in that it is under this area of the law that the parties' respective rights are sorted out. It does this in the following ways.

Granting a decree of specific performance on terms

A decree of specific performance is an order of the court requiring a person to carry out his obligations.

In *Grist v Bailey [1967] Ch 532,* the claimant agreed to buy the defendant's house. There was a tenant in the house and both the claimant and the defendant mistakenly believed that this tenant was protected under the Rent Acts and could not be removed. Without a tenant, the house was worth £2,250 but with a protected tenant it was worth only £850. This was the amount the claimant agreed to pay. The tenant then moved out of the house and the defendant refused to go ahead with the sale at the lower price, claiming the contract was void for common mistake. The claimant sued for specific performance.

It was held that, at common law, the mistake was not operative so the contract was valid. The court, however, refused to grant a decree of specific performance as this would have been unfair on the defendant. Instead it dismissed the claimant's action on terms that the defendant would enter a new contract to sell him the property at the proper vacant possession price.

Grant rescission on terms

In *Cooper v Phibbs (1867) LR 2 HL 149*, it was held that the contract for the lease of the fishery which was in fact owned by the 'lessee' was void for common mistake. The court ordered the fishery to be returned to the true owner on condition that he first compensated the person who had thought he owned it for all the work he had done in improving the property.

Refuse a decree of specific performance

An order of specific performance is entirely at the court's discretion and will not be granted, even if the contract is valid at common law, if it would cause injustice.

In a case we dealt with earlier, *Wood v Scarth*, where the lease was supposed to be subject to a £500 premium, the contract was held to be valid at common law. The mutual mistake was not operative. However, the court refused to grant the claimant specific performance as this would have been unfair on the defendant. All that the claimant could do would be to claim damages for breach of contract. He could not demand the tenancy of the public house.

Allow rectification of the written contract

If the parties have made an oral agreement, which is later put into writing but the written document does not reflect what was agreed orally, the court may order the written contract amended to bring it into line with the verbal agreement.

In *Craddock Brothers Ltd v Hunt [1923] 2 Ch 136*, there was an oral agreement for the purchase of a house under which it was agreed that an adjoining yard was not to be included in the sale. When the contract was put in writing and the conveyance drawn up, the yard was included.

It was held that the written contract and the conveyance would be amended to exclude the yard from the sale and thus bring the written contract into line with the previous oral agreement.

10 – Duress and undue influence

A contract must be entered into freely and voluntarily. Therefore, if the 'agreement' to contract was obtained as a result of threats or coercion against one of the parties by the other, there will not be true consent. In these circumstances the law provides relief to the innocent party by means of the common law doctrine of duress and the wider, more flexible, equitable doctrine of undue influence.

Whether the contract is made as a result of duress and undue influence, it will be held to be voidable by the innocent party. The burden of proof is on the person alleged to have exerted duress or undue influence to show that it did not induce the contract.

Duress

This is a common law concept and operates when one person has entered into a contract with another as a result of that other's coercion. Initially, the doctrine of duress applied only where the innocent party was subjected to physical violence, the threat of such violence or unlawful constraint. There was no remedy if the duress related to goods or property.

Relatively recently, however, the courts have widened the scope of duress in recognition that economic duress or wrongful commercial pressure could also affect a person's consent and could therefore mean that the contract was not freely entered into.

This wider concept of economic duress was first stated by Kerr J in *Occidental Worldwide Investment Corporation v Skibbs A/S Avanti, The Sibeon and The Sibotre [1976] 1 Lloyd's Rep 293*. Because of a recession in the shipping industry, charter rates had fallen substantially. The defendants, charterers of two ships belonging to the defendants, wanted to renegotiate the rates of hire, claiming, falsely, that unless this was done, they would go bankrupt. They also said that, as they had no substantial assets, it would not be worthwhile for the ship owners to sue them.

The owners reduced the rates of hire, feeling that, if they did not, the charterers would break the contract and, because of the recession in the industry, their ships would have been idle. This would have meant that the owners would not be able to meet their own charges and mortgage costs. This fact was known to the charterers.

Later, the defendants withdrew both ships from the charter and the charterers sued, claiming breach of contract. The owners argued that they had agreed to charge the lower hire charge because of the charterers' duress.

It was held that duress could include economic duress but that ordinary commercial pressure of itself was not enough. There had to be such pressure that 'the consent of the other party was overborne by compulsion'. In this case, it was held that the owners' argument that there had been duress failed as their will and consent had not been overborne. The claimants' tactics were ordinary commercial pressure. The defendants were therefore liable in breach.

Kerr J said that the question is whether or not the agreement was entered into voluntarily. To establish this it has to be asked:

(a) Did the party alleging duress make any protest at the time?
(b) Did he make it clear that he intended to pursue the matter further or did he regard the issue as closed?

Later cases have tried to explain the distinction between legitimate business pressure and duress. Kerr J's test was looked at again in *North Ocean Shipping Co Ltd v Hyundai Construction Co Ltd, The Atlantic Baron [1979] QB 705*, in which it was confirmed that duress occurs when there is coercion of the other party's will. In this case, the defendants agreed to build a supertanker for the claimants. The price was payable in five instalments in US dollars. After the payment of the first instalment, the value of the dollar fell and the defendant threatened that, unless the price for the contract was increased by 10%, they would stop work on the ship.

The claimants felt they had no choice but to agree to this demand as, at the time, they were negotiating a valuable contract for the charter of the ship. Their agreement, however, was made 'under protest'. Furthermore, when the supertanker was finished, the claimants had another ship being built by the defendants. The claimants did not want to jeopardise this second contract so they waited until this second ship was finished before suing to recover the extra 10% they had paid for the supertanker.

It was held that there had been economic duress but the claimants had waited too long before they made their claim. Because of this delay they had constructively affirmed the agreement so could not recover the extra money they had paid.

This decision in this case highlights the problems faced by someone who is put under economic duress. If the claimants had brought an action immediately, although they could have recovered the extra 10%, they could also have jeopardised the contract for the second ship. By trying to avoid this problem, they lost their claim for the money paid under duress. This dilemma has not been resolved by subsequent cases on the point.

The test of 'coercion of the will' was confirmed in *Pao On v Lau Yiu Long [1979] 3 All ER 65*, a case we looked at in the section on consideration. The facts were that the claimants had agreed to take shares in Fu Chip but also agreed not to release 60% of these shares onto the market for a year. They then threatened to refuse to go through with the purchase of the shares unless the defendants, shareholders in Fu Chip, agreed to indemnify them against any fall in the value of the shares during that year. Thinking that there was little risk of this, the shareholders agreed but when the share price fell they refused to pay the indemnity arguing, amongst other things, that their agreement had been obtained by economic duress.

It was held that this was simple economic pressure and not coercion of the will which would show lack of consent. Lord Scarman said that, for duress, it 'has to be shown that the payment made on the contract entered into was not a voluntary act'. To decide whether there was coercion of the will it has to be asked whether:

(a) the victim protested;
(b) at the time of the alleged coercion, the victim had an adequate and effective legal remedy or not;
(c) the victim had been independently advised; and
(d) the victim took steps to avoid the contract once the duress had ended.

This approach, however, could be regarded as too wide in that payment in these cases is, in fact, voluntary but made because the victim feels he has no other choice. This point was addressed in *Universe Tankships Inc of Monrovia v International Transport Workers' Federation, The Universe Sentinel [1983] 1 AC 366*. The defendant trade union threatened to have the crew of the claimants' ship break their contract of employment and prevent the ship, The Universe Sentinel, leaving port. The ship would be released only if the owners paid a large sum of money into the Union's welfare fund. If the threat had been carried out it would have ruined the owners financially so they paid.

It was held that this was illegitimate business pressure. The claimants' consent to pay was negated by the economic duress exerted by the defendants. The claimants, therefore, could recover the money.

Lords Diplock and Scarman accepted that it is not necessary to show destruction of the will to prove duress. In this case, the claimants had an intention to enter into the arrangement but although the act was voluntary, it arose '... *from the realisation that there is no other practical choice open to [them] ... the victim's silence will not assist the bully if the lack of any practical choice but to submit is proved'* (Lord Scarman).

So, for economic duress there are two ingredients:

- a coercion of the will to such a degree as the victim has no practical choice but to comply; and
- pressure which the law regards as illegitimate.

Coercion of the will

In the *Universe Tankships* case, the ship owners had no practical alternative but to pay the money demanded. The pressure forcing them to pay was legitimate (the union acting on behalf of its members) but because they had no reasonable alternative but to do as demanded, they could recover the money.

Pressure

Pressure means that the victim has been put in such a position that he feels that he has no choice but to comply with the demands made – that he has no practical alternative. The victim's consent is not freely given; he has no choice but to agree. In *Pao On*, the shareholders' agreement to indemnify was freely given as they assumed that there was little risk of the share price dropping and so they were running only a slight risk. There was, therefore, no coercion.

In contrast, in *Dimska Shipping v International Transport Workers' Federation, the Evia Luck [1992] 2 AC 152*, the court looked at both the pressure exerted and at its effect on the individual and found that there was duress.

In this case, the defendants stopped its members from allowing the claimants' ship to leave dock until the claimants (the ship's owners) agreed to give back pay to the crew; to make a new contract of employment with the crew, giving them higher rates of pay; and to give guarantees for future payments.

Eventually the claimants agreed to these terms and signed the contract, having lost over £100,000 as a result of delays in loading and sailing and in giving back pay.

It was held that the claimants could avoid the contract and recover the money paid as this was illegitimate business pressure.

The same principle was applied in *Universe Tankships*.

Another example of economic duress occurred in *Atlas Express Ltd v Kafco (Importers and Distributors) Ltd [1989] 1 All ER 641*. The claimants, road hauliers, contracted with the defendants to deliver cartons of basketware to Woolworths' stores throughout the country. The claimants' manager overestimated the number of cartons which could be carried on each load and so agreed too low a rate per carton transported. When they realised their mistake, the claimants told the defendants that they would be unable to make any more deliveries unless the defendants agreed a substantially higher price for the job.

The defendants were a small organisation which was largely dependent on their contract with Woolworths. Believing they could not find another carrier at such short notice and fearing the loss of the Woolworths' contract, they reluctantly agreed to pay the new price.

After the deliveries had been completed, the defendants refused to pay the extra money and the claimants sued. It was held that the defendants were entitled to refuse to pay. They had had no option but to accept the revised price even though this was harmful to their interests. The claimant had put illegitimate pressure on the defendants. This was economic duress.

The pressure must be illegitimate

In the *Atlas Express* case, the threat to break the contract was held to be illegitimate as the results of a breach would have been disastrous to Kafco. However, it will not be illegitimate to threaten to take genuine civil proceedings against the other party, as the person making the threat would be entitled to do this. It will also not be illegitimate to threaten to exercise contractual rights.

In *CTN Cash & Carry Ltd v Gallaher Ltd [1994] 4 All ER 714*, the claimants bought cigarettes from the defendants who mistakenly delivered them to the wrong address from where they were stolen. The defendants invoiced the claimants for the cigarettes and threatened to exercise their contractual right to remove the claimants' credit facilities if they refused. The claimants paid but then brought this action to recover the money alleging that it had been obtained through economic duress.

It was held that the defendants' methods were 'unattractive' but did not constitute economic duress. They had a contractual right to withdraw the credit facilities and so were not exerting illegitimate pressure. Furthermore, when the defendants made the threat they honestly believed that the money was due to them, so they were not trying to extort money which they did not believe was their due.

Steyn L J accepted that the distinction between proper and improper pressure was a difficult one to make. The issue of the defendants' good faith was relevant in *CTN Cash & Carry*, so it would seem that even a lawful threat which is made unreasonably and so shows bad faith in the person making it could be regarded as illegitimate pressure.

The matter was again discussed in *R v Attorney General for England and Wales [2003] UKPC 22*. In the Gulf War, the defendant, a soldier in the SAS, had been on a mission called Bravo Two Zero, behind enemy lines. He was told, in effect, that he could not write a book about his experiences and was asked to sign a confidentiality agreement. Failure to sign would result in him being sent back to his unit as an ordinary soldier with a resultant drop in pay and status. Such a demotion was normally only imposed for a disciplinary offence or because a soldier was not regarded as fit to serve in the SAS. The soldier was not allowed to read the contract in advance but was given time to think. He signed the agreement but later left the army and emigrated to New Zealand, where he contracted to write a book on his Bravo Two Zero experiences. The Attorney General brought this action claiming breach of the confidentiality agreement and asking for an injunction to stop publication of the book.

It was held that pressure had been exerted on the defendant and this amounted to a compulsion of the will. The threat of demotion meant that he had, in effect, no choice but to sign. However, the court held that this pressure was not illegitimate as the Ministry of Defence had a lawful right to remove the defendant from the SAS.

Lord Hoffman said that economic duress requires the court to look at two issues:

- the nature of the pressure applied; and
- the nature of the demand that the pressure is used to enforce.

The threat to do an unlawful act will normally be illegitimate but duress can still be found where the threat is to do a lawful act, as where the threat is to report a crime unless payment is made.

In this case, it was held that the demand to sign the confidentiality agreement was justifiable as there was a valid concern that publications relating to the SAS could undermine this unit's effectiveness.

The contract therefore was free from duress and was enforceable.

In summary, business pressure will be legitimate and will not constitute economic duress where:

- the threat is to exercise a legitimate right and is made in good faith (*CTN Cash & Carry*);
- where the 'victim' had free choice (*Pao On v Lau Yiu Long*); and
- where the pressure is ordinary commercial pressure (*Siboen and Sibtree*).

The business pressure will be illegitimate and thus constitute economic duress where:

- there is coercion (*Universe Tankships v ITWF*);
- the victim's will is overborne by compulsion (*The Atlantic Baron*);
- the victim had no choice but to agree (*Universe Tankships v ITWF and Dimska v ITWF*); and
- there is an unjustifiable threat to break the contract (*Atlas Express*).

The position with regard to economic duress is unclear and uncertain. It is still being developed by the courts.

Undue influence

The limits on the common law doctrine of duress led to the development of undue influence in equity. Undue influence arises where one party, the stronger, is in a position to dominate the will of the other, the weaker. In these circumstances, if the weaker party has agreed to enter a contract because of the influence exerted by the stronger, the weaker party may be able to end the contract because of this improper pressure.

There are two categories of undue influence:

- actual undue influence; and
- presumed undue influence, which may arise either where there is a special relationship between the parties or there is a relationship of trust and confidence between them.

Actual undue influence

For this claim to succeed it has to be shown that influence existed and had been exercised and that the transaction resulted from it.

In *Bank of Credit and Commerce International SA v Aboody [1990] 1 QB 923,* Mrs A, who was 20 years younger than her husband, had for many years signed documents relating to his business without reading them. On one occasion when she was asked to sign another document the bank's solicitor suggested that she should obtain legal advice before signing. Her husband overheard this, argued with the solicitor and reduced Mrs A to tears. She signed the document without having taken any legal advice. The document was a contract guaranteeing her husband's company's debts to the bank by granting security over the matrimonial home. The company became insolvent and the bank brought this action to recover its security.

The Court of Appeal held that Mr A had unduly influenced his wife. He had kept relevant matters from her and his bullying manner had led her to sign documents simply because she wanted peace. However, the transaction was not to Mrs A's 'manifest disadvantage' as she would have benefited had the company survived so the contract with the bank would not be set aside.

In the case of *CIBC Mortgages plc v Pitt [1993] 4 All ER 433,* however, it was held that it was not necessary to show 'manifest disadvantage' in cases involving actual undue influence. In this case, Mr P persuaded his wife, the defendant, to sign a contract mortgaging their jointly owned family home to the claimant in order to discharge the existing mortgage and to buy a holiday home. Mr P, who was in substantial debt, failed to keep up the mortgage repayments and the claimant sued to obtain possession of the house.

The House of Lords held that Mr P had used undue influence on his wife so she could set aside the agreement with him even though she had suffered no manifest disadvantage (thus overturning *Aboody* which gave this as a requirement). However, CIBC Mortgages was not affected by the undue influence as Mr P was not its agent and the claimant had no actual notice of the undue influence. There was nothing to show that the transaction was not just a normal loan to a married couple for their joint benefit. So the mortgage to the claimant could not be set aside and the firm could obtain possession of the property.

Proof of a manifest disadvantage to the victim was not necessary in cases of actual undue influence.

Presumed undue influence where there is a special relationship

Where there is a special fiduciary relationship between the parties, equity presumes undue influence unless the contrary is proved. For such a presumption to rise, the relationship must be one where confidence is placed in one of the parties, which confidence:

- gives that person authority over the other; or
- creates an obligation in the person with authority to offer or recommend that the other seeks, professional advice.

In other words, undue influence will be presumed where the relationship between the parties is such that the stronger party can take advantage of the weaker. The stronger party has to show that such unfair advantage was not taken either because the weaker party took independent advice or used their own free will.

Undue influence will be presumed in relationships such as:

- parent/child
- solicitor/client
- guardian/ward
- trustee/beneficiary
- doctor/patient
- religious adviser/disciple.

In *Allcard v Skinner (1887) 36 Ch D 145*, the claimant joined a religious order and, in accordance with its rules of poverty, gave about £7,000 to the head of the order during the eight years she was a member. She left the order and, six years later, sued to recover the money she had paid.

It was held that the money had been obtained by undue influence and so the agreement to pay was voidable. However the money was not recoverable as the claimant had waited too long to make her claim and was therefore taken to have affirmed the contract.

Although the list of relationships where undue influence will be presumed is not conclusive, those between a husband and wife or a bank and its customer are not regarded as special relationships in this context as it is assumed that, in these cases, the other party is able to exercise their own judgement or to seek independent advice. Such relationships, however, may give rise to a claim of undue influence if this can be shown on the facts of the case.

Presumed undue influence where there is a relationship of trust and confidence

The presumption of undue influence may also apply where one party, because of the trust and confidence placed in them by the weaker party, is able to take unfair advantage of that weaker party. In other words, there will be a presumption of undue influence where:

- one person relied on the guidance and advice of another;
- that other knew of the reliance;
- that other obtained a benefit from the transaction;
- the transaction so obtained gave unfair advantage to the other person; and
- it caused injury to the weaker party.

In these circumstances, the dominant party has to show that no dominance was practised in bringing about the transaction and that the weaker party relied on their own judgement. The presumption of undue influence will arise when the transaction is suspicious and 'calls for an explanation'. In *Allcard v Skinner* it was said that the gift had to have been 'so large as not to be reasonably accounted for on the grounds of friendship, relationship, charity or other ordinary motives on which ordinary men act'. It does not have to be 'manifestly disadvantageous' although it is difficult to imagine circumstances when a transaction that is not disadvantageous will raise suspicions or will be the subject of a later complaint.

In *Lloyds Bank Ltd v Bundy [1975] QB 326*, the defendant, an elderly farmer, gave the claimant a guarantee of his son's overdraft, mortgaging the farm to the bank as security. The farmer had relied exclusively on the bank's assistant manager and had been given no opportunity to seek independent advice. The defendant's son ran into financial difficulties and the assistant manager persuaded the farmer to grant a further charge over the farm. Eventually, the son's company failed and the bank brought this action to take the farm.

The Court of Appeal held that the guarantee and charges should be set aside. The contracts were voidable for undue influence. The farmer had looked to the bank for financial advice and had placed confidence in it and it was in the bank's interests to obtain the guarantee and charges. The bank should have ensured that the defendant received independent legal advice.

The House of Lords said that, for a presumption of undue influence, it had to be shown that:

- there was a relationship where one party exercises dominance over the other; and
- the transaction was manifestly disadvantageous to the weaker party.

This case was followed in *National Westminster Bank plc v Morgan [1985] 1 All ER 821*. Here, a couple in financial difficulties mortgaged their jointly owned house to the bank. The wife was visited by the bank manager who, despite her lack of confidence in her husband's business, persuaded her to sign the mortgage. She was not independently advised nor was she told (and did not realise) that the mortgage extended to her husband's business debts. The loan was not repaid and later the husband died. The bank then began proceedings to take possession of the house. The wife pleaded undue influence.

The House of Lords held that there was no undue influence and that the mortgage was binding on Mrs Morgan. There was no relationship of trust between her and the bank manager and so there was no duty to insist on her obtaining independent advice. The transaction was not obviously to her disadvantage as it could have been a means of saving her home. She wanted the loan and, despite her misunderstanding as to its exact extent, knew what she was doing.

The court held that undue influence of itself was not sufficient to avoid a contract. It also had to be shown that the transaction was of manifest disadvantage to the weaker person and that there was domination by one of the parties over the other.

Later cases, however, relaxed the requirements set out in the *Morgan* case. As stated earlier, the requirement of 'manifest disadvantage' is no longer an absolute requirement. Furthermore, in *Goldsworthy v Brickell [1987] 1 All ER 853*, it was held that dominance was also no longer an absolute requirement. Undue influence could be shown where there is an abuse of a relationship falling short of actual domination. In this case, the claimant, who was 85 years old, let his farm to the defendant, a neighbouring farmer, whom he trusted and upon whom he relied entirely. The claimant also agreed to give the defendant a favourable option to buy the farm when the claimant died.

It was held that the agreement to give the option could be set aside. The relationship between the parties raised a presumption of undue influence because of the degree of trust and confidence between them and the claimant had not given the agreement full and informed thought. The court, however, rejected the *Morgan* argument that there had to be dominance by one of the parties. Dominance, it said, is just one form of undue influence. Abuse of a relationship of confidence falling short of dominance could also result in undue influence.

The position now, therefore, is that for a presumption of undue influence to arise in cases where there is no special relationship, there has to be a relationship of confidence between the parties and this gives rise to a transaction which calls for an explanation because it looks suspicious even if it is not manifestly disadvantageous to one of the parties.

Undue influence and third parties

So far, we have looked at the effect of undue influence on the contract between the parties. However, in many cases, a person may be persuaded to enter into a guarantee or surety contract with the creditor as a result of undue influence by another party. This often happens in the context of a husband/wife relationship where the wife, acting under emotional pressure or following a misrepresentation or misunderstanding fostered by the husband, signs a charge in favour of a bank or other creditor over the matrimonial home in order to secure a loan for the husband, usually for his business. The bank has not behaved improperly but in certain circumstances the courts have allowed the wife to set aside the contract. This applies equally where the emotional pressure occurs between co-habitees or other types of relationship based on trust and confidence.

The court addressed this issue in *Barclays Bank plc v O'Brien and another [1993] 4 All ER 417*. Mr O'Brien, who wanted to use the family home as security for his business debts, told his wife, who was the joint owner of the property, that the security was for a £60,000 overdraft. In fact, the true amount was £135,000. Mrs O'Brien was asked to go to a branch of the bank to sign the necessary documents. This was not the branch she usually used, but the manager of her usual branch had given instructions that the implications of the transaction should be explained to her. He had also left a letter for Mrs O'Brien concerning the contract she was being asked to sign suggesting that she obtain independent advice. There was some confusion at the branch the wife attended and her branch manager's instructions were not followed.

When Mr O'Brien's business failed, the bank tried to enforce the security and obtain possession of the house. Mrs O'Brien argued that the contract should be set aside on the grounds of her husband's misrepresentation.

The House of Lords held that the contract should be set aside as the bank had *constructive notice* of a possible irregularity in the arrangement. The bank was aware that the parties were married and was therefore put on notice of this chance of there being an irregularity. It had failed to warn the wife of the risks she was running and had not advised her to obtain independent legal advice. Lord Browne-Wilkinson said that, in order to avoid being fixed with this constructive notice, the bank should:

- at a meeting not attended by the husband, inform the wife of the extent of her liability;
- warn the wife of the risks involved; and
- advise her to take independent legal advice.

Failure to take these steps may enable the wife to have the transaction set aside.

So, from this case, it can be seen that constructive notice will arise where:

- the transaction is such that there is a substantial risk of misconduct by the husband where the wife is acting as surety for his debts; and
- the transaction is not, on the face of it, to the financial advantage of the wife.

In *CIBC Mortgages v Pitt [1993] 4 All ER 433*, the charge on the matrimonial home was taken out jointly by the husband and wife to discharge the first mortgage on their house and to buy a holiday home. When the claimant tried to enforce the security and take possession of the property, the wife argued that the agreement should be set aside as she had been induced to agree to it by the undue influence of her husband.

It was held that this agreement would not be set aside as the security had appeared to be a straightforward advance to the couple for their joint benefit and therefore the claimant would not be taken to have constructive notice of any possible irregularity.

By contrast, in *Credit Lyonnaise Bank Nederland NV v Burch [1997] 1 All ER 144*, the defendant employee agreed to her employer's request to guarantee his company's overdraft and to take out a charge on her flat as security. This charge exposed her to unlimited liability for an unlimited time. She was unaware of the full extent of the company's debts. The claimant advised her to obtain independent legal advice but she did not do so. The company failed and the bank tried to enforce its security.

It was held that the claimant failed in its action. The charge was set aside. The transaction was so clearly against the defendant's interests and to her disadvantage that 'it would cause a bank manager to raise his eyebrows more than a little when he was engaged in entering a contract with a young employee which involved guaranteeing her employer's indebtedness in the sum of £27,000 and mortgaging her home to the bank'. The transaction must have looked very suspicious, so the bank could not claim it had taken reasonable steps to avoid being fixed with constructive notice of the employer's undue influence.

A process for dealing with surety arrangements, applicable not just to banks but to any lender entering such contracts and applying to all borrowers, not just wives, was given in the case of *Royal Bank of Scotland v Etridge (No 2) [2001] UKHL 44*. In this case, again involving a wife standing surety and charging her interest in the matrimonial home for her husband's debts, the House of Lords confirmed the point that the husband/wife relationship did not give rise to an irrebuttable presumption of undue influence. It is a question of fact in each case and will arise where it can be shown that advantage had been taken of the weaker party to persuade that party to enter the transaction.

Lord Nicholls set out the procedure to be followed in all future cases of this type, giving lenders guidelines as to how they could avoid being fixed with constructive notice of undue influence or misrepresentation. In order to avoid such liability, the lender has to take reasonable steps to satisfy itself that the borrower has been informed in a meaningful way of the implications of the proposed transaction. This can be achieved by relying on a letter from a solicitor that the borrower had been appropriately advised. This solicitor must be provided with all the relevant information by the lender.

The lender is put on enquiry and must take these steps whenever a wife offers to stand as surety for her husband's debts. This, however, would not be the case:

- if the money was advanced jointly unless the lender was aware that the loan was being made solely for the husband's business purposes. The lender is always put on enquiry where the loan is to a company in which both parties have an interest even where the wife is a shareholder, director or company secretary. The shareholding and the identity of directors does not provide an accurate guide as to who has *de facto* control of the company's business; or
- where the relationship between the surety and the debtor is non-commercial but not where the person standing surety is providing a commercial service. Such lenders charge a fee for the service and can look after themselves, being fully understanding of the risks involved in giving a guarantee.

In giving the independent advice, the solicitor should see the client in a face-to-face meeting without the husband being present and should:

- explain the nature and possible consequences of the transaction and the seriousness of the risk involved;
- discuss the wife's understanding of the value of the property being charged together with her own financial means;
- discuss the husband's financial position, including matters such as his indebtedness and the amount of the debt for which the charge is being made; and
- clearly advise the wife that she has a choice whether or not to proceed with the transaction.

Ultimately, however, it is up to the wife to decide whether or not to go ahead with the transaction, following the solicitor's reasoned advice even if the solicitor believes that the deal is not in the wife's interests. Reasoned advice should be given to her to this effect. The solicitor should only cease to act for the wife if there are exceptional circumstances where it is 'glaringly obvious' that the wife is being 'grievously wronged'.

Unless it knows otherwise, the lender is entitled to assume that the solicitor has given the necessary advice and can proceed with the transaction without fear of it being set aside later. However, it is not enough for the lender merely to instruct a solicitor to attend to the formalities of signing the charge without giving instructions also to advise the wife. If the appropriate advice is not given or is deficient the wife could sue the solicitor.

In *Padden v Bevan Ashford (a Firm) [2011] EWCA Civ 1616*, the claimant was told by her husband, a financial consultant, that he had taken money from a client and, to avoid being sent to prison, had to return that money to the client. In order to do this they had to sell the matrimonial home. The husband's solicitor told the wife to seek independent advice 'for the sake of formality' but to ignore any advice she was given not to sign.

The claimant went to the defendants and, in the half-hour meeting they had, stated that she intended to go ahead with the transaction for the sake of her children and to avoid the husband being imprisoned. The solicitor advised her not to sign but did not arrange any further meetings with her. The husband and wife then went to another branch of the defendant's firm and signed the various documents for the sale of the house and of various other assets in front of another solicitor. This solicitor gave no advice but merely witnessed the signature. He also certified that the consequences of the transaction had been explained to the wife, that he was satisfied that she understood their nature and that, to the best of his knowledge, she had consented without undue influence or misrepresentation.

The husband was later convicted of fraud and was imprisoned for six years. The claimant sued the solicitors in damages for giving negligent advice in relation to the transaction.

It was held that, in cases where a client seeks advice from a solicitor about a significant transaction which is, at least on the face of it, for the sole financial benefit of another who is in a close personal relationship with the client, the solicitor has a duty to question and advise the client in detail. Merely advising them not to enter the transaction is not sufficient to discharge the solicitor's duty. In the *Padden* case, the solicitor should have:

- explored why the wife was willing to risk all her assets to protect a husband who was a fraudster;
- told the wife to discover all the relevant facts; and
- advised her that, in the light of her husband's fraud (which was more extensive than he had admitted to her) it was unlikely that she would be bale to save him from prison.

The solicitors, therefore, had not complied with their duty to the client and were liable to her.

Remedies for duress and undue influence

Both duress and undue influence render a contract voidable. The victim, therefore, can have the contract set aside (rescinded). Rescission will not be granted, however, where:

- the claimant has affirmed the contract or has waited too long before trying to have the contract avoided. As we have seen in *Allcard v Skinner* above, the victim waited six years before trying to recover the money she had had handed over because of the undue influence of her spiritual adviser. The court held that she had left it too late and that rescission was not possible. In the case of duress, the action has to be brought as soon as the duress has ended, otherwise the victim will lose the right to have the contract avoided; or
- the parties cannot be restored to substantially their original position; or
- innocent third parties have acquired rights in the subject matter of the contract before an attempt to avoid is made.

11 – Illegal and void contracts

The validity of a contract may be affected by the fact that it is illegal either in its formation or its performance or by the fact that it is void by statute or at common law because it offends public policy. The effect of these on a contract is determined by the wrong the law is trying to control.

We will look at contracts which are illegal by statute or at common law and then at contracts which the law treats as void on the grounds of public policy.

Public policy addresses the social, moral and economic values of society. The concept is used to regulate behaviour either by reinforcing existing social values or by encouraging constructive change. Judges argue that their decisions reflect society's attitudes and are intended to avoid undesirable social or economic consequences. One of the problems with this, however, is that as policy varies with changes in public opinion and ideas of morality, the application of public policy can give rise to uncertainty. For example, in *Cowan v Milbourn [1866–67] LR 2 Ex 230*, it was held that a contract to lease a hall for a meeting of atheists was illegal and void. However, in *Bowman v Secular Society Ltd [1917] AC 406*, it was held that such a contract was not illegal, thus recognising the changed attitudes of society to matters such as atheism.

As a general rule, and in order to maintain as great a measure of certainty as possible, judges tend to limit the application of public policy by following previous precedents and by adopting the view that making new law is the role of Parliament not the courts. The power to change law on the grounds of public policy, however, is still within the judges' remit.

Illegal contracts

The courts will not enforce contracts which have an illegal purpose, whether they are criminal in intent or are harmful to society, being against public policy. Contracts may be illegal by statute or at Common Law.

Contracts made illegal by statute

An Act of Parliament or an order or regulation authorised by Parliament may expressly or impliedly prohibit certain contracts. In *Mohamed v Alaga & Co [1998] 2 All ER 720*, the claimant, a leading member of the Somali community in the UK, made an oral agreement with the defendant solicitors by which the defendants promised to pay him half the fees they received from the Legal Aid Board for asylum applications made on behalf of Somali refugees he introduced to the firm. He also agreed to provide translation services for the applicants he introduced.

The solicitors later refused to honour this agreement so the claimant sued the firm for breach of contract.

It was held that the contract was illegal, being in breach of rules made under the Solicitors Act 1974 which prohibited solicitors from entering such agreements and making payment for this kind of service. The fact that the claimant was unaware of this prohibition was irrelevant to his claim for payment for introducing clients. However, the translation service he provided could be separated from the illegal aspect of the arrangement and, given the fact that he was blameless, he was entitled to compensation for this.

If a contract is affected by legislation, the court will look at the reason why the provision was made. If it was to prevent such contracts altogether, a contract made in violation of the statute will be illegal and void. However, if the purpose of the act is to raise revenue, non-compliance may not affect the contract. In *Re Mahmoud and Ispahani [1921] 2 KB 716*, the sale and purchase of linseed oil was prohibited by the Seeds, Oils and Fats Order 1919 unless both parties had a licence from the Food Controller. The claimant, who had a licence to sell, sold oil to the defendant who fraudulently stated that he too was licensed. The defendant later refused to accept delivery of the oil and, when sued, pleaded the illegality of the contract.

It was held that, despite the claimant's innocence of the defendant's position, his action failed. The Order clearly and unequivocally prohibited contracts unless both parties were licensed. The contract was void.

In contrast, in *Smith v Mawhood (1845) 14 M&W 452*, statute required amongst other things that sellers of tobacco had to be licensed. The claimant sold tobacco to the defendant although he had no licence to do so. The defendant did not pay and, when he was sued, argued that he was not liable as the contract was illegal and void because the claimant was not licensed.

It was held that the claimant succeeded in his action. The object of the statute was not to make unlicensed sales of tobacco void but rather to raise money for the state.

Again in *Archbolds (Freightage) Ltd v S Spanglett Ltd [1961] 1 QB 374*, contrary to legislation, carriers contracted to transport goods without obtaining the necessary licence for the relevant vehicle to do so. In using the vehicle for this purpose, the carriers were committing a criminal offence. The customer was unaware that the vehicle was unlicensed. The carrier failed to deliver the goods and, when the customer sued, argued that the contract was illegal and void.

It was held that the customer succeeded in his action. The purpose of the licensing requirement was to help in the administration of road transport not to prevent such contracts being made. Furthermore, the claimant was unaware of the carriers' illegal performance of the contract.

However, if the innocent party knew or knowingly participated in the illegal performance of the contract, there may be no claim allowed by the court. In *Ashmore, Benson, Pease & Co Ltd v AV Dawson Ltd [1973] 1 WLR 828*, the claimants made a contract for the defendants to transport a 25-tonne tube to a port. The lorry on which the tube was to be carried had a weight limit of 20 tonnes and it was illegal for it to carry loads in excess of this weight. The claimants' transport manager supervised the loading of the tube onto the lorry. On its journey to the port, the lorry overturned and the tube was damaged. The claimants sued for compensation.

It was held that the claimants' action failed. Their manager had participated in the illegal performance of the contract.

Some legislation actually implies that sanctions are to be imposed on the parties to the agreement but that the agreement itself remains enforceable even though it was made in breach of the statutory requirement. In the case of *Hughes v Asset Managers plc [1995] 3 All ER 669*, the Prevention of Fraud (Investments) Act 1958 required anyone dealing in securities, whether as principal or agent, to be licensed. The appellants gave the respondents, who were licensed under the Act, £3 million to invest in certain shares. A month later the value of the shares dropped and the appellants told the respondents to sell, which they did through an unlicensed dealer. The appellants lost £1 million on the transaction and sued the respondents for this sum claiming that, the sale was void as it had been made by an unlicensed dealer.

It was held that the purpose of the Act was to protect the public by imposing criminal sanctions on people who either as employee or agent dealt in securities without a licence. Its purpose was not to invalidate the deals themselves or to penalise the other parties. The contract, therefore, was not void, so the appellants lost their action.

Contracts illegal at common law

A contract to commit a crime or one which is contrary to generally accepted moral standards may be prohibited at common law and be declared illegal and void. The categories of such contracts are decided on by the judges and are based on the concept of public policy, which, as said earlier, is flexible and can change with changes in society. Judges are, however, reluctant to create new heads of public policy, generally applying existing law in this area.

Contracts which are recognised as being illegal at common law include:

Contracts to commit a crime or tort (a civil wrong)

A contract to commit a crime or tort is illegal and unenforceable.

In *Miller v Karlinsky (1945) 62 TLR 85*, the defendant employed the claimant at a weekly wage of £10 plus expenses. These expenses included the income tax payable on his wages. The defendant failed to pay and the claimant sued to recover ten weeks' wages and expenses.

It was held that the contract was illegal as it defrauded the Revenue. The claimant was not entitled to recover the wages or expenses as all these payments were tainted with the illegality of the original contract.

In *Salvesen v Simons [1994] 490 IRLR 3*, in a contract of employment, part of the employee's remuneration was paid into a partnership which in fact provided no services to the employer. When the employee was sacked, he brought this action for unfair dismissal.

The Employment Appeal Tribunal held that the arrangement could mean that the employee could set off business expenses against his salary and thus evade tax under PAYE. This was a fraud on the Revenue. The employment contract was therefore held to be illegal and void and the claimant lost his action.

If, however, the payment involves genuine and acceptable tax avoidance rather than evasion, the contract will be upheld. For example, in *Lightfoot v D & J Sporting Ltd [1996] 1 IRLR 64*, the claimant was helped in his work by his wife and it was agreed with his employers, the defendants, that over one-third of his income should be paid to his wife. This reduced the claimant's income tax and national insurance contributions. The claimant was later dismissed and both he and his wife were given P45s. When he sued in unfair dismissal, the defendants denied liability claiming that, because of the agreement relating to the wife, the contract of employment was illegal and void.

The Employment Appeal Tribunal held that this was a valid method of tax reduction which had been or would be, disclosed to the Revenue. The fact that the effect of an agreement was to reduce a person's tax liability did not of itself make the contract of employment illegal and void. The contract of employment was valid therefore the claimant could sue in unfair dismissal.

The illegality extends to any contract of indemnity for loss caused by a deliberate wrong. In *Gray v Barr [1970] 2 QB 626*, the defendant had an insurance policy covering him against liability for causing death. He shot dead his wife's lover and, when he was sued by the lover's wife who was awarded damages, he claimed indemnity under this policy. It was held that he was not entitled to indemnity as it would be against public policy to allow a person to be indemnified against the consequences of a crime they had intentionally committed. In effect, of course, this meant that the lover's wife could not obtain the damages she was awarded as the defendant had no resources.

So, as a general rule, not only is a contract to commit a crime or a tort illegal and void, so is any related civil claim. The two exceptions to this are:

- where the crime is one of strict liability (i.e. liability without proof of fault); and
- where the claim is made under a policy of motor insurance.

Contracts leading to corruption in public life

Any contract which leads to corruption in the administration of the state, such as one to buy, sell or procure a public office, favour or honour, is illegal and void and will be unenforceable.

In *Parkinson v Royal College of Ambulance [1925] KB 1*, a secretary of the defendant, a charity, promised to procure a knighthood for the claimant in return for a suitable donation. The claimant gave the charity £3,000 but when he did not receive a knighthood he sued to recover the money.

It was held that his action failed. The contract amounted to corruption in public life.

Contracts promoting sexual immorality

Even though a particular act may not be a crime or a civil wrong, if the contract under which the act was performed promotes sexual immorality, it will be contrary to public policy and therefore void.

In *Pearce v Brooks (1866) LR 1 Exch 213*, the defendant, a prostitute, hired a carriage from which, to the knowledge of the claimant's firm, she was going to ply her trade. She returned the carriage in a damaged state and the claimant sued her for the cost of hire and for compensation which was payable under the terms of the contract.

It was held that, although the contract between the parties was not of itself illegal, given that fact that the claimant knew the purpose of the hire, the whole contract was tainted with illegality. The claimant, therefore, could not recover either the hire charge or the cost of damage to the carriage.

Contracts against the interests of the state

A contract against the interests of the state, such as one with an enemy alien, is illegal and void, as are contracts in breach of a friendly country's laws. The interests of the state in these circumstances outweigh freedom of contract.

In *Foster v Driscoll [1929] KB 470*, an English partnership was formed to smuggle whisky into the USA during Prohibition. The agreement was held to be illegal and void because, as a matter of public policy, the court was not prepared to uphold a contract which was in breach of the laws of a friendly country.

Contracts prejudicial to the administration of justice

A contract not to prosecute a crime is illegal as being against the administration of justice. However, a contract not to sue for an infringement of a civil right could be enforceable. In *Fisher & Co v Apollinaris (1875) 10 Ch App 277*, for example, a contract not to bring an action for infringement of a trade mark was held to be valid and enforceable. The offence committed was private in nature and did not relate to a matter which harmed the public generally.

It follows, that if the agreement is designed to defeat a law intended to protect society generally, it could be held to be illegal and unenforceable. In *John v Mendoza [1939] 1 KB 141*, the defendant was made bankrupt owing money to the claimant and others. The defendant asked the claimant to say that the money owing to him had been given as a gift and said that, in return, he would pay the claimant in full, regardless of the claims of the other creditors. Acting on this promise, the claimant did not prove in the defendant's bankruptcy. It was later discovered that the defendant could pay in full all the creditors who had proved in the bankruptcy. He did this and the bankruptcy order was annulled. However, he did not pay the claimant who then brought this action.

It was held that the action failed. As he had not proved in the bankruptcy, the claimant had lost all rights to recover the debt. The defendant's promise to pay him in full was unenforceable as it was designed to defeat the bankruptcy laws.

The effects of illegality

The effects of illegality depend on whether the contract was either illegal as formed or illegal in the way it was performed.

Contracts which are illegal as formed

Where the actual creation of the contract is illegal, neither party can sue or be sued.

In *Re Mahmoud and Ispahani (1921)* which we dealt with earlier, the fact that the seller of the linseed oil had been misled by the buyer's false claim that he was licensed did not affect the court's decision that the contract was void, as it was in breach of the statute requiring both parties to be licensed. The seller's action against the buyer therefore failed as the contract was totally unenforceable.

Contracts which are illegal as performed

This arises where a valid, legal contract is performed by one of the parties in a way prohibited by law. In these circumstances, the party who performed the contract illegally has no rights under the contract.

In *Anderson v Daniel [1924] 1 KB 138*, in a contract for the sale of artificial fertiliser, the seller, in breach of a statutory requirement, failed to give the buyer an invoice containing information about the percentage of certain chemicals in the product. The buyer failed to pay for the goods but when the seller sued it was held that his action failed as the way in which he had performed the contract was illegal.

In these cases, the court will look at the purpose of the statute in deciding the rights of the parties to see whether the law intended to invalidate the contract as a whole or merely to penalise the conduct of the offending party. We saw in the case of *Hughes v Asset Managers plc [1995] 3 All ER 669* that it was held that the purpose of the legislation was to protect the public by imposing criminal sanctions on people who dealt in securities without a licence. The statute was not aimed at invalidating the contract itself or at penalising the parties to it other than the one who made the deal without being licensed.

For a contract which is legal as formed but illegal in its performance to be invalidated, however, the illegality must be sufficiently closely tied in with the contract. For example, in *21st Century Logistic Solutions Ltd (in liquidation) v Madysen Ltd [2004] EWHC 231*, the claimant company, which was registered for VAT in the UK, had been formed to defraud Customs and Excise by buying goods free of VAT from overseas suppliers and selling them in the UK charging VAT. The company's owner did not declare the sales. The defendants bought a consignment of goods from the company but refused to pay arguing that the sale contract was tainted with illegality and was therefore void. The claimant's liquidator sued.

It was held that the contract between the claimant and the defendants was a straightforward, lawful contract for the sale of goods which enabled the claimant's owner to commit fraud by failing to account to Customs and Excise. There was not a sufficient closeness between the claimant's fraudulent intention and the sale of goods to the defendants to taint the sale with illegality. The illegal act depended on the success of the sale of the goods but the illegal act was sufficiently separate from the contract so as not to make it illegal.

The defendants therefore had to pay for the goods which they had bought.

Recovery of money or property passed under an illegal contract

As a general rule, money paid or property transferred under an illegal contract cannot be recovered (as we saw in *Parkinson v Royal College of Ambulance*). There are, however, exceptions to this rule where property can be recovered:

- *If the transferor can make a claim for recovery without relying on the illegality.* In other words the transferor may succeed in recovering money or property if the claim can be made by relying on rights other than those in the illegal contract. In *Bowmakers Ltd v Barnet Instruments Ltd [1945] KB 65*, war-time regulations required all sellers of machine tools to be licensed. The claimants, who did not have such a licence, hired machine tools to the defendants under a hire-purchase agreement. This contract was illegal. The defendants failed to keep up with the H-P instalments and, in fact, sold some of the tools to a third party. The claimants brought this action, not on the illegal H-P contract, but in conversion, the defendants having wrongfully dealt with the claimants' property. It was held that, although the H-P agreement was illegal, the claimants' action succeeded as it was based on the ownership of the tools not on the illegal contract.
- *If the parties are not equally at fault.* If the claimant can show that, although the contract was unlawful, he had entered it because of the other's fraud, duress or undue influence, he may be able to recover his property from the defendant. For example, in *Atkinson v Denby (1861–73) All ER Rep Ext 2294* the claimant offered to pay his creditors five shillings in the pound. This was agreed by all the creditors except the defendant, who said that he would accept it only if the claimant paid him £50. The claimant, worrying that unless the

defendant was a party to the arrangement it would fail, agreed to this demand. It was held that the claimant could recover the £50 as he had been coerced into defrauding the other creditors. The £50 was then available to be distributed to the creditors generally. In *Hughes v Liverpool Victoria Legal Friendly Society [1916] 2 KB 482*, a shopkeeper took out policies with the defendants on customers who owed him money. When the shopkeeper let these policies lapse, an agent of the defendants persuaded the claimant, who had no financial interest whatsoever in the subjects of the insurance, to take over the policies. Under the Life Assurance Act 1774, it is illegal to insure the life of a person in whom you have no financial interest. It was held that, although the contract of insurance was illegal, the claimant could recover the premiums she had paid as she had been persuaded to take out the policies by the fraud of the defendants' agent.

- *If the transferor genuinely repents the illegality*. The transferor can recover property if there is genuine, rather than convenient, repentance. In *Bigos v Bousted [1944] 2 All ER 579*, in breach of the Exchange Control At 1947, the claimant agreed to give the defendant £150 of Italian currency, to be handed over to the defendant's wife and daughter in Italy, in return for payment of £150 in England. The defendant gave share certificates as security for this payment. When the claimant did not supply the Italian money, the defendant demanded the return of the share certificates which the claimant refused, instead suing to obtain the £150 which she alleged the defendant owed her. The defendant counter-claimed for the return of the certificates arguing that, although the initial contract was illegal under the 1947 Act, he had repented of the illegality. It was held that the defendant's counter-claim failed. His repentance was the result of the illegal contract failing and was not genuine. Had the Italian currency been made available in Italy he would have accepted it. His repentance, said the court, was 'but for want of power to sin'. Not only must repentance be genuine to succeed, it also has to be shown that the claimant has only partly, rather than substantially, performed the contract. In *Kearley v Thomson (1890) 24 QBD 742*, the claimant, a friend of a bankrupt, paid the defendant £40 to stay away from the friend's public examination and not to oppose discharge from bankruptcy. The defendant, who had been likely to oppose discharge, did stay away but, before an application for discharge was made, the claimant brought this action to recover his £40, claiming that he had changed his mind and repented the illegality. It was held that the claimant failed. The illegal scheme had already been substantially carried out so the repentance was too late. In contrast, in *Taylor v Bowers (1876) 1 QBD 291*, the claimant, who was being pressurised by his creditors, assigned some machinery to A in order to put it out of his creditors' reach. A sold the machinery to the defendant. When the claimant called a creditors' meeting the machinery was not shown as part of his assets. He tried to persuade them to take less than they otherwise would. The creditors refused. The claimant then brought this action to recover the machinery from the defendant. It was held that the claimant succeeded. The fact that the creditors had refused to accept his proposal meant that his fraud on them had not been carried out.

- *If the transferor belongs to a class which the statute was designed to protect*. If certain contracts are made illegal to protect a class of people, a member of that class may be able to sue on the illegal contract. In *Barclay v Pearson [1893] 2 Ch 154*, a newspaper competition was held to be illegal under the Gaming Act 1802. The Act was passed to protect people who entered lotteries against those who organised such schemes. It was held that, as the people who entered the newspaper's competition were the class of people the Act was passed to protect, they could recover their entry fee, although they could not obtain any prize money.

Void contracts

Contracts made void by statute or common law do not involve moral wrongdoing. Rather, they are made void and unenforceable on the grounds of public policy as leading to undesirable social or economic consequences. Public policy, as mentioned earlier, is a difficult and variable concept, given the fact that it can change in line with changes in social attitudes.

Contracts can be declared void by statute or at common law.

Contracts made void by statute

ANTI-COMPETITIVE CONTRACTS

An agreement which prevents, restricts or distorts competition has long been regarded as being contrary to public policy. The law is contained in the Competition Act 1988, the Enterprise Act 2002 and the Treaty on the Functioning of the EU 2009 (TFEU), Articles 101 and 102.

Under the Competition Act 1988, agreements between undertakings, decisions by associations of undertakings or concerted practices which may affect trade and have as their object or effect the prevention, restriction or distortion of trade are void unless granted exemption by the Director-General of Fair Trading or by the relevant EU body. The Act also prohibits abuse by one or more undertakings of a dominant position in a market which may affect trade in the UK. In other words, the Act applies to conduct which does or may, affect competition.

The major provisions in the Competition Act are based on the prohibitions in TFEU, Articles 101 and 102 and both sets of rules apply only where the agreement etc has an appreciable effect on competition having regard to the share of the relevant market affected (in the Competition Act – the UK; in TFEU – the EU). Arguably a share of 5% or less of the market will not be regarded as appreciable, so the majority of the cases held void at common law, which we will deal with later, will not have a sufficiently appreciable effect to be prohibited by the legislation. in other words, the legislation is concerned with the economy as a whole, whereas the common law rules are concerned with relationships between parties and with activities which have an effect only between those parties.

A party who is affected by an anti-competitive practice may complain to the Office of Fair Trading or, if there is an EU dimension, to the EU Commission. If there is a finding against the offending body, this body will be subjected to a fine of up to 10% of its UK turnover. To recover compensation for any loss caused by the anti-competitive activity, however, the action must be brought in the courts. In practice, a party who has suffered loss will wait for the OFT to investigate and make a finding of infringement and then bring their claim to court, relying on this finding. This will mean that they will not have to bring their own evidence to show infringement but will rather rely on the OFT report. This is known as a 'piggyback' claim and was introduced in the Enterprise Act 2002. The 2002 Act also extended the jurisdiction of the Competition Appeals Tribunal to permit it to rule on actions for damages based on a competition infringement decision by the OFT or the EU Commission. This innovation was designed to deal with the fact that some ordinary courts are unfamiliar with competition issues and that this may cause difficulties in assessing causation and quantification of damages.

The Enterprise Act also created a criminal offence for people engaged in cartels and who dishonestly engage in such prohibited activities as price-fixing or limiting supply or production. For conviction on trial by indictment the sentence is a maximum of five years' imprisonment and/or an unlimited fine.

Contracts void at common law

Contracts to oust the jurisdiction of the courts

A contractual provision to remove the right of one or both of the parties to bring an action in court is void.

In *Baker v Jones [1954] 1 WLR 1005*, the rules of the British Amateur Weightlifters' Association stated that the only body with the power to interpret its rules was the Central Council of the Association, whose decisions would be final.

It was held that this provision tried to oust the jurisdiction of the courts and was therefore against public policy and void.

A provision which requires the parties to go to arbitration before going to court, however, is valid. The Arbitration Act 1996, governing this area of the law, allows an appeal to the court from an arbitration where there was some material irregularity affecting the tribunal, the arbitration proceedings or the award. A material irregularity is something that will cause substantial injustice to the applicant (e.g. where the tribunal acts outside its powers or does not deal with relevant issues).

There is also an appeal to the courts on a question of law arising out of an arbitration award, provided all the parties to the action agree or leave to appeal is granted by the court. The parties, however, may expressly agree to exclude the court's jurisdiction in these circumstances.

For any appeal to the court, available appeals and reviews within the arbitration process itself must have been exhausted.

12 – Contracts in restraint of trade

A clause or term in an agreement restricting a person's freedom of contract to carry on in the future any trade or business that person wishes, may fall within the doctrine of restraint of trade. Such clauses, known as covenants, are found mainly in:

- contracts of employment
- contracts for the sale of a business
- exclusive trading contracts (*solus* agreements).

These covenants are dealt with by the courts on the basis of public policy and their effect, therefore, has altered over time. For example, in the eighteenth century, general restraints (covering the whole of the UK) were void, but reasonable partial restraints (covering specific areas of the country) could be upheld. A judge said: 'What does it signify to a tradesman in London what another does in Newcastle?' In other words, at that time, given the fact that transport and communications between the various parts of the UK were poor, an attempt to stop someone trading anywhere in the country would be far wider than necessary to give the covenantee (the person in whose favour the covenant was given) genuine protection.

As communications improved, however, the courts adapted the policy and removed the distinction between general and partial restraints. The position now is that all restraints of trade are *prima facie* (on the face of it) void but will be allowed if they can be justified as reasonable. In other words, it is in the interests of the public that there should, in general, be no restrictions on employment or trade. Even though the parties have agreed on the restraint the court will treat it as void unless it can be shown to be reasonable in the interests of the parties and in the public interest.

The courts, of course, will deal with the issue only if the covenantor (the ex-employee or the seller of the business) breaks the promise. In these circumstances, the burden of proving that the restriction is reasonable lies on the covenantee (the ex-employer or the buyer of the business to whom the promise was given). It is up to the covenantor to show that the promise was unreasonable in the public interest.

Restrictions in contracts of employment

Here, employees covenant that, after leaving the employment, they will not compete with their former employer either by working for a competitor of this employer or by setting up a similar business of their own. As with all restraints of trade, such a covenant is *prima facie* void, but it can be upheld if it can be justified as reasonable. It has to be shown that:

- the former employer had an interest worthy of protection;
- the restraint is no wider than necessary to protect this valid interest; and
- the restriction is not against the public interest.

It is more difficult to show that a restriction in a contract of employment is reasonable than it is to show reasonableness in a contract for the sale of a business. This is because, in the latter situation, the parties are in a more equal bargaining position than in employment contracts where unfair terms can be imposed on an individual by a more powerful employer. Also, if a restriction bound an employee, the employer would be put in an unfairly advantageous position in relation to salary negotiation or disputes over working conditions. The employee would not have the choice of changing employment. In relation to sales of a business, the buyer will usually have paid for the goodwill and so, if the seller were to set up an identical business nearby, the buyer would lose part of what he paid for. Were such clauses not allowed it would be difficult for people to sell their business.

The courts, therefore, are more stringent in their approach to covenants in contracts of employment.

To enforce a restrictive covenant in an employment contract, as stated above, it has to be shown that the following apply.

Interest worthy of protection

An employer cannot protect himself from competition from a former employee, nor can he prevent this employee from using the skills obtained in his employment. The employer has to show that the employee has obtained some proprietary interest belonging to the employer such as trade secrets or influence over clients. In *Herbert Morris Ltd v Saxelby [1916] 1 AC 688*, the defendant had spent all his life working for the claimants, manufacturers of hoisting machinery in the UK. A clause in his contract of employment prevented him from working in a similar business in the UK or Ireland for seven years after leaving the claimants' employment. It was held that this clause was void. The defendant was not in possession of any trade secrets or influence over clients and if the clause was upheld it would mean that the employee would be forced to work and use the skills developed in his employment exclusively for the benefit of the employer. An employee cannot be prevented from using his skills elsewhere. Again, in *Leng & Co Ltd v Andrews [1909] 1 Ch 763*, in a journalist's contract of employment he covenanted not to work for another newspaper within 20 miles of the employer's business as the employers wanted to protect their 'sources of information'. It was held that this was not an interest worthy of protection. However, in *Forster & Sons Ltd v Suggett (1918) 35 TLR 87*, the defendant, who had been employed by the claimants, manufacturers of glass and glass bottles, had been instructed in certain secret manufacturing processes. In his contract of employment, the claimant covenanted that, for five years after leaving his employment, he would not carry on or be interested in the manufacture of glass bottles or any other business relating to glass making as carried on by the claimants. The restriction covered the whole of the UK. It was held that the claimants had trade secrets which were interests worthy of protection. The employee had acquired substantial knowledge of these, so the restriction was reasonable and the claimants could stop the defendant competing with them.

An employer is also entitled to protection from having his customers or clients enticed away from him by employees where the employees had the opportunity to become closely acquainted with these customers in such a way that they were able to exert influence over them. In *Home Counties Dairies Ltd v Skilton [1970] 1 All ER 1227*, in his contract of employment the defendant milkman covenanted that, for one year after leaving the claimants' employment, he would not serve or sell milk or dairy produce to anyone who had been a customer of the claimants during the six months preceding the termination of his employment. The employee left his job and started working for one of the claimants' competitors, following the same milk round he had previously worked. It was held that the claimant had an interest worthy of protection in that the defendant had influence over and could solicit their customers. The one-year duration was a reasonable time. The claimants were granted an injunction to stop the defendant working for their competitors.

The restriction must be no wider than necessary to protect the employer's interests

Excessive area

If the area is excessive then there is a strong inference that the covenant is unreasonable. The excessiveness or otherwise of the area covered is a question of fact depending on the surrounding circumstance. In *Empire Meat Co Ltd v Patrick [1939] 2 All ER 85*, the employee of a retail butcher covenanted in his contract of employment that, on leaving his job, he would not be employed in or carry on the business of, retail butchery within five miles of his employers' place of business. It was held that this was too wide a restriction as the employers' trade was drawn from a much smaller area. The restraint, therefore, was void. Again, in *Mason v Provident Clothing & Supply Co Ltd [1913] AC 724*, an agent, who was employed to canvass for orders in the Islington area of London, was restricted from working in a similar business within 25 miles of London. It was held that, as the area of restraint was 1,000 times larger than the area of employment this restriction was unreasonable and void.

However, in *Fitch v Dewes [1921] 2 AC 158*, a solicitor's managing clerk in Tamworth, who had acquired influence over the solicitor's clients, was restricted from working in a similar business within seven miles of Tamworth town hall after leaving the solicitor's employment. This was held to be reasonable, as the solicitor's clients were drawn from a wide area around Tamworth. In *Littlewoods Organisation Ltd v Harris [1978] 1 All ER 1026*, the defendant, a divisional director of the claimants, a mail-order business, covenanted in his contract of employment that, for 12 months after leaving his job, he would not work for Great Universal Stores (GUS), Littlewoods' main competitor. In the course of his employment, the defendant gained detailed knowledge of Littlewoods' bi-annual catalogue, such a document being vital to the success of a mail-order business. The defendant left Littlewoods and, within 12 months, took up a post with GUS. Littlewoods sued to obtain an injunction to stop him taking up this job. It was held that Littlewoods had an interest worthy of protection, the contents of the catalogue being a trade secret. The 12-month period of restraint was reasonable. However, as the restraint referred to the defendant working for GUS without any territorial limit, it was held that this was too wide. Littlewoods' business was limited to the UK, whereas GUS had a world-wide operation. The court decided that the covenant could be construed as covering only GUS's mail-order business in the UK and could be enforced by injunction to that extent.

Reasonable duration

A restriction must be reasonable in duration. In *Fitch v Dewes*, no limit on the restriction was mentioned in the covenant so this was interpreted as being life-long. It was held that this was reasonable as a solicitor's clients tended to be life-long. Again it is a question of fact in each case. It depends on the nature of the business as to whether or not the length of time the restraint is to operate is reasonable.

The restriction must not be unreasonable in the public interest

This is a question for the judge to decide. It will depend on matters such as the work in which the employee is engaged and the judge's perception of its value to society. In *Hensman v Traill (1980) 124 SJ 776*, a doctor who was a partner in a general practice, was restricted for five years after leaving the practice from engaging in similar work within a seven-mile radius of the original practice. It was held that the restriction was too wide and that it was against the public interest to deprive the community of the services of this doctor.

The interpretation of what is meant by the public interest can sometimes be difficult to justify. In *Wyatt v Kreglinger and Fernau [1933] 1 KB 793*, a wool broker retired and was given a pension by his former employers, the defendants, conditional on him not re-entering the wool trade or doing anything detrimental to the defendants. The pension was paid for nine years but the defendants then stopped paying it. The broker sued in breach of contract. It was held that the claimant failed in his action. The restriction was too wide and it was against the public interest to deprive society of the services of an experienced wool tester. The claimant therefore lost his pension.

The courts will not uphold indirect means used to restrain employees from carrying out their trade as they wish

In *Kores Manufacturing Co Ltd v Kolok Manufacturing Co Ltd [1959] Ch 108*, the parties to the action both manufactured the same products and occupied adjoining premises. They made an agreement that neither would, without the other's consent, 'at any time employ any person who during the past five years shall have been a servant of yours'. The claimants' chief chemist wanted to move into the defendants' employment but the claimant refused to consent and brought this action for an injunction to stop breach of the agreement. It was held that the action failed. It was unreasonable in that it was in excess of what was necessary to protect the parties. This indirect approach to try to restrain employees was invalid and the contract was void.

Restrictions imposed on the sale of a business

The courts are more willing to allow these restrictions as the parties are dealing on a more equal footing that they are in contracts of employment. To be valid, however, these restraints must still satisfy the same requirements as those in contracts of employment.

There must be an interest worthy of protection

The main interest worthy of protection in these cases will be where the seller has sold the goodwill in the business in question. In these circumstances it would be reasonable for a person who has bought a business, together with its goodwill, to be allowed to stop the seller from setting up a similar business in the vicinity and thus negate the benefit of paying for the goodwill. Without such a restriction, sales of businesses would be difficult. There must, however, be a genuine sale of the business and of the goodwill. The restriction must be more than merely a bare attempt to prevent competition. In *Vancouver Malt and Sake Brewing Co Ltd v Vancouver Breweries Ltd [1934] AC 181*, the appellants had a licence permitting them to brew beer on their premises, although in practice they never did. Their product was sake. The respondents also held a beer brewing licence and did brew beer from their premises. The appellants sold the goodwill of their business, other than in relation to sake, to the respondents and undertook not to brew beer for 15 years. It was held that, as the appellants had never brewed beer, they had no goodwill to sell. The restriction amounted merely to an agreement not to compete and was therefore illegal and void. Furthermore, the restriction must be no wider than necessary for protection. In *British Reinforced Concrete Engineering Co Ltd v Schelff [1921] 2 Ch 563*, the defendants sold their business of manufacturing and selling 'Loop' road reinforcements. There were several other types of road reinforcement on the market. In the contract of sale, the defendants undertook not to compete with the claimants in the manufacture or sale of any road reinforcements. They broke this agreement. It was held that, as the defendants had sold only the 'Loop' reinforcement business, the claimants were entitled to protection for this business alone. The restriction was much wider than was necessary for protection and was therefore void.

THE RESTRICTION MUST BE REASONABLE IN AREA AND DURATION

In *Nordenfelt v Maxim Nordenfelt Guns and Ammunition Co Ltd [1894] AC 535*, N had a worldwide business for the manufacture and sale of guns and ammunition. When he sold the business he covenanted that, for 25 years, he would not, except on behalf of the purchasing company, '... engage ... either directly or indirectly in the trade or business of a manufacturer of guns, gun mountings or carriages, gunpowder, explosives or ammunition or in any business competing or liable to compete in any way with that for the time being carried on by the company'. The restriction was worldwide. It was held that the worldwide restraint was valid as N had sold a worldwide business. However, the phrase '... or in any business competing or liable to compete in any way with that for the time being carried on by the company' was too wide. If the company decided to diversify from the manufacture of military hardware into a completely different area of work, N would have been prevented from competing here too. The company had only paid for the business and goodwill of the military hardware business. This clause was severed from the contract, but the rest were upheld.

THE RESTRICTION MUST NOT BE UNREASONABLE IN THE PUBLIC INTEREST

In *Nordenfelt*, it was held that the restraint was reasonable in the public interest as it retained a very important business for the UK.

Solus agreements

These are agreements between a supplier and a retailer whereby the retailer agrees to sell only the products of the supplier in return for the supplier giving some benefit such as a reduction in the price charged for the goods. They may also be part of a mortgage or lease. For example, an oil company may give a loan to a garage to enable that garage to improve its facilities taking a mortgage over the garage premises and making it a condition of the mortgage that the garage will sell only the oil company's petrol until the loan has been repaid.

As these are limitations on freedom of contract they are *prima facie* void and, if one of the parties wishes to enforce the undertaking he will have to show that there is an interest worthy of protection, that the restriction is reasonable and that it is not against the public interest.

In *Petrofina (GB) Ltd v Martin [1966] Ch 14*, the defendant agreed that, for 12 years, he would sell only Petrofina petrol, in return for which Petrofina gave him a discount on the price of the fuel. The defendant also agreed that, if he sold the business he would make the sale conditional on the buyer entering a similar agreement with Petrofina. The defendant broke the agreement and started selling other companies' petrol. Petrofina brought this action to obtain an injunction to prevent further breaches.

It was held that the action failed as the agreement could not be justified. The defendant's obligation to sell the business only to a person who would enter a similar *solus* agreement with Petrofina was unreasonable as it would make the garage business unsaleable. Also, the 12-year period for which the agreement was to run was unreasonably long.

This area of law was reviewed in *Esso Petroleum Co Ltd v Harper's Garage (Stourport) Ltd [1968] AC 269*. The defendants owned and operated two garages. It entered into two *solus* agreements with Esso. The agreement relating to the first garage was to last for 4 years 5 months and that relating to the other for 21 years. In return for these agreements, the defendants were given a rebate on the price of the petrol. After a time, the defendants attempted to break the agreement as they found that they could get a greater discount from other suppliers. Esso sued.

The House of Lords held that the agreements were within the doctrine of restraint of trade and so were *prima facie* void unless justified as reasonable. The 4 years 5 months was held to be reasonable, the 21-year restraint was unreasonable and void. The court accepted that the oil company had an interest worthy of protection in that the *solus* agreement secured their presence in the area and gave them guaranteed outlets for their petrol. It also enabled them to plan their production more efficiently.

The court also said that, in deciding the reasonableness of such agreements, the public, rather than the parties', interest was the soundest basis for making a decision. Both parties, being in business, had negotiated from a position of relatively equal bargaining strength. The agreement must have suited both parties when it was negotiated and it was only when, later, the garage discovered it could obtain better discounts elsewhere that it tried to break the contract.

In giving its judgment, the Lords referred to a report on *solus* agreements by the Monopolies and Mergers Commission in 1965. The report had recommended that a *solus* tie for a maximum of five years benefited the public in that, amongst other things, it kept prices down. Any longer than five years, however, took the agreement beyond what was reasonably foreseeable in the industry.

The court also said that the doctrine of restraint in these cases applied only where, as in the *Esso* case, there was an agreement to give up an existing right or freedom to trade. However, if a retailer takes on a limited right where none existed before, the *solus* tie will be valid. In other words, if a person buys a business which is already subject to a *solus* tie, that tie will be valid, but if a person who is already trading limits his freedom by entering into a *solus* agreement, that tie will be *prima facie* void.

An attempt to use this distinction to validate a restrictive covenant was made in *Alec Lobb (Garages) Ltd v Total Oil Great Britain Ltd [1985] 1 WLR 173*. In this case, Alec Lobb garages were in financial difficulties so, in 1969, they leased their garage to the defendants for 51 years at a premium of £35,000. Total then granted a sub-lease to Alec Lobb for 21 years at a low rental, with a mutual right to end the lease at seven and then 14 years. The sub-lease contained a *solus* agreement requiring the garage to sell only Total petrol. In 1979, Alec Lobb sued to have the lease set aside, arguing that the *solus* agreement was an unreasonable restraint of trade and was therefore void.

Total argued that, once the garage had been leased to them, Alec Lobb had no interest in it. When the garage took on the sub-lease, they were acquiring a limited right where none had existed before. The *solus* agreement should be held to be valid as being outside the doctrine of restraint of trade.

The court, however, relied on the decision in *Amoco Australia Pty Ltd v Rocca Bros Motor Engineering Co Pty Ltd [1975] AC 561* in which the Privy Council stated that a lease and leaseback were a single transaction. Therefore, in the *Alec Lobb* case, the court looked at the transaction as a whole and held that the lease and leaseback were part of one deal. Alec Lobb was giving up an existing freedom and so the *solus* tie was subject to the doctrine of restraint and had to be justified as reasonable if it was to be enforced. The claimants also argued that the agreement should be set aside as an unconscionable bargain.

It was held that the agreement was reasonable in the parties' interests in that it had released Alec Lobb from financial difficulties and had benefited the company by giving it £35,000 which was good consideration for the promise. The fact that there were mutual break clauses in the contract showed that the garage had not been subjected to unfair pressure. The agreement was also in the interests of the public in that it kept the garage in business and trading as a petrol station.

The *solus* agreement, therefore, was held to be valid and binding and Alec Lobb lost its action.

Restraint of trade in other contracts

The doctrine of restraint applies to all businesses which, for example, have exclusive dealing arrangements.

In *Schroeder Music Publishing Co Ltd v Macauley [1974] 1 WLR 1308*, Macauley, a young songwriter signed a five-year contract with Schroeder whereby he gave Schroeder full and exclusive world copyright in all his music for the period of the contract. Macauley was to receive royalties on any of his compositions which Schroeder exploited, but Schroeder was under no obligation to publish or promote any of his work. If Macauley's royalties exceeded £5,000 the contract was to be automatically extended for a further five years. Schroeder was free to terminate the contract at any time by giving one month's notice but Macauley had no such right. Macauley asked the court to declare the contract void.

It was held that the contract fell within the doctrine of restraint and so had to be justified as reasonable. The parties were not dealing on an equal footing and the contract was so heavily weighted in Schroeder's favour that it was unreasonable and void. Macauley had to transfer all his rights in his music to Schroeder, but they had given no obligation in return, nor did they have to provide Macauley with any remuneration or give him any other rights. The fact that this type of contract was standard in the music industry did not prevent it from being held void when the parties were negotiating on such obviously unequal terms. Its effect was potentially to prevent a person earning a living and giving the public the benefit of his abilities.

In relation to commercial agents, the Commercial Agents Regulations 1993 (SI 1993/3053) deal with restrictive clauses in that they limit the use of such clauses to the geographical area and/or the group of customers and the type of goods which are covered in the agency contract. They also limit the duration of such clauses to two years after the ending of the agreement. Furthermore, the Regulations provide that, in their implementation, enactments and rules of law are preserved so, it would seem, the restriction must also be reasonable as between the parties to the contract as required by the common law.

The effects of a covenant in restraint of trade

If a covenant in restraint of trade cannot be justified as being reasonable between the parties or not unreasonable in the public interest or if there is no interest worthy of protection, it will be declared void.

If the entire contract is based on the void restriction, the whole contract will fail. In *Wyatt v Kreglinger and Fernau* the entire contract was based on the claimant's promise not to engage in the wool testing business in return for a pension. This restriction was held to be against the public interest in that it deprived society of the services of an experienced wool tester. Therefore, the whole contract was held void and the claimant lost his action to enforce the payment to him of a pension.

If, however, the offending restrictive covenant is only part of the contract and if it is possible to remove it without affecting the contract as a whole, the court may sever the offending clause, leaving the rest of the contract enforceable. In deciding whether such severance is possible, the courts use what is sometimes called the 'blue pencil test' – can a line be drawn through the offending part without altering the basic contract? If it can, the offending clause will be struck out but the rest of the contract will stand.

For example, in *Nordenfelt v Maxim Nordenfelt Guns and Ammunition* (see above), the restriction imposed on Nordenfelt in the contract for the sale of his business tried to prevent him from carrying on any business relating to guns and similar matters and also to '... any business competing or liable to compete ... with that for the time being carried on by the company'. The restriction relating to guns etc. was valid as this was the business the company had bought. The end of the clause, relating to 'any other business' however, was held void and was severed from the contract. It did not affect the contract as a whole.

If, however, such severance is not possible, the whole contract has to fail. In *Attwood v Lamont [1920] 3 KB 571*, the claimants owned a department store in Kidderminster. The business of the store included tailoring, outfitting and drapery. The defendant was the head cutter and manager of the tailoring department. In his contract of employment, he covenanted that, on leaving his employment, he would not at any time carry on the trade of tailor, dressmaker, general draper, milliner, hatter, haberdasher or outfitter within ten miles of Kidderminster. The list of forbidden occupations covered the whole of the claimant's business.

The court held that this was a single indivisible covenant intended to prevent any competition. The covenant was too wide and was therefore void. The claimants asked the court to sever all but the reference to tailoring but the court refused to do so as such severance would alter the effect of the contract. The whole covenant was void.

As a general rule, the courts will not rewrite a covenant to make it reasonable. So, in *Mason v Provident Clothing and Supply Co Ltd*, the court refused to substitute the words 'in Islington' for the phrase 'within 25 miles of London' to make the restriction valid.

In some cases, however, the courts have been more flexible in their approach to restraint clauses. In *Goldsoll v Goldman [1915] 1 Ch 292*, the defendant sold the claimant his business dealing in imitation jewellery in the UK. In the sale contract, the defendant covenanted that, for two years, he would not deal in real or imitation jewellery in the UK, France, the USA or Spain or within 25 miles of Potsdammerstrasse, Berlin or St Stephens Kirche, Vienna.

The court held that the reference to real jewellery and to places other than the UK should be struck out and the remaining part of the covenant enforced.

It is difficult to reconcile this case with *Attwood v Lamont*. One point of distinction is that Attwood related to an employee covenant, which the law treats quite stringently, whereas *Goldsoll*, being a contract for the sale of a business, was dealt with more flexibly.

In practical terms, clauses in restraint of trade, whether in employment contracts or contracts between businesses, should be drafted carefully to ensure that they are reasonable in both parties' interests and are a genuine and acceptable attempt to protect trade secrets and/or influence over clients, or, in the case of a the sale of a business, to represent the goodwill that has been sold.

Attempts merely to stop competition will not be acceptable to the courts and will be struck out.

13 – Discharge of the contract

Discharge of a contract means that the contract has ended. This can happen in four ways:

- by performance
- by agreement
- by condition subsequent
- by breach.

Discharge by performance

A contract is discharged when both parties have completed their side of the bargain. For example, a contract for the sale of a car will be discharged by performance when:

- the car has been handed over and complies in all respects with the terms of the agreement; and
- the buyer has paid the agreed price.

If the car has a faulty engine, the seller will not have fully performed their obligations and therefore the contract has not been discharged. The buyer's right to sue under the contract remains.

In other words, as a general rule, for a contract to be discharged by performance, the performance must be precisely and exactly as required by the contract.

In *Sumpter v Hedges [1898] 1 QB 673*, the claimant was a builder who contracted to construct two buildings for the defendant for £565. He did work to the value of £333 but then abandoned the project. The defendant had to complete the work himself which he did using some of the materials the builder had left on the site. The builder brought this action claiming payment for the work he had actually done.

It was held that the builder was not entitled to be paid for the work he had done as he had not precisely and exactly performed what he had contracted to perform. The defendant had had no choice but to accept this partial performance. The unfinished building was of no use to him and he was under no obligation to keep it in this state. He had no choice but to accept the partial work. However, he had had a free choice whether or not to use the materials the builder had left on the site, so he had to pay the builder for these.

There are, however, circumstances in which a person who has only partly performed his side of the bargain may nevertheless obtain discharge from further liability and/or claim rights under the contract. These circumstances can arise as detailed below.

There is voluntary acceptance of partial performance

As we saw in *Sumpter v Hedges*, the defendant had no choice but to accept the partial performance but he could choose whether or not to use the materials left on the site by the builder.

Where the contract is divisible

For example, where the contract provides for delivery of goods in instalments and payment is to be made on delivery of each instalment. In this case, the buyer will have to pay for the instalments delivered even though the seller later defaults and does not deliver the full amount agreed in the contract.

One of the parties is responsible for preventing the other from fully completing the contract

In *Planche v Colburn (1831) 8 Bing 14*, the claimant contracted to write a book for a series to be published by the defendant. He was to be paid £100 on completion of the book. After the claimant had undertaken research and had written part of the book, the defendant told him that the series had been discontinued and the book was no longer needed.

It was held that the defendant had prevented the claimant from fully completing his side of the contract therefore the claimant was entitled to reasonable remuneration for the amount of work he had undertaken. The court assessed the award to be made on a *quantum meruit* basis (i.e. 'how much is it worth?'). This amounted to a quasi-contractual claim, operating independently of the original contract.

Where there has been substantial performance

In these circumstances, the other party has to pay the agreed contractual amount less the cost of putting right the faulty work. In *Hoenig v Isaacs [1952] 1 All ER 176*, an interior decorator was employed to decorate and furnish the client's flat for £750. When the work was finished there were slight defects, costing £55 to put right. The client refused to pay.

It was held that, as the decorator had substantially performed the contract, he was entitled to full payment less the cost of remedying the defect.

In deciding whether or not there has been substantial performance, the court will look not only at the cost of the defects but also at their nature. In *Bolton v Mahadeva [1972] 2 All ER 1322*, the claimant contracted to install a central heating system in the defendant's house for £560. After the system had been installed it was found that it emitted 10% less heat than it should have and that a defective flue had caused fumes to come into the living room. These defects could be put right for £174. The defendant refused to pay.

It was held that the claimant was not entitled to recover his fee. The defects were too serious for him to be able to claim substantial performance.

Discharge by agreement

In effect, this discharges one contract by replacing it with another. Such discharge can be either bilateral or unilateral.

Bilateral discharge

If a contract is made by agreement it can also be ended by agreement, such an agreement being itself a binding contract. This will occur where the contract is wholly or partly executory (i.e. yet be to be performed) on both sides.

The discharge can take one of three forms:

- termination of the original contract – the consideration of each of the parties is to release the other from their contractual obligations;
- termination of the original contract and substitution of a new agreement – again, the release of each other and the acceptance of the new agreement provides consideration; and
- variation of the original contract – each party provides consideration by agreeing to the variation.

Unilateral discharge

Where the contract has been wholly performed by one of the parties, any release of the other has to be:

- by deed; or
- supported by fresh consideration (i.e. by showing accord (agreement) and satisfaction (fresh consideration)).

Discharge by agreement may take any form unless the original agreement had to be in, or evidenced in, writing. The variation must then be in that form. A contract can be discharged by deed without the need for consideration.

Discharge by condition subsequent

A contract may provide for its own discharge on the happening of a particular event. For example, a contract of employment may be ended by either the employer or the employee giving the agreed notice. A lease of property may be ended by notice.

In *Head v Tattersall (1871) LR 7 Exch 7*, the claimant bought and paid for a horse from the defendant. The horse was 'guaranteed to have hunted with the

Bicester hounds' and there was an understanding that the claimant could return it by the following Wednesday if it did not conform to the description. Before the end of this period and through no fault of the claimant, the horse was injured. It was then discovered that it had never hunted with the Bicester hounds. The claimant returned the horse and claimed to recover the purchase price.

It was held that the claimant succeeded in his action. The option to return the horse was a condition subsequent. It made no difference that the horse was injured.

Discharge by frustration

Discharge by frustration occurs when further performance of the contract becomes impossible or is deprived of its commercial purpose, by an event which is beyond the control of either party. A contract can be frustrated in a number of ways.

Personal incapacity

In *Condor v Barron Knights [1966] 1 WLR 87*, the claimant was a drummer with the defendant pop group with whom he had a contract to work seven nights a week when work was available. After an illness, the claimant was told by his doctors that he should work a maximum of only four nights a week. The defendants, therefore, had to find a replacement who could work as many nights as required. The claimant was dismissed from the group. He sued in breach of contract.

It was held that the action failed. The contract was one of personal services and, as the claimant's illness meant that he could not fulfil his obligations, the contract was frustrated.

The incapacity of one of the parties, however, must mean that further performance of the contract is not possible. So, in *Storey v Fulham Steel Works (1907) 24 TLR 89*, it was held that the claimant's six months of illness in a five-year contract was not sufficient to frustrate the contract.

If the contract is not of a personal nature, death or incapacity of one of the parties will not frustrate it. In *Phillips v Alhambra Palace Co [1901] 1 KB 59*, a troupe of performers was engaged to appear at a music hall by one of the partners in the defendant firm. Before the date of the performance, however, the partner who had made the appointment, died. The remaining partners claimed that this frustrated the contract. It was held that the contract with the performers was not of a personal nature with the dead partner and so it was not frustrated.

Destruction of subject matter

In *Taylor v Caldwell (1863) 3 B & S 826*, the defendant hired out a music hall to the claimant for a series of concerts. Six days before the first concert the music hall burnt down. The claimant sued for the costs of advertising and other expenses incurred in promoting the concerts. It was held that the destruction of the subject matter of the contract meant that the contract was frustrated. The defendant was not liable to pay any of the claimant's expenses.

Non-occurrence of an event

In *Krell v Henry [1903] 2 KB 740*, a contract for the hire of a room overlooking Edward VII's coronation procession's route was held to be frustrated when the coronation was cancelled because the King had developed appendicitis. Although, as the claimant argued, the room could still be used, the whole purpose of the contract was to view the coronation procession and this was not now possible.

If, however, the agreement does not depend exclusively on the event which does not occur, the contract will not be frustrated. In *Herne Bay Steamboat Co v Hutton [1903] 2 KB 123*, the claimant hired a boat from the defendant to take paying passengers around the fleet which had assembled at Spithead for a royal review following Edward VII's coronation. The purpose of the hire was to enable people to look at the fleet and to see the King reviewing it. The fleet assembled before the review was cancelled because of the King's appendicitis. Because of the cancellation, the defendant argued that the contract for the hire of the boat was frustrated. This argument was rejected by the court. The boat could still have been used to take passengers around the fleet. The contract did not depend exclusively on the King's review.

A change in the law

In *Metropolitan Water Board v Dick Kerr & Co [1918] AC 119*, the defendants were constructing a reservoir for the claimants but had to stop when, under emergency wartime powers, the government banned construction work. It was held that the contract was frustrated.

However, this supervening illegality must affect the contract in a fundamental way. In *Tamplin (FA) Steamship Co Ltd v Anglo-American Petroleum Products Co Ltd [1916] 2 AC 397*, a ship was chartered for five years from December 1912. In 1915, the government requisitioned the vessel to be used as a troop carrier. The government paid compensation for this requisition and both the owner and charterer wanted to be able to claim this money. The owners argued that the contract was frustrated and that the ship had to be returned to them, whereas the charterers argued that, as they were willing to keep paying the agreed hire charge, the charter should be regarded as continuing.

It was held by the House of Lords that the requisition of the ship did not amount to frustration of the charter party. In view of the time still left to run on the contract and the possibility that there could be many months after the requisition ended during which the ship could be used, the interruption was not enough to frustrate the charter.

An inordinate and unexpected delay

In *The Evia (No. 2) [1983] 1 AC 736*, in November 1979 the claimants, ship owners, chartered a ship to the defendants for 18 months. In September 1980 the ship unloaded its cargo in Basra, Iraq but then the Iran–Iraq war broke out and the Shatt-al-Arab waterway, leading from Basra to the sea was closed. This meant that the ship was trapped and it was still trapped in 1982 when the claimants sued the defendants for breach of the charter party.

The House of Lords held that this inordinate and unexpected delay, not caused by the fault of either party, had frustrated the contract so the defendant was not liable.

Again, in *Jackson v Union Marine Insurance Co Ltd (1874) LR 10 CP 125*, the contract was frustrated when a ship, chartered by the defendants to sail from Liverpool to San Francisco, ran aground shortly after leaving Liverpool and took over eight months to be re-floated and repaired. The length of time meant that the contract was frustrated in the commercial sense.

In certain circumstances, however, a contract will not be frustrated despite what has happened. This can happen in the following circumstances.

Substitute performance is possible

In *Tsakiroglou & Co Ltd v Noblee Thorl GmbH [1962] AC 93*, the claimants bought a consignment of groundnuts from the defendants who were to ship them from Port Sudan to Hamburg. Although both parties contemplated that the ship would use the Suez Canal this was not a term, either express or implied, in the contract. When the Egyptian Government closed the canal, the sellers did not deliver the groundnuts, claiming that the contract had been frustrated by this closure.

It was held that the contract had not been frustrated. The goods could have still been shipped to Hamburg via the Cape of Good Hope. Given the fact that the contract did not require shipment through the canal and that the groundnuts would not have deteriorated on the longer journey, the contract was still viable and therefore the sellers were liable in breach of contract.

Less commercially viable

In *British Movietone News v London and District Cinemas [1952] AC 166*, the parties made a contract for the claimants to supply newsreels to the defendants' cinemas. These were very popular with the public as they were the only source of visual information about the progress of the war between 1939 and 1945. When the war ended, the newsreels became much less popular and the defendant argued that, as there was no longer a need for them, the contract was frustrated.

It was held that the fact that the contract was no longer commercially viable was not enough to frustrate it. The defendants remained bound by their obligations.

Self-induced frustration

Parties cannot argue frustration if they were responsible for the event which prevented performance of the contract or which deprived it of its commercial purpose.

In *Maritime National Fish Ltd v Ocean Trawlers Ltd [1935] AC 524*, the ship which Maritime chartered from Ocean Trawlers could be used only with an otter trawl. It was an offence to use such a trawl without a government licence. Maritime was granted three licences which it used for three other ships. Because of this, Maritime could not use the ship it had chartered from Ocean Trawlers and argued that the contract was frustrated.

It was held that as Maritime had freely chosen not to licence Ocean Trawlers's ship, their inability to use it was a direct result of their own act. The contract could not be held to be frustrated and Maritime was liable to pay the charter fees.

Foreseeable circumstances

In *Amalgamated Investment and Property Co Ltd v John Walker and Sons Ltd [1976] 3 All ER 509*, the purchasers were negotiating to buy a warehouse from the sellers who knew that the purchasers intended to develop the property and that planning permission would be needed. The purchasers asked the sellers if the property was of any special historical or architectural interest and the sellers, speaking honestly, said that it was not. Unknown to both parties, however, the Department of the Environment planned to list the building. On 26 September, the purchasers contracted to buy the building for £1.7 million. On 27 September, the warehouse was made a listed building and its value dropped to £210,000. The purchasers refused to complete the transaction. The sellers sued.

The purchasers' argument that there had been a common mistake was rejected. There was no mistake as to the nature of the building at the time of the contract. In the alternative, the purchasers claimed that the contract had been frustrated. This argument also failed as both parties were aware that the building was at risk of being listed. The purchaser had to pay the price agreed in the contract.

Express provision for the frustrating event

In this case the contract will not be frustrated when that event occurs. This will not apply if the supervening event is illegality.

The effects of frustration

Until 1943, when a contract was frustrated, the consequences were covered by the common law and 'loss lay where it fell'. In other words, money already paid could not be recovered unless there was a total failure of consideration. There was no remedy where the failure of the consideration was only partial nor was there compensation for a party which had incurred expenses in reliance on the contract before the frustration occurred.

Because of these limitations, the Law Reform (Frustrated Contracts) Act 1943 was passed to deal with the effects of frustration. The Act provides that:

- money paid before frustration is recoverable;
- money payable before the frustration ceases to be payable whether or not there has been total failure of consideration;

- if one of the parties to whom such money has been paid or is payable has incurred expenses in performance of the contract before it was frustrated, the court may award such expenses up to the limit of the money paid or payable; and
- if nothing had been paid or was payable before discharge but one of the parties had already received a valuable benefit under the contract, the court may order this party to pay a 'just sum' for this benefit. A valuable benefit appears to mean that one of the parties has received an end product, not just a service.

Note that the Law Reform (Frustrated Contracts) Act 1943 does not apply to contracts such as:

- voyage charterparties;
- contracts of insurance;
- contracts for the sale of specific goods which perish before the risk passes to the buyer (as stated in s. 7 of the Sale of Goods Act 1979 – in this case, the common law rules apply); and
- contracts which actually cover the rights and liabilities of the parties in the event of frustration.

Discharge by breach of contract

A breach occurs when one of the parties to a contract fails or refuses to perform their side of the bargain. The remedy available depends on whether it is a breach of:

- condition
- warranty or
- innominate term.

As we have seen, if there is a breach of *condition*, the innocent party has the right to:

- treat the breach as a repudiation of the contract by the other party and regard the contract as ended. If, for example, the contract is for a sale of goods, the innocent party can recover the purchase price and, if he has suffered loss, sue for damages; or
- treat the contract as continuing and merely sue for damages.

If the breach is a breach of *warranty*, the innocent party's only action is a claim in damages but the contract continues.

If the breach is a breach of an *innominate term*, the court will look at the effect of the breach and award a remedy accordingly. So, if the effect of the breach is serious, the court will treat the contract as repudiated and therefore at an end; if the effect is not so serious it will award the innocent party damages only.

These breaches all occur after performance of the contract has started. In some cases, however, the breach occurs before the time for performance has arrived. This is known as *anticipatory breach*. Anticipatory breach was considered in

Hochster v de la Tour (1853) 2 E & B 678. In April, the claimant was engaged as a courier for the defendant, the work to commence in June. In May, however, the defendant told the claimant that his services would not be required. The claimant sued in breach of contract. It was held that the action succeeded and the claimant was entitled to damages even though the time for performance had not yet arrived.

If there is an anticipatory breach, the innocent party has a choice of actions but once they have elected to pursue a course of action, they cannot change their mind. They can:

- either accept the breach and treat the contract as repudiated and claim damages immediately; or
- treat the contract as continuing, perform their side of the bargain and claim the original contract price. To be entitled to do this, however, the innocent party must show that there is a legitimate interest in the contract continuing.

In *White and Carter (Councils) Ltd v McGregor [1962] AC 413*, McGregor, a garage owner, contracted with White and Carter, who supplied litter bins for a local authority. They paid for the bins by displaying advertisements for the garage on them for three years. The same day that the agreement was made, McGregor changed his mind and said he did not want to go ahead with the contract. White and Carter refused to accept this repudiation and displayed the advertisements for three years as originally agreed. At the end of this period they sued McGregor for the full contract price.

It was held that White and Carter were entitled to the full amount. McGregor had committed an anticipatory breach but they were entitled to treat the contract as continuing. There was no obligation on them to accept the breach as terminating the contract as, at such short notice, they could not have let the advertising space to anyone else (even though they had not actually started work on McGregor's advert). White and Carter had a legitimate interest in and reason for treating the contract as continuing.

The decision in this case has been criticised. Its application was limited in *Hounslow Borough Council v Twickenham Garden Developments Ltd [1971] Ch 233*. Here, the defendants contracted with the claimants to do work on the claimants' land. When the claimants later cancelled the contract there was a dispute as to whether they had a contractual right to do this so the defendants carried on working on the property. The claimants brought this action asking the court to grant an injunction requiring the defendants to stop trespassing on the claimants' property. The defendants argued that, under the principle established in *White and Carter*, it was entitled to refuse to accept the anticipatory breach and to continue with the work. The claimants argued that *White and Carter* could be distinguished in that the continued performance in that case could take place without the other party's cooperation whereas, in the present case, the defendant needed the claimants' permission to go onto the land.

It was held that the claimants succeeded and an injunction would be granted. The right given in *White and Carter* could be exercised only where the innocent party has a legitimate interest, financial or otherwise, in performing the contract and only where the contract can be completed without the other party's cooperation. In the *Hounslow* case, neither of these points applied.

The situations where the innocent party can validly choose to refuse to accept the anticipatory breach as repudiating the contract are very limited. In the majority of cases, acceptance of the breach and an action in damages would be the usual course of action. Furthermore, there is a danger in refusing to accept the anticipatory breach as ending the contract means that it may be frustrated before the time for performance arrives. This happened in *Avery v Bowden (1856) 26 LJQB 3*, in which a ship was to load a cargo of corn at the port of Odessa in the Crimea within 45 days. When the ship arrived at Odessa, the charterer told the captain that there was no cargo and advised him to sail home. The captain refused to leave, hoping that the charterer would find a cargo but, before the 45-day period expired, the Crimean War broke out between the UK and Russia so any trade with Russia became illegal. In other words, the contract was frustrated. The ship owner sued the charterer for damages for breach of the charter party but the action failed. The captain had refused to accept the charterer's anticipatory breach as ending the contract and, before the time for performance had arrived, the contract had been discharged by frustration. The defendant, therefore, had a good defence to the action.

If, however, there is an anticipatory breach and the innocent party validly elects to treat the contract as continuing, they must continue to carry out their side of the bargain. They will otherwise have committed a breach of contract and the other party will escape liability. In *Fercometal SARL v Mediterranean Shipping Co SA [1989] AC 788*, a ship was chartered to carry a cargo from a named port. Under the charter the ship was to be ready to load on or before 9 July. If this did not happen, the charterers could cancel the contract. Later, the ship owners asked for a four-day extension to enable them to pick up another cargo but the charterers refused and, cancelling the charter, chartered another ship to carry the cargo. The ship owners refused to accept this anticipatory breach; when their ship arrived at the named port on 8 July they informed the charterers that it was ready to load. This was not true: the ship was not ready. The charterers loaded their goods onto the other vessel they had obtained. The ship owners sued the charterers in damages for dead freight (the fact that the ship would sail without carrying a cargo).

It was held that, although the ship owners were entitled to refuse to accept the charterers' anticipatory breach, if they did so they had to fulfil their own contractual obligations. Failure to do this (i.e. by not having the ship ready to load on 9 July) meant that the charterers escaped liability for their anticipatory breach. The ship owners had themselves broken the contract which they had earlier affirmed by refusing to accept the repudiation. This affirmation meant that the contract was still in existence, so the charterers could rely on the clause entitling them to cancel the agreement because of the failure by the owners to have the ship ready for loading on the agreed date.

If the innocent party accepts the anticipatory breach and chooses to treat the contract as ended and sues for damages, he must attempt to mitigate his loss. In other words, he must try to find another customer. If it would have been possible to find such a new customer but the innocent party does not do so, the damages they will be awarded against the party in breach will be reduced by the amount they could have obtained under the new contract. In *Clea Shipping Corporation v Bulk Oil International Ltd (The Alaskan Trader) (No 2) [1984] 1 All ER 129*, a ship, The Alaskan Trader, was chartered. After the ship developed a number of faults and had to have extensive repairs, the charterers, in breach of contract, told the owners that they were ending the charter. Ignoring this, the owners refused to accept the repudiation, carried on with the repairs and, when these were completed, told the charterers that the ship was ready. In other words, the owners refused to accept the anticipatory breach and insisted they had the right to payment for the period of the charter.

It was held that an innocent party can refuse to accept an anticipatory breach as ending the contract only if they have a legitimate interest in the contract continuing. In this case, the claimant could have accepted the repudiation and chartered the ship to another company. There was no right to claim the charter money. The only right was to claim damages for any losses incurred after the charterers' breach, these damages reflecting what the owner could have received by mitigating their loss.

If the innocent party has suffered no loss as a result of the anticipatory breach, the damages awarded will be nominal.

In *Maredelanto Cia Naviera SA v Bergbau-Handel GmbH (The Mihalis Angelos) [1971] 1 QB 164*, a ship was chartered to load ore at Haiphong, Vietnam and to carry the ore to Hamburg. Under the contract, if the ship was not ready for loading by 20 July, the charter party would be cancelled. On 17 July, the ship was still in Hong Kong unloading a cargo from a previous charter. At that time, Haiphong harbour had been bombed and no cargo was available to load. The charterer told the ship owners that they no longer wanted the ship. In other words, they committed an anticipatory breach. This breach was immediately accepted by the ship owners. In fact, the ship was still in Hong Kong on 23 July so the charter party would have been cancelled anyway.

In assessing the damages, the court took account of the fact that the ship owners could not have performed the contract on 20 July. This, it was held, was a fact that had to be looked at in assessing the damages. The ship owners had suffered no loss as the contract could have been validly cancelled anyway. The claimants were awarded only nominal damages.

Finally, a breach can also occur if one of the parties acts in such a way as to prevent themselves from performing the contract. This person will be regarded as having impliedly repudiated the contract. This may be either during the contract or before it is due to be performed.

14 – Remedies for breach of contract

If there is a breach of contract, the innocent party has a number of remedies. The main ones are:

- damages
- specific performance and
- injunction.

Damages

An action in damages is a common law remedy and is available as of right if there has been a breach of contract. The purpose of damages is to compensate the injured party.

Compensation for any loss suffered

A party who has not suffered any loss as a result of the breach will be awarded nominal damages.

In *Beach v Reed Corrugated Cases Ltd [1956] 1 WLR 807*, the claimant, who had a 15-year contract with the defendants at a salary of £5,000 pa, was wrongfully dismissed after four years. He sued, claiming as damages the salary he would have earned had he remained in employment. The claimant had a large personal fortune.

He won his case but, as the purpose of damages is to compensate, not to allow a person to make profit, the amount he was awarded was reduced by the amount of tax he would have paid on the salary he would have earned and on his own personal income. The damages, therefore, were set at £18,000.

In commercial contracts, damages are assessed as at the date of breach but sometimes the court takes account of events which happened after the breach occurred. For example, in *Golden Strait Corporation v Nippon Yusen Kubishika Kaisha (The Golden Victory) [2007] UKHL 12*, the owners of a ship chartered it to the defendants for the period July 1998 to December 2005. Under cl. 33 of the charter, either party had the right to cancel if war or hostilities broke out between named countries including the USA, the UK and Iraq. In breach of contract, the charterers repudiated the contract in December 2001. The owners accepted this repudiation and claimed damages, the matter being referred to arbitration. The arbitrator found in the owners' favour but, before an assessment of damages had been made, the second Gulf War broke out in March 2003.

The charterers argued that, in assessing damages, account should be taken of the fact that, had the contract continued, they would have been able to cancel the charter in March 2003 under cl. 33, so damages should only be assessed as arising from December 2001 to March 2003. The owners, however, argued that damages should be assessed as at the date of breach and that, although the possibility of cl. 33 coming into force should be taken into account, the actual occurrence of the war was not relevant.

A majority in the House of Lords held that the basic principle of damages is to put the innocent party in the position he would have been in had the contract been performed. The anticipatory breach had deprived the owners of nothing from March 2003 onwards so the damages awarded reflected this. The principle that damages are to compensate the innocent party overrides the need for certainty. Lord Bingham, however, dissented arguing that in commercial contracts the element of certainty is paramount. Damages should be assessed as at the date of breach and should not take account of subsequent events, especially those happening a substantially long time after the breach.

The principle at issue, therefore, was when should damages be assessed? The general rule has been that, to ensure certainty in commercial contracts, the assessment should be at the date of breach. Sometimes, however, subsequent events may be taken into account.

Damages awarded must not be too remote

Damages must flow as directly as possible from the breach and be a natural and foreseeable consequence of that breach. This principle was established in *Hadley v Baxendale (1854) 9 Exch 341*. The driveshaft of Hadley's mill broke, so he employed Baxendale, a carrier, to take it to London to be used as a model for a new one. Baxendale delayed. During this time the mill was idle as Hadley, unlike other mill owners, had no spare drive shaft. Hadley sued Baxendale for his loss of profits during the delay.

It was held that, as Baxendale did not know that Hadley had no spare drive shaft, he could not foresee that his delay would cause a loss of profits. This loss, therefore, was too remote and Hadley could not recover it.

In this case, the basic principles for remoteness of damage in contract were established. It was said that damages for breach will be awarded for:

- loss arising directly and naturally from the breach; and
- loss which was within the reasonable contemplation of the parties at the time of the breach as the probable consequences of the breach.

Any other loss will be compensated for only in the case of a 'special loss' (i.e. if the defendant knew or should have known when the contract was made, about the special circumstances causing the loss).

The way in which these rules are applied was shown in *Victoria Laundry (Windsor) Ltd v Newman Industries Ltd [1949] 2 KB 528*. In this case, the laundry was expanding its business and had ordered a new boiler from the defendants, delivery to be on 5 June. The laundry also had a 'highly lucrative' contract to dye surplus clothing for the armed services. The defendants were unaware of the dyeing contract. The new boiler was needed for this too. The defendants did not deliver the boiler until 8 November by which time the laundry had lost the dyeing contract. The laundry sued the defendants claiming damages for:

- loss of profits from the delay in the expansion of its business; and
- loss of profits from the dyeing contract.

It was held that although damages could be recovered for the first loss, they would not be awarded for the loss of the dyeing contract as the defendants could not have known about this contract and its likely loss.

In *Czarnikow Ltd v Koufos (The Heron II) [1967] 3 All ER 686*, Koufos, a ship owner, contracted to carry a cargo of sugar to Basra where, as he knew, there was a sugar market. He also knew that Czarnikow, the charterers, were sugar merchants but did not actually know that Czarnikow intended to sell the sugar as soon as it was unloaded in Basra. In breach of contract, Koufos's ship deviated from its course and arrived in Basra nine days late, by which time the price of sugar in the market had fallen by £4,000. Czarnikow sued.

It was held that Czarnikow could recover the £4,000 as damages. Koufos, knowing that Czarnikow Ltd were sugar merchants and that there was a market for sugar in Basra, should have realised that:

- the sugar would be sold as soon as it arrived; and
- the price of sugar fluctuates.

The £4,000 loss was in the ordinary course of events and within the reasonable contemplation of the parties.

It does not have to be shown that the party in breach knows how much loss might be suffered, just that he is or should be, aware of the type of loss that would be suffered because of the breach of contract.

In *H Parsons (Livestock) Ltd v Uttley Ingham Ltd [1978] 1 QB 791*, the claimant, the owner of a pig farm, contracted with the defendants to supply and erect a bulk storage hopper to store pig nuts. Under the contract, the hopper had to be fitted with a ventilated top. The ventilator had been sealed while the hopper was being transported but the defendants forgot to open it once they had erected the unit. As a result, some of the nuts went mouldy. The claimant used the nuts. As a result of eating the mould, the pigs contracted a rare intestinal disease and over 250 of them died. Parsons sued the defendants.

It was held that the claimant could be compensated for the damage to the nuts and for the loss of the pigs. It was in the parties' contemplation that if the animals were fed the nuts they would fall ill and the disease was just 'a more extensive example of a contemplatable loss'. Some loss could reasonably have been anticipated. The fact that the full loss was more than might have been expected did not excuse the defendant from liability for it.

Damages for special loss will be awarded only if the defendant knew or should have known about the special circumstances which gave rise to the loss when the contract was made. So, if it is possible that some exceptional loss will be incurred if the contract is broken, this fact should be made clear to the other party from the outset if a claim for this loss is to be successful in the event of a breach.

In *Simpson v London & Northern Railway Co (1876) 1 QBD 274*, Simpson, a manufacturer of cattle food, sent samples of his products via the railway company to an agricultural show in Newcastle where he had taken a stand. Simpson stressed to the company that the samples had to arrive by a certain date. Simpson travelled to Newcastle to display his goods but the railway company delayed and the samples did not arrive until after the show had ended.

It was held that Simpson was entitled to special damages to cover his loss of profit and the waste of his time.

In contrast, in *Horne v Midland Railway Co (1873) LR 8 CP*, Horne had contracted to sell over 4,500 pairs of boots to the French army at a price well above the normal market price. He shipped the goods via the defendant railway company but the company delayed in delivering them and the buyer refused to accept delivery, time being of the essence in his contract with Horne. Horne sued the railway company for his loss of profits.

It was held that Horne could recover the market price of the boots but not the extra profit he would have made under the contract. The defendant was not aware of this exceptional profit and so could not be made liable for it.

There are a number of approaches the court can take in assessing the damages to be awarded. Damages may reflect the loss of the bargain and put the claimant, as far as possible, into the position he would have been in had the contract been performed. As we have seen in *Beach v Corrugated Cases*, the damages were awarded to put the claimant into the position he would have been in had he not been improperly dismissed (i.e. the salary he would have earned less the tax he would have paid – his 'take-home' pay).

Damages can also be awarded to put the claimant in the position he would have been in had the contract not been made. These are known as reliance damages and could cover, for example, expenses incurred in performance of the contract by the innocent party before the other party's breach. In *Anglia Television Ltd v Reed [1972] 1 QB 60*, the claimants contracted with the defendant for him to play the lead in a television play they were going to produce. The claimants incurred expenses in preparing for filming but then the defendant repudiated the contract and, as the claimants were unable to find a substitute actor, they had to abandon the whole project, losing £2,750.

It was held that Anglia was entitled to recover the whole of this wasted expenditure from Reed. It was money they had spent in reliance on the contract which he had broken.

It is possible to claim both loss of bargain damages and reliance damages. In the case of *Millar Machinery Co Ltd v David Way & Son (1935) 40 Com Cas 204*, machinery was delivered which did not comply with the contract. The buyer was able to recover:

- the price of the machinery;
- the net loss to the business from the breach (loss of bargain); and
- expenses of installing the machinery (reliance damages).

Mitigation of loss

This can be done, for example, by trying to make a deal with someone else. So, if a firm which has contracted to buy goods breaks the contract and says that it does not want them, the seller should try to find another purchaser thereby reducing his losses. In assessing damages for breach of contract the court will take account of the possibility of reducing the loss and, even though the innocent party has not tried to mitigate, will reduce the sum awarded by the amount this party could have obtained had there been mitigation.

In *Yetton v Eastwoods Froy Ltd [1967] 1 WLR 104*, the claimant, who was paid £7,500 p.a., was wrongfully dismissed with five years of his contract left to run. He tried unsuccessfully to obtain a similar job, turning down work which he would have obtained but which paid only £2,500 p.a. He sued his former employers for damages for breach of contract.

It was held that the claimant was right to look for similarly paid work for the first few months of unemployment but after that he should have followed up lower-paid jobs. The damages, therefore, were assessed at £7,500 p.a. for the first 18 months of his unemployment but, after that time, it was held, he could have found work at £3,000 p.a. Damages for the remaining period of the original contract were reduced to take account of the amount he could have earned.

Emotional suffering and loss of enjoyment

As a general rule, damages for such non-pecuniary losses are not available in ordinary commercial contracts. They are normally awarded only where a major and distinct purpose of the contract or of the term which has been broken, is to give the claimant enjoyment or freedom from distress or a feeling of security and this has been communicated to the other party. In other words, whether such damages will be awarded depends on the nature of the contract.

In *Jarvis v Swan's Tours Ltd [1973] QB 233*, the claimant booked a holiday with the defendant company having read in their brochure that it included a 'house party' together with various activities and entertainments. The actual holiday was not as described. In the first week there were only 13 people at the hotel and in the second week the claimant was the only guest. The claimant sued in breach of contract.

It was held that the claimant would be awarded the cost of the holiday together with damages to compensate him for 'disappointment, distress, upset and frustration'.

Damages will also be awarded to a claimant who has suffered mental distress and lack of security because of the other party's default. In *Heywood v Wellers (a Firm) [1976] QB 446*, in breach of their instructions, the defendant solicitors failed to obtain an injunction to stop a man molesting the claimant. The man molested her again.

It was held that the claimant was entitled to damages for her disappointment, mental distress and upset suffered as a result of the defendants' breach. Further, the solicitors lost their counterclaim for their charges. They had completely failed to perform their contract.

It is also possible to claim for non-pecuniary loss even where the sole object of the contract is not to provide enjoyment or peace of mind, provided that these are important elements in the contract.

In *Farley v Skinner [2001] UKHL 49*, the claimant was thinking of buying a house near Gatwick Airport. The defendant, a surveyor employed by the claimant, was specifically asked to report on aircraft noise. The defendant negligently said that this was not a problem. Following this report, the claimant bought the house and spent money improving it. He then discovered that the house was below a stacking point for aircraft flying into the airport which caused considerable noise. He sued the surveyor.

It was held that, even with the noise, the claimant had paid a reasonable price for the house. However, the claimant was awarded £10,000 damages for distress. Although this was not the main object of the contract and the aim of the contract with the surveyor was not to provide pleasure, relaxation or peace of mind, the question of the noise was an important part of the contract as shown by the specific request to the surveyor to report on it.

Non-pecuniary loss, however, will not be compensated in a breach of commercial contracts as these are entered into for profit. In these cases it is necessary to show that the breach has caused financial loss. Mental distress caused by the breach will not be considered as a head of damages. Nor will damages be awarded for mental distress caused by a breach of a contract of employment. In *Bliss v South East Thames Regional Health Authority [1985] IRLR 308*, the claimant, an orthopaedic surgeon, claimed damages for the mental distress and anxiety he was caused when he was suspended for refusing to be examined by a psychiatrist. It was held that such damages could not be recovered.

The same principle applies where an employee has been wrongfully dismissed – no damages will be awarded for any mental distress suffered as a result of this breach of contract.

Speculative damages

Difficulty in assessing loss will not deter the court from awarding damages. For example, in *Chaplin v Hicks [1911] 2 KB 786*, the claimant had won the early stages of a beauty contest. In breach of contract, the organisers stopped her from competing in the final stages. She sued.

It was held that, despite the fact that the various imponderables involved made an assessment difficult, the court would not be deterred from making an award. The claimant was awarded £100 damages

Agreed damages and penalties

Damages for breach of contract may be fixed in advance in the contract. These are known as **liquidated damages**. To be enforceable they must be a genuine pre-estimate of the loss that would have been incurred in the event of a breach. If they are not regarded as being a genuine pre-estimate, but rather as a means of deterring a breach and punishing the party who breaks the contract, they will be a penalty. The courts will refuse to enforce a penalty and will instead compensate for the actual loss suffered.

The distinction between liquidated damages and penalties was discussed in *Dunlop Pneumatic Tyre Co Ltd v New Garage and Motor Co Ltd [1915] AC 79*. In this case, under a price-fixing agreement, the defendants agreed, amongst other things, not to sell the claimants' tyres at less than a price fixed by the claimant. The contract provided that if the agreement was broken, the defendants would pay the claimants £5 for every tyre sold at below the minimum price. The defendants broke the agreement and the claimants sued for these agreed damages.

It was held that the claimants succeeded. The £5 damages were liquidated damages. Although £5 was a large sum compared to the actual loss suffered, the reason for the charge was to prevent a price war, which would have harmed Dunlop, and to maintain balance in the industry. The £5 represented a genuine pre-estimate of Dunlop's possible indirect losses.

Lord Dunedin explained the distinction between liquidated damages and a penalty. He said that a fixed sum in an agreement will be a penalty if:

- it is extravagant in relation to the greatest loss that could be proved to result from the breach;
- the breach is in not paying money and the amount of damages is a greater sum than was owing;
- the same sum is payable on the occurrence of a number of different events, some serious, some not so serious; and
- difficulty in assessing loss does not stop a sum being regarded as a genuine pre-estimate of loss.

The court will look at the effect of such a clause when making its decision. It does not matter whether the parties call the clause liquidated damages or a penalty or whether they agree that the amount payable is a reasonable pre-estimate. So, in *Cellulose Acetate Silk Co Ltd v Widnes Foundry (1925) Ltd [1933] AC 20*, a clause in the contract between the parties stated that, in the event of late performance, a 'penalty' of £20 per week would be payable.

It was held that this sum was not excessive in relation to the losses that could be incurred if performance was late and awarded the £20, ignoring the fact that it had been described as a penalty. The court looked at the reality of the case.

The courts will examine the contract and look at what the parties expected the loss to be when they entered the agreement. The assumption is that, in commercial contracts, as the parties are dealing at arm's length, they should, as far as possible, be bound by the terms of their agreement.

The rules about penalties apply only where the money is payable on breach of contract. If payment is to be made in circumstances other than breach, the rules will not apply and the stronger party will be able fully to recover what, if it was payable in the event of a breach, would be a penalty and unenforceable.

Time limit on claims

Claims for damages for breach of contract must normally be brought within six years.

Specific performance

An order of specific performance is an order by the court to require a person to carry out their obligations. It is an equitable remedy and is granted at the court's discretion. In other words, unlike damages, there is no automatic right to specific performance if a contract is broken.

An order of specific performance will be made only when damages would not be adequate. For example, if a seller of goods breaks the contract, the court will generally not grant the buyer an order of specific performance unless the goods are rare or unique.

In *Sky Petroleum Ltd v VIP Petroleum Ltd [1974] 1 WLR 576*, at a time when an oil embargo meant that petrol was in short supply, the claimant was granted an order of specific performance requiring the defendant to honour a contract to supply petrol. Damages in this situation would not have been an adequate remedy.

Land or an interest in land, is always regarded as unique, so an order of specific performance will be granted for the enforcement of contracts relating to this subject matter.

As a general rule, however, the courts will not grant specific performance for contracts involving personal services on the grounds that such an order could not be supervised, although it is sometimes granted against employers. The issue of the court's ability to supervise is one that the court usually factors into its decisions. This can be relevant even where damages are not adequate, especially where the contract is long-term rather than one where there is an end-product which the court could check.

In *Co-operative Insurance Society Ltd v Argyll Stores (Holdings) Ltd [1997] 3 All ER 297*, the claimants, who were developing a shopping centre, gave a 35-year lease to the defendants to operate a Safeway supermarket on the premises.

This store was vital to the success of the shopping centre as it encouraged business for other, smaller, shops. With 20 years left on the lease, the defendants, in breach of contract, closed the store as it was losing money. The claimants asked the court for an order of specific performance to require the supermarket to continue with the tenancy for the rest of the lease.

The House of Lords refused to grant the order. Even though assessing the loss from the breach that the claimants would suffer over the next 20 years was very difficult, given the 'knock-on' effect on smaller businesses, the court would not order specific performance as this would require constant supervision by the court. Also, the effect of requiring an uneconomic business to keep running could be to cause the defendant's loss; this would be out of proportion to the loss caused to the claimants by the breach of contract.

An order will also not be made to enforce a contract to lend money nor one to build or repair property unless:

- the building work was clearly defined;
- the claimant had a substantial interest in the performance of the work;
- damages would be insufficient to cover the claimant's interest; and
- the defendant had possession of the land so that another builder could not take over the work.

In *Wolverhampton Corporation v Emmons [1901] 1 KB 515*, the claimant sold development land to the defendant under a contract whereby the defendant was to demolish houses on the site and then build new property on it. The defendant demolished the existing houses. They then submitted and had approved plans for the new properties, but failed to build them.

It was held that the claimants would be granted specific performance as:

- the plans for the new properties were clearly defined;
- the claimant was losing potential rates on the new property so damages would be insufficient; and
- the defendant was in possession of the land so that claimant could not employ another builder.

Injunction

Like an order of specific performance, an injunction is an equitable remedy and so will be granted only at the court's discretion rather than being available 'as of right'.

There are two types of injunction: prohibitory and mandatory.

Prohibitory injunction

This stops a person from doing something in breach of contract. It will only be granted to enforce a negative promise. In contracts of employment, as we have seen, an injunction may be granted to prevent an employee acting in breach of a restrictive covenant prohibiting the employee from taking trade secrets to a competitor (as in *Forster & Sons v Suggett*) or from taking customers from the ex-employer (as in *Home Counties Dairies Ltd v Skilton*).

However, an injunction will not be granted if it would prevent an employee working altogether. In *Warner Brothers v Nelson [1937] 1 KB 209*, the defendant, whose stage name was Bette Davis, contracted with the claimants to work exclusively with them for a specified period and not to work for anyone else during this time without Warner Brothers' consent. Without obtaining this consent, Nelson entered a contract with another film company.

It was held that Warner Brothers could be granted an injunction to stop Nelson breaking her contract. The argument was that, although the injunction limited her freedom to act as she wished, it did not prevent her finding other work outside the film industry.

This case has been criticised as it forced Nelson to work for Warner, which went against the general principles of equity. In fact, in later cases involving similar facts, an injunction has not been granted. In *Page One Records Ltd v Britton [1967] 3 All ER 822*, an injunction was refused when it was shown that it would have forced the defendant, acting on behalf of the Troggs pop group, to engage Page One as their agent and manager or to wind up the pop group altogether.

This more realistic approach can be seen again in *Warren v Mendy [1989] 1 WLR 853*, in which the claimant, a boxing promoter and manager of a particular boxer, was refused an injunction to stop the boxer he managed being given advice by the defendant. The injunction was requested to prevent the defendant from inducing the boxer to break his contract with the claimant. The reason for the refusal was that, if the injunction were to be granted, it would indirectly force the boxer to keep working under the claimant's management.

As with contracts in restraint of trade, however, the court takes a somewhat more relaxed approach to the question of injunctions if the issue is one between companies and involves a commercial contract.

Mandatory injunction

This requires a person to take positive steps to undo something which has been done in breach of contract. For example, a person who has built on land in breach of a contractual obligation not to do so can have a mandatory injunction granted against him, requiring him to demolish the building. Such an order would be granted only if, in the circumstances, it would produce a fair result between the parties after the court has weighed the advantages to the claimant against the detriment to the defendant.

In *Wrotham Park Estate Co Ltd v Parkside Homes Ltd [1974] 2 All ER 321*, the defendant built houses on his land in breach of a restrictive covenant. The neighbours, in whose favour the restrictive covenant operated, but who had suffered no financial loss by the breach, sought a mandatory injunction. If granted, this injunction would have required the defendant to demolish the houses.

The court refused to grant the injunction as it would be a waste of houses which were much needed. Instead, the neighbours were awarded damages. On the ordinary measure of damages, as they had suffered no financial loss, the neighbours would have received nominal damages. The court, however, decided that it would be equitable to award the amount the court considered could have been demanded had the neighbours been paid to consent to breach of the restrictive covenant. This was assessed as 5% of the profit the defendant had made from the breach of the covenant.

Claims in equity

Unlike a common law action for damages, a claim in equity must be brought as soon as possible. Failure to do so will mean that the claimant will have lost the possibility of an equitable remedy. This is known as the doctrine of laches and is an application of the equitable maxim that 'delay defeats equity'.

In *Leaf v International Galleries [1950] 2 KB 86,* the innocently misrepresented attribution of a painting was discovered only five years after the purchase. The purchaser sued to have the contract rescinded (an equitable remedy) but it was held that too long a time had elapsed and the action failed.

Quantum meruit

This is a quasi-contractual, rather than equitable, remedy. *Quantum meruit* roughly means 'How much it is worth?' A claim can be made on a *quantum meruit* basis when:

- the claimant is prevented from fully completing his side of the agreement by the other party's breach. In *Planche v Colburn* (see above) the claimant was prevented from completing his book by the defendant's breach. He was awarded compensation on a *quantum meruit* basis for the work he had done before the series for which he was writing was discontinued;
- one party voluntarily accepts partial performance of the contract (see *Sumpter v Hedges [1898] 1 QB 673,* where, in completing the partly built house, the defendant voluntarily chose to use the materials the builder had left on the land);
- the contract does not state how much is to be paid nor does not make full provision for payment;
- there is a contract to sell a minor necessaries, such as foodstuff; and
- if, unknown to both parties, the contract is void. In *Craven-Ellis v Canons Ltd [1936] 2 KB 403,* the claimant was appointed and carried out work, as managing director of the defendants. It later turned out that, unknown to both parties, the claimant's contract of employment was void.

It was held that he could recover payment for the work he had done on a *quantum meruit* basis.

As can be seen from the above, unlike damages, which aim to compensate for loss caused by breach of contract, *quantum meruit* aims to grant pay for performance where there is no contractual provision to provide for such payment.

In *British Steel Corporation v Cleveland Bridge & Engineering Co Ltd [1984] 1 All ER 504*, during negotiations for a contract which both parties believed would be agreed, the defendants asked the claimants to start the work, which they did. Eventually, however, no contract was agreed. The claimant was entitled to be paid on a *quantum meruit* basis for the work they had done.

However, if the defendant does not undertake the work at the defendant's request but rather on a voluntary basis (possibly to encourage future negotiations) then a *quantum meruit* claim will not be allowed. The work will have been done at the defendant's own risk.

PART 2

Boilerplate Clauses for Drafting Commercial and Consumer Contracts

1 – Introduction

This part of the book is concerned with the drafting and interpretation of written contracts. Frequently, and especially in the commercial context, contracts are written. We shall be looking at standard provisions which arise in such contracts and how they should be interpreted.

First, we consider a very basic point, which needs to be considered whenever a contract is being negotiated and especially where it intended that the contract shall ultimately be set out in a standard form contract.

A contract is a legally binding agreement. As detailed in the first part of this book all that is required is offer, acceptance, consideration, certainty and an intention to be legally bound. There is nothing in law which requires the contract to be reduced into writing. Very few contracts must be written, but common sense dictates that the more significant a contract is, the more likely it is to be written. Of those which have, legally, to be written, there are:

- contracts for the sale of land;[1]
- negotiable instruments, such as cheques and other bills of exchange;[2]
- consumer credit agreements, such as contracts of hire purchase and consumer loans;[3]
- guarantees;[4] and
- assignments of patents.[5]

Perhaps curiously, there is no general requirement that an insurance contract needs to be written, though obviously it will invariably be reduced into writing if only because an insurer wants to be quite clear as to when he can refuse to pay on a claim. Nor is there a need for a contract of employment to be written. An employer must send an employee a written statement of terms within eight weeks of his commencing employment, but failure to do so has no impact on the validity of the contract itself. The absence of writing does not render the contract void.[6]

Conclusion of the contract

In regard to the making of any contract probably the most significant case is that of *Olley v Marlborough Court Hotel*.[7] Mr and Mrs Olley had checked into the Marlborough Court hotel. In their room there was a disclaimer of liability for their possessions on the part of the hotel. Because of the negligence of a hotel employee, some of their possessions were stolen. The question which the court had to decide was whether the disclaimer of liability was effective. This depended on precisely when the contract had been made. It was held that this had occurred when Mr and Mrs Olley had checked in at the hotel reception. Terms cannot be put into a contract after that contract has been made, therefore the disclaimer was ineffective.

The significance of this in the commercial context cannot be understated. Within a business there are usually to be found two groupings of people who have completely different mindsets. Firstly, there are the salesmen who get their adrenalin rush (and, perhaps more importantly, their commission!) from closing a deal. Then there are the administrators who are more concerned with getting things done in a proper and effective way. Salesmen need to understand that once a contract has been created, it is impossible to insert further clauses into that contract. Often a business will spend large amounts on expensive lawyers to draw up their standard terms of business, which will include carefully drafted exclusion or limitation provisions, only for a salesman to conclude a contract without having incorporated his company's standard terms.

Two devices to avoid this problem are first for the salesman always to ensure that he is not actually concluding the deal himself and secondly to refer to the contract's being subject to the company's standard terms in every piece of correspondence. The salesman can refer to the agreement's being 'subject to contract'. It is worth noting that such terminology is semantically ridiculous. If an agreement is subject to contract it is not a legally binding agreement and, if it is a legally binding agreement, it cannot be subject to contract. Thus, while on the face of it, the estate agent's notice 'sold subject to contract' is a complete nonsense: everyone knows what it means. There has been an agreement, but such agreement has to be reduced into writing. In the commercial context it is therefore an extremely useful term to use.

Problems caused by not having a written contract

There are a number of practical difficulties which can flow from a contract's not being reduced into writing. A seller might have difficulty in enforcing payment. The absence of writing means that a dispute comes down to his word against that of the other party. Similarly, recovery of payments might be difficult if the other side becomes insolvent.

The absence of writing means that a party has probably removed his entitlement to limit his potential liability by means of a well-drawn limitation or exclusion clause. Thus his liability if things go wrong could be unlimited.

By not having a written contract, a party may well deprive himself of the right to be given notice before the termination of an ongoing contract. There is a risk that the other side could simply withdraw from an agreement without warning.

Finally, there may arise otherwise-avoidable disputes. A clearly written contract leaves less room for argument as to its terms and the obligations of the parties.

Peace of mind should follow from a written contract.

Incorporation of terms

It is important at this point to observe that terms can be incorporated into a contract by reference (e.g. this often occurs with train tickets and car park tickets). The ticket may state that the contract is subject to standard terms which may be seen at the booking or cash office. This is not ideal but it is better than nothing. However, the approach must be to make reference to the terms as frequently as possible. Include them on websites. Ensure they are in brochures. Put them or at least refer to them, on the backs of invoices and purchase orders. Try to get the other party to show that he has accepted the rules. Include tear-off slips or similar on letters so that the recipient is encouraged to acknowledge that he has accepted the rules. When taking bookings by telephone, always ensure that a question is asked as to whether the person placing the order has the seller's rules in front of him.

Professional advice

This book is not intended as a substitute for legal advice and should not be treated as such. Legal advice should always be sought before taking action based on the information provided. While the aim of the text is to provide an introduction to standard terms used in commercial contracts, there will be circumstances where proper professional advice should be taken. Hopefully, however, there should be a better awareness as to when such advice should be taken.

The same basic principles are applicable to all business contracts. However, some contracts are subject to special and idiosyncratic rules and, as such, fall outside the scope of this course.

For example, special rules apply in the following types of contracts:

- those providing for the sale and purchase of a business;
- those involving land, including leases and licences;
- those concerned with franchising, agency and distribution agreements;
- those concerned with employment; and
- those involving insurance.

Formation of a contract

As stated above, contracts can take any form. They can be made:

- in writing
- orally
- by conduct.

These are known as **simple contracts**. In deciding whether an agreement is such a contract, the court will look at the essential elements required. These are:

- offer;
- acceptance;
- consideration;
- certainty; and
- an intention to enter into a legally binding agreement.

In other words, the courts usually look at the substance rather than the form of the agreement. As stated above, by law, some contracts have to be in writing and others have to be evidenced in writing and, as a rule of thumb, the more important the contract, the more likely it is to be reduced into writing by the parties.

A contract can also be contained in a deed. This is known as a **specialty contract**. Such a contract is valid even though it may not be supported by consideration. A gratuitous promise set out in a deed is enforceable.

The battle of the forms

A situation which often arises in the context of commercial contracts is where both parties have their own standard terms. This is known colloquially as 'the battle of the forms'. In such circumstances, on whose terms is the contract made? Suppose one party, the offeror, makes an offer on its standard terms. If 'acceptance' by the offeree is qualified, this will constitute a revocation of the original offer and be a fresh offer in itself. The initial offer is, therefore, at an end. Performance of the contract by the initial offeror will constitute acceptance.

Putting this another way, a buyer asks for a quotation using a form setting out his terms and conditions. The seller then responds on a form setting out his own, but contradicting, terms. The buyer then places an order on the original terms. The seller accepts, but on his terms. Whose terms apply? The buyer's request for a quotation was an offer. It was, however, brought to an end by the seller's contradicting terms. What the seller was doing was making a counter offer. The buyer's then placing the order was itself a counter offer, bringing the second offer to an end. On performance, which itself was an acceptance by the seller, the contact was made. The contract was therefore on the seller's terms.

For all that this is a common commercial situation there is remarkably little case law. Probably the leading case is *Butler Machine Tool Co Ltd v Ex-Cell-O Corporation Ltd.*[8] Butler offered to sell machine tools to Ex-Cell-O subject to Butler's standard term and conditions. These included a price-variation provision. Ex-Cell-O purported to accept the offer but on its own standard terms and conditions. These did not include a price-variation provision. Butler acknowledged the order by returning a tear-off slip from Ex-Cell-O's 'acceptance'. After the delivery of some tools, Butler sought to increase the price originally agreed to take account of increased costs. Ex-Cell-O refused to pay. It was held that the situation had to be analysed in terms of offer and acceptance. Ex-Cell-O's 'acceptance' was not an acceptance at all. It was a counter-offer, which amounted to a rejection. Acceptance had been by the return of the tear-off slip to Butler. The contract was on Ex-Cell-O's terms. There was, therefore, no price-variation provision in the contract. It was held that Butler could not vary the price.

Basically, if an offer is made on terms, acceptance is only valid on those terms. If 'acceptance' is on other terms it is no more than a counter-offer. A response on the original terms is, again, merely a counter-offer. To be effective, terms must be unconditionally agreed. It is important to ensure that 'our' terms form the basis of our contracts.

General considerations when entering into a contract

Negotiation should have been completed by the time drafting begins

Beware – often a contract may be made before a legal department is asked to draft the documentation. Salesmen must be warned! Mark all communication 'subject to contract'. This is especially important with quotations and similar proposals. A long form of a 'subject to contract' is:

> *These heads of agreement are subject to contract and are not intended to be legally binding. Neither do they represent a complete summary of the contractual or commercial aims of the parties. However, they express the desires and understanding of the parties subject to obtaining legal and other professional advice and executive approval. Once executive approval has been given, these heads of agreement shall form the basis of negotiation of a detailed agreement, but, save for the mutual obligation of confidentiality contained in clause ... hereof (which both is and is intended to be, legally binding) neither party shall become legally obligated to the other unless and until such an agreement is formally executed by both parties and has become effective in accordance with its terms.*

A letter of intent is not legally binding

As stated previously, before a valid contract can be concluded there must be an intention on the both parties to be legally bound. Thus, if an agreement is couched in conditional terms (e.g. as the draft precedent above) it is not legally binding.

A letter of comfort is not legally binding

A document cannot be a guarantee unless it is reduced into writing and is signed as required by the Statute of Frauds 1677. In *Kleinwort Benson Ltd v Malaysian Mining Corporation*,[9] it was held that a letter of comfort was not a contractual document.

It is not necessary for the contract to include every possible safeguard and to cover every possible eventuality

Keep sight of the wider picture. Over-concentration on a specific detail can result in the ignoring of what actually the contract is intended to achieve.

Drafting should seek to achieve clarity and certainty of expression

The draftsman should not simply rely on 'heads of terms'. These may give a superficial feeling of comfort to the contracting parties but it is unlikely that a court would be willing to enforce them because it will probably be clear that they are not intended to be the final agreement.

The parties should seek to void a confrontational and adversarial approach to drafting

Sometimes lawyers can be confrontational but this is not a sensible approach. The contract is intended to be mutually beneficial. The ultimate aim must be to achieve a balance between the interests and desires of both parties.

Concentrate on the main points which are to be achieved

Undue attention to trivia can obscure these. One party might feel he has negotiated a really good price for goods which he is buying but then overlook the required delivery date.

Use plain English

Short sentences are preferable to long ones. Say precisely what you mean. In one celebrated case a judge referred to a contract as a 'bisynallagmatic' agreement – but who knows what one of those is? (The word actually means an agreement between two sides.) If that is the case, why not just say so? Sometimes what might subjectively seem to a writer to be semantic brilliance can result in unnecessary obfuscation.

- *If a standard clause can achieve what the draftsman wants then it is a waste of time trying to express an idea in an alternative way.* Often lawyers use the term 'boilerplate' in a pejorative sense. But if a standard clause can achieve a desired result, there can be no point in seeking to express the underlying thought in a different way.
- *The draftsman must always be aware of the impact of the law generally upon the contract.* For example, the traditional common law approach of freedom of contract has been impacted by the Unfair Contract Terms Act 1977 and the Unfair Terms in Consumer Contracts Regulations 1999.
- *It is essential to be aware of the impact of taxation.* If necessary, expert advice should be taken in this regard.
- *The draftsman should not seek to achieve elegance at the expense of clarity.* For example, it is often clearer to repeat proper names rather than use pronouns.

- *The detailed drafting should not be left until the last minute.* There is the danger that a contract-threatening dispute may arise over something which has not been considered at an early stage.
- *Care should be taken over what is said and written.* One must be vigilant that promises are not made which subsequently cannot be kept.
- *Work pursuant to a contract.* This should, as far as possible, be kept to a minimum until the formal contract is signed.

Renegotiation of contracts

Because of changing circumstances, it is sometimes necessary to renegotiate an existing contract. Such renegotiation will be allowed by the courts provided there has been no fraud or improper pressure.

This was the point of the case of *Williams v Roffey Bros & Nicholls (Contractors) Ltd.*[10] A builder, Roffey, was contracted to renovate some council houses. The contract contained a substantial liquidated damages provision. If Roffey did not get the work completed on time, he would lose some of the payment due to him under the contract. Roffey was contracted with Williams, a sub-contractor carpenter. He had contracted to do the carpentry work at a rate that was substantially under-priced. He could no longer afford to continue with the work. Roffey promised Williams an additional payment of £10,300 if he would perform his contract. When the work was completed, Roffey refused to pay. It was held that he should honour his promise. Purchas LJ said: 'I consider that the modern approach to the question of consideration would be that where there were benefits derived by each party to a contract of variation even though one party did not suffer a detriment this would not be fatal to establishing sufficient consideration to support the agreement. If both parties benefit from an agreement it is not necessary that each also suffers a detriment.'

However, it has to be said that while this case caused some consternation at the time it was decided, it has not been much followed as was discussed in the earlier part of this book.

For example in *Re Selectmove Ltd*,[11] a company had got into arrears with its corporation tax payments. The (then) Inland Revenue agreed to accept payment in instalments. It was held that the agreement to pay in instalments was not sufficient consideration to justify the Revenue's deferral of the tax due. The company was already under an obligation to pay. Accordingly, when the company defaulted, the Revenue could petition for the winding up of the company.

Renegotiation may be possible only as long as there is no fraud or economic duress.

Economic duress arises where illegitimate business pressure is exerted. For example, in *Universe Tankships of Monrovia v International Transport Workers Federation (The Universe Sentinel)*,[12] the threat by the Federation to stop its members working on the Universe Sentinel unless its owners paid money into the union's fund was held to be illegitimate business pressure and, therefore, economic duress. The owners had to pay the money demanded to be able to use its ship but were allowed to recover it once the threat had ended.

So, in order to renegotiate effectively, any pressure exerted must be legitimate and not improperly coercive. Such legitimate business pressure was found in *Pao On v Lau Yiu*.[13] In this case, the Privy Council set out the nature of economic duress. Lord Scarman stated: 'there is nothing contrary to principle in recognising economic duress as a factor which may render a contract voidable provided always that the basis of such recognition is that it must amount to a coercion of will, which vitiates consent. It must be shown that the payment made or the contract entered into was not a voluntary act'.

In *CTN Cash & Carry Ltd v Gallagher Ltd*,[14] a renegotiation was successful because the threat used by Gallagher (that it would exercise its contractual right to withdraw credit facilities granted to CTN) was valid business pressure even though, in the Court of Appeal, Steyn LJ described it as *'unattractive'*.

If the pressure to renegotiate is to more than ordinary commercial pressure and amounts to coercion, the 'victim' who has paid under such pressure can recover the money by avoiding the contract. He must, however, act as soon as the pressure ends. Failure to act promptly will result in the court refusing to allow him to recover anything, however improper the threat had been and whatever the reason for the delay. The effect of this is shown in the case of *North Ocean Shipping Co Ltd v Hyundai Construction Co Ltd (The Atlantic Baron)*.[15]

It is, therefore, possible to renegotiate a contract, but for the results of such renegotiation to be enforceable, care must be taken to use only legitimate business pressure. For even more certainty of enforceability, fresh consideration should be provided.

Negotiating the contract – tactical tips

- Terms must be communicated before or at the time the contract is made. (What about the shrink-wrapped computer package stating that 'opening this package indicates your acceptance of these terms and conditions'?)
- There are, however, two instances where this does not apply:
  - Where there has been a regular course of dealing between the parties on standard terms (*Spurling v Bradshaw [1956] 1 WLR 461*).[16]
  - Where there customary trade terms habitually used (*British Crane Hire v Ipswich Plant Hire [1974] 1 All ER 1059*).[17]
- If alterations are made to standard documents, make sure they are written in at the time and not afterwards.
- Unusual and onerous terms may have to be brought fairly and reasonable to the attention of the other party not hidden in the small print *(Interfoto Picture Library v Stiletto Visual Programs [1988] 1 All ER 348)*.[18]

Third-party rights – the key factors

- There is no need for the third party to have given consideration.
- The third party does not need to agree to the terms; they need not even be aware of them.
- The two contracting parties can decide whether or not to give rights to a third party.
- The third party has no right to challenge that decision as being unfair.
- To have rights, the third party must be expressly identified in the contract by name, as a member of a class or as answering a particular description. There is, however, no need for the third party to be in existence when the contract is made.
- Rights can also be excluded. For example, the RIBA contract for appointment of architect: '*For the avoidance of doubt nothing in this agreement shall confer on any third party any benefit or the right to enforce any term of this agreement.*'

The relationship between a contract for the sale of goods and a manufacturer's guarantee

At this point it is useful to look at the relationship between the implied terms in a contract for the sale of goods and the guarantee or warranty given by a manufacturer.

Someone buys a new car. It is a top of the range model from a reputable manufacturer. There is a manufacturer's guarantee for 60,000 miles or three years, whichever comes first. After being driven for 37 months and 15,000 miles of very ordinary motoring, the gearbox needs to be replaced.

The owner takes the car back to the garage where he bought it and is told that because the guarantee has expired, there is nothing that can be done. Is this the end of the story? In other words, what is the effect of the guarantee?

A guarantee in these circumstances constitutes a contract between the purchaser of the goods and the manufacturer. The main contract is, of course, between the purchaser and the garage from which he bought the car. So this is a completely different contract. What, in effect, it promises is that if, within its terms, the selling garage carries out a repair of the car to which it relates, the manufacturer will indemnify the garage. Or, if the car is taken to another dealership and the dealership repairs the car, the manufacturer will indemnify the dealership.

But consider now the contract between the customer and the garage. This is a completely different contract. Implied in this contract are terms that the car must be of satisfactory quality and fit for purpose.[16] Do you consider that a car which needs to have its gearbox replaced after a mere 15,000 miles satisfies these implied conditions?

The customer's remedy now is against the garage from which he bought the car for straightforward breach of contract.

Obsolete practices in drafting

There is little to be said for some old-fashioned practices in drafting in regard to punctuation, terminology and verbosity. These will now be considered.

Punctuation

Traditionally, legal documents were written in Latin, a language in which punctuation did not feature. When English became the language of the law, lawyers carried this practice forward. Over the years punctuation became more acceptable by lawyers, but there are still some who refuse to use it. However, punctuation is today a critical part of the English language and to eschew its use is both archaic and ridiculous.

For example, consider the following combinations of words and consider how many different meanings can be given to them by the use of punctuation:

- What is this thing called love
- A woman without her man is nothing

Admittedly these are rather silly examples, but they make a point about the significance of punctuation. A comma, a question mark, an exclamation mark or a full stop can significantly change the meaning of the words to which they are added.

Terminology

Some words have dropped out of common use and should no longer be employed in drafting. For example, 'forthwith' might be replaced by 'immediately'. 'In as much as' can be replaced by 'since'. 'Pursuant to' can be replaced by 'under'. 'Hereinafter' should give way to 'below'.

Verbosity

The significant point here is for the writer to reflect on what he is writing.

It is not unknown for the writer of a letter to 'beg to enclose' a document with his letter. Begging has almost died out amongst lawyers today, so there is no need to 'beg to enclose'. Perhaps the draftsman might then say that 'we enclose herewith', but a moment's thought will reveal that if it is 'enclosed' it is 'herewith', and if it is 'herewith' it is 'enclosed', so why not just say 'we enclose'? To do otherwise is to waste the time of both the writer and the reader.

Sometimes a document will begin with the words: 'This memorandum of agreement.' Why not just say: 'This agreement?'

Similarly, the document might state: 'now it is hereby agreed that'. This is verbosity for the sake of it. It is far better to say: 'It is agreed that.'

Notes

1 Law of Property (Miscellaneous Provisions) Act 1989.
2 Bills of Exchange Act 1882.
3 Consumer Credit Act 1974.
4 Statute of Frauds 1677.
5 Patents Act 1977.
6 Employment Rights Act 1996.
7 [1949] 1 KB 532.
8 [1979] 1 All ER 965 CA.
9 [1989] 1 All ER 785.
10 [1990] 1 All ER 512.
11 [1994] BCC 379.
12 [1983] 1 AC 366; [1982] 2 All ER 67.
13 [1979] 3 All ER 65.
14 [1994] 4 All ER 714.
15 [1979] QB 705; [1978] 3 All ER 1170.
16 Sale of Goods Act 1979, s. 14.
17 See, e.g. *Spurling v Bradshaw [1956] 1 WLR 461*.
18 See, e.g. *British Crane Hire v Ipswich Plant Hire [1974] 1 All ER 1059*.
19 See *Interfoto Picture Library v Stiletto Visual Programs [1988] 1 All ER 348*.

2 – The layout of a commercial contract

The parties and the commencement date

Note the commencement date may be different from the date of signing.

Recitals

These set out the background to the transaction including the reasons behind it. Be careful here. This is not part of the agreement but may be used in interpreting the agreement. Traditionally, recitals would be fairly extensive, but today they tend to be kept to a minimum by most draftsmen.

Definitions

Sometimes it is sensible to draft these as one goes along and then draw them together at the end of drafting. These form part of the substantive agreement because invariably they provide that specific terms shall mean specific things.

Examples of definitions include:

'... shall mean ...'

This is probably the simplest form of definition. However, there is a danger that certain matters which are intended to be brought within the definition might inadvertently be omitted.

'where the context so admits ... shall mean ...'

This sort of definition should be avoided if possible because of the risk of ambiguity.

'In this agreement taxation shall include income tax, corporation tax and value added tax.'

This is a sensible type of definition especially where, for example, there is a contract for the purchase of goods or services in circumstances where the buyer wants to be sure that the price stated in the contract is the price which he will have to pay and no more. For example, a definition of taxes might be along the following lines:

'Taxes' shall include all present and future taxes, charges, import duties, levies, deductions withholding or fees of any kind whatsoever or any amount payable on account of or as security for any of the foregoing, payable at the instance of or imposed by any statutory, governmental, international, state, federal, provincial, local or municipal authority, agency, body or department whatsoever, in each case whether in the United Kingdom or elsewhere, together with any penalties, additions, fines, surcharges or interest relating thereto and the expressions 'taxes' and 'taxation' shall be construed accordingly.

Similarly, suppose that a draftsman is seeking to define 'regulation'. For example, when a buyer wants to ensure that goods which he is buying comply with all the legal obligations which the government of his country imposes and is likely to enforce, he might choose something along the following lines:

'Regulation' includes any regulation, rule, official directive, request or guideline (whether or not having the force of law but, if not, being one which is customarily complied with by persons carrying on a comparable business) of any governmental body, agency, department or regulatory, self-regulating or other authority or organisation.

Substantive clauses

These form the main body of the contract. Ideally they should enable a reader to see what the contract is about and this at a first reading if possible. Often a contract can be made easier to read if lists are removed and instead put into schedules.

Schedules

These are somewhere where a list can be more easily read than if it was set out in the substantive clauses. These should be used freely.

Appendices

These consist of documents referred to in the contract. They can be extremely useful, especially where reference is made, for example, to trade conditions which might change from time to time. The reproduction of such a document in an appendix is clear evidence of the document as it was at the date of the execution of the contract.

Signatures

There is a distinction between a contract being under hand and under seal. A simple contract has only a six-year limitation period. A contract by deed carries a 12-year limitation period.

Counterparts and copies

In the old days, when contacts were handwritten by clerks on parchment, the contract itself would be written twice on the same piece of parchment and then cut in a wavy line across the middle so that one part could go to each of the contracting parties. The authenticity of the documents could then be proved by bringing the two parts together. The two parts were then known as the part and the counterpart respectively. However, language changes in its meaning and, with the advent of first typewriters and then word processors, the practice today is to refer to any executed copy of a contract as a counterpart. The wavy line dividing the two parts of the traditional parchment contract gave rise to the word 'indenture'. (The letters DENT in the middle of the word come from the same Latin stem as denture or dentist. The reference is to the 'teeth' on the part and the counterpart.) References to indentured apprentices refer to the contract of apprenticeship being contained in an indentured document (i.e. one written twice on a single piece of parchment, one executed copy going both to the master and to the apprentice).

3 – Commencement of the contract

Agreement 'subject to contract'

In English law, such an expression is not intended to bring about a binding contract. It is no more than a set of heads of agreement. However, care should be taken in certain other jurisdictions. In some countries, such an agreement may be legally binding.

Date of commencement

In the absence of express agreement to the contrary, the contract commences on the date of signature. However, there is no reason why commencement should not be retrospective or deemed to be at some time in the future.

Partial commencement subject to competition law approval

Provisional commencement is sometimes used to avoid illegality which could result from breaches, for example, of domestic competition law.

Conditions precedent

Often an agreement will be said to come into force subject to certain conditions precedent. These fall into three broad categories:

1 Financial conditions (e.g. opening of letters of credit or giving of bonds).
2 Regulatory conditions (e.g. obtaining consent from government bodies).
3 Technical matters (e.g. acceptance of specifications by a government body).

Where a number of conditions precedent are to be satisfied, it is sensible to provide that: 'notwithstanding signature by the parties, this contract shall not come into force until all of the following conditions precedent have been satisfied ....'

Deeds – Examples of Execution and Attestation Clauses

Contractual agreements can be set out in a simple contract or in a deed. The main distinctions are:

(a) that for a simple contract to be legally enforceable there must be the presence of consideration, whereas consideration is not necessary for a deed; and
(b) that the limitation period for bringing legal proceedings in respect of a breach of contract is six years, though if the contract is contained in a deed this is extended to 12 years.

In witness of which this document has been [duly] [signed/sealed as a deed] and delivered the day and year first before written.

[COMPANY HAVING A SEAL]

THE COMMON SEAL *of* ***[XYZ] PLC*** *was affixed in the presence of:*

Director ....

Director/Secretary ....

[COMPANY WITHOUT SEAL]

SIGNED as a Deed for [XYZ] PLC:

[Director] and ***Director*** ....

[Director/Secretary] ***Director/Secretary***...

[INDIVIDUAL]

SIGNED as a DEED and DELIVERED *by [name of maker] in the presence of:*

Witness: ....

Address: ....

Occupation: ....

Signature clauses

IN WITNESS whereof this Agreement has been entered into the day and year first above written.

SIGNED BY)
for and on behalf of)
[ ])
in the presence of:)

SIGNED BY)
for and on behalf of)
[ ])
in the presence of:)

SIGNED BY)
for and on behalf of)
[ ])
in the presence of:)

AS WITNESS the hands of the duly authorised representatives of the parties hereto on the day and year first before written.

SIGNED BY)
duly authorised for and on behalf of)
[ ])
in the presence of:)

SIGNED BY)
duly authorised for and on behalf of)
[ ])
in the presence of:)

AS WITNESS the hands of the parties or of their duly authorised representatives the day and year first before written.

SIGNED BY)
duly authorised for and on behalf of)
[ ])
in the presence of:)

SIGNED BY)
duly authorised for and on behalf of)
[ ])
in the presence of:)

Examples of counterpart clauses

This agreement shall be executed in two counterparts, one counterpart to be retained by each of [X] and [Y].

This agreement may be entered into in any number of counterparts and by the parties to it on separate counterparts, each of which when so executed and delivered shall be an original, but all the counterparts shall together constitute one and the same instrument.

Examples of conditions precedent

Simple form of condition precedent
This agreement shall not come into force and effect until the occurrence of the effective date except for Clauses [ ] which shall come into force and effect on the date of this agreement.

Example of automatic termination if condition precedent does not occur
If the effective date has not occurred on or before [ ] 2014 or such later date as the parties agree, this agreement (except for Clauses [ ]) shall cease to have effect.

Setting out the conditions precedent
Notwithstanding signature by the parties, this agreement shall not come into force until all of the following conditions precedent have been fulfilled: [Specify]

Automatic termination if conditions not satisfied

- *If the contract does not come into force within [ ] months of the date of signature of the agreement each party shall be free to withdraw from this agreement.*
- *Upon such withdrawal this agreement shall thereupon terminate and neither party shall be under any liability to the other by reason only of such termination.*

Definition clause

All but the most simple of contracts will be likely to contain a definition clause. In regard to commencement, there might be a provision along the following lines:

Effective date

- *'Effective date' means the business day on which the conditions are satisfied (or waived as the case may be) in accordance with this agreement.*
- *The effective date of this agreement shall be the date upon which [X] shall approve this agreement and notify such approval to [Y], which approval [X] shall notify to [Y] without delay.*
- *This agreement shall come into effect on the date hereof.*

Time is of the essence

As a general rule in English law, time is not of the essence in regard to contracts. For example, in contracts for the sale of goods neither the time of delivery nor the time of payment is of the essence unless expressly stated to be so or made to be so by means of a notice served during the contract itself. A party to a contract can serve a notice where there has been a failure on the part of the other party to perform a particular term to time. However, it is possible to make it such by means of an express term:

- *Time shall be of the essence in regard to this agreement.*
- *Time shall be of the essence in relation to all matters arising hereunder or pursuant hereto.*

When such a term is included in a contract, any failure to perform strictly in accordance with its provisions permits the other party to bring the contract to an end without even the need to give notice.

It is worth giving serious thought to telling a supplier why you need work to be done by a particular date and any losses that you could fall under personally in the event of that work not being done. Commercially, this concentrates the supplier's mind on his obligations. Legally, it lays him open to substantial damages in the event of any breach.

Periods of time

Often a contract will refer to matters such as a period of time. For example:

'X shall within one month pay ....'

In interpreting such a provision, great assistance is to be gained from a piece of legislation. Under s. 61, Law of Property Act 1925:

> *'In all deeds, wills, orders and other instruments executed, made or coming into operation after the commencement of this Act, unless the context otherwise requires:*
>
> *(a) "Month" means calendar month*
> *(b) "Person" includes a corporation*
> *(c) The singular includes the plural and vice versa*
> *(d) The masculine includes the feminine and vice versa.'*

Perhaps it is wise to avoid possible uncertainty by referring to days rather than months etc.

Fixed-term contract

Ideally, the precise date of termination should be identified or otherwise be ascertainable from the contract.

Such a clause should allow for earlier termination (e.g. because of breach, insolvency etc).

Renewable term contracts

Distinguish between contracts which continue until brought to an end by notice and contracts which expire unless renewed.

Some agreements may automatically terminate on the happening of a specified event.

Termination by notice

- Termination by notice may be either for cause or without cause (i.e. merely for convenience). The contract should set out for how long an agreement will last and under what circumstances, if any, it can be terminated prior to the set expiry date.
- Frequently in contracts for rental, distribution, licensing or agency there are provisions for termination by notice without cause.
- There should be appropriate provisions for return or destruction of records, software etc., repayment of licence fees etc.
- Where termination is by notice without cause, it may be desirable that it is subject to a specified notice period.
- However, where termination is by notice with cause, it is desirable that it should take effect immediately.
- The one exception to this is where notice is subject to a 'cure period' (i.e. a period during which the breach can be corrected by the party in default).

- In such cases there may be a distinction between breaches arising from failure to pay sums due (which should be treated severely) and breaches for which a longer cure period may be allowed.
- Do you want to be able to terminate in the event of the other party's becoming insolvent?

Effect of termination

It should be considered whether termination should allow both parties to walk unscathed away from the agreement.

Alternatively, there might be some provision for compensation for work in progress at the date of termination or the return of any advance payments made.

It may be that certain provisions should remain in force despite the termination of the agreement.

Termination for breach or insolvency

If either party ('the first party')

(a) commits or allows to be committed any breach of this agreement and does not remedy such breach within 20 days after written notice from the other party requiring such remedy; or

(b) has an administrative receiver or a receiver appointed of the whole or any part of its assets or any order made or resolution passed for its administration or winding-up (unless as part of a scheme of reconstruction or amalgamation) or compounds with or convenes a meeting of its creditors or allows, permits or does anything analogous to any of the foregoing under the law of any jurisdiction occurs in relation to the first party then in any such event the other party may by written notice to the first party determine this agreement but without prejudice to any right of action of the other party in respect of any antecedent breach of this agreement by the first party.

Termination by notice

This agreement will continue indefinitely unless terminated by either party upon not less than one month's written notice to the other in accordance with the following provisions.

On and after the termination date specified in the notice of termination, [X] shall complete all outstanding or incomplete transactions as if the agreement were still in force but will not initiate or effect any new transaction or perform any new service for [Y] on or after that date. [Y] shall pay any fees or other sums accrued or due at the date of termination. [Y] shall bear any additional expenses of [X] necessarily incurred in terminating the agreement and any losses necessarily incurred in settling or concluding outstanding obligations.

Simple termination by notice

This agreement may be terminated by either party giving 15 days' written notice to that effect to the other party.

Termination by notice with outstanding fees to be paid

This agreement shall continue indefinitely unless terminated by either party in accordance with the following provisions.

[X] is entitled to terminate this agreement forthwith upon written notice being received by [Y], without penalty but without prejudice to the completion of outstanding transactions and the payment of any fees or other sums accrued or due at the date of termination.

Termination by notice with compensation payable

This agreement may be terminated by either party by three months' notice to the other party. [X] may also terminate the agreement forthwith by notice to [Y], but in such case [Y] shall be entitled to three months' fees in lieu of notice.

Termination on breach

This agreement shall terminate:

(a) upon 15 days' written notice by either party to the other; or
(b) forthwith on written notice by one party if the other shall be in material breach of the provisions of this agreement.

Termination by notice but with right of indemnity continuing

This agreement may be terminated forthwith by either party by giving written notice to the other party, such termination to be effective, unless otherwise specified in the notice, on receipt by the other party of such notice, subject to any outstanding transactions being settled and any commissions or fees accruing to [X] (including any additional expenses incurred in connection with such termination) being paid. Any notice of termination by [Y] must be addressed to the company secretary of [X]. [Y] agrees that the indemnity provisions set out in clause [ ] will survive any such termination of this agreement and remain in full force and effect.

Effect of termination

Termination of this agreement shall not affect any rights or liabilities which have accrued prior to the date of such termination.

The provisions of clause [ ] shall survive the expiry or termination of this agreement and continue in full force and effect.

Upon termination of this agreement, each party shall return to the other party (or destroy if so agreed) all confidential information relating to the other party and certify in writing to the other party that there has been compliance with the requirements of this clause.

Upon termination of this agreement for whatever reason, [X] and its employees and agents shall be irrevocably licensed to enter [Y's] premises and recover [ ], which [Y] acknowledges are the property of [X].

Duration

This agreement shall run for a period of [ ] years from the date upon which [X] shall approve this agreement provided that after one year it shall be subject to termination by either party upon giving 90 days' notice in writing, such notice to be sent by recorded delivery letter, provided that if this agreement is terminated under this clause within a period of [ ] years from the date of its coming into effect, then [X] shall be entitled to receive all fees due to it in terms of clause [ ] in respect of a period of [ ] days after the date that such notice of termination is given.

Continuing effect of agreement

It may be necessary for some terms (particularly those fixing obligations of confidentiality) on one or both of the parties to continue notwithstanding the general termination of the contract.

The provisions of this clause shall survive any termination of this agreement and shall continue in full force and effect.

The provisions of this agreement, insofar as the same shall not have been performed at completion, shall remain in full force and effect notwithstanding completion.

Continuing authority

The authorities herein contained are continuing ones and shall remain in full force and effect until revoked by termination of this agreement as hereinafter provided, but such revocation shall not affect any liability in any way resulting from transactions initiated prior to such revocation.

Amendments

This agreement may be amended, varied or altered only by written consent by both the parties hereto.

The seller reserves the right to vary [any of the terms of this agreement] by written notice to the buyer. The variation shall be deemed to take place 10 working days after the date of deemed delivery of the notice and all orders placed thereafter shall be governed by the terms of this agreement as varied.

No variation permitted

No act, course of conduct, failure or neglect to act or acquiescence on the part of the seller shall result in the seller being taken to have waived or be precluded whether temporarily or permanently from enforcing and relying on:

(a) any provision of this agreement; or
(b) any breach by another party to this agreement of any obligation under it or under the general law; or
(c) any right of the seller under the general law including a right arising out of a breach such as one described in paragraph (b) above.

4 – Confidentiality and disclosure confidentiality agreements

Central to many commercial contractual documents is a confidentiality agreement, sometimes referred to as a **non-disclosure agreement** (NDA). It is critical that such an agreement is properly drawn.

Define what information is intended to be confidential

It is both desirable and necessary to define that information which is to be subject to obligations of confidentiality. It could relate simply to technical information (e.g. regarding the product being sold) or to more general commercial information or perhaps a general catch-all provision relating to all information. With regard to the latter, a party must be careful not to be fixed with a confidentiality agreement which covers matters which are not secret at all. Notwithstanding the existence of a confidentiality agreement, the courts will not enforce it in regard to information which has ceased to be confidential (e.g. where such information has entered the public domain). A party who is being made subject to a confidentiality agreement should be careful to exclude:

- information of which he is already aware;
- information which is already within the public domain (e.g. records available for inspection at Companies House, the Land Registry etc.) or which becomes so available after the making of the contract;
- information of which he becomes subsequently aware from a source outside the scope of the confidentiality agreement; and
- information of which he becomes aware as a result of his own research.

With regard to all the above, it may be sensible to maintain records to show to which information it relates and how the information was acquired. In particular, it may be useful to ask the recipient of information to acknowledge receipt of specific papers and other confidential information. This receipt should be dated. A record should also be maintained of other information which is disclosed in a more informal manner such as in discussions and conversations, noting when and where such disclosure occurred.

Define the parties to be fixed with confidentiality obligations

The party who is to be fixed with obligations will wish to be as certain as possible not only as to what those obligations are, but also who is to be fixed with the obligations. Often employees of the person receiving the information will become parties to the confidential information. The larger the matter to which the contract relates, the wider the raft of persons to whom information may need to be disclosed. For example, in the sale of a company, advice may need to be taken from accountants, solicitors, tax advisers etc. It is a matter of convenience that information should be able to be forwarded in such circumstances without the need to go back to the discloser for further consent, not least because such a request might well alert the discloser to further leverage which he might exercise to maximise his profits under the contract. Moreover, the greater the number of persons involved in the process of negotiation, the more difficult it becomes to comply with requirements regarding matters such as the number of copies of information being made and the persons to whom such copies may be circulated.

However, the party disclosing information should be anxious to ensure that anyone receiving it will be fixed with the duty of confidentiality and that the party to whom disclosure is made will be liable for any breach by a recipient of the information.

In drafting a confidentiality agreement, a balance must be drawn between the desire of the party to whom disclosure is made to be able freely to consult on and review the matters disclosed and the risk of his breaching the confidentiality agreement if a consultee should make a prohibited disclosure.

It is reasonable for a party to whom disclosure is being made to accept responsibility for breaches by himself or his employees. However, it may not be so reasonable should the disclosure be made by a third party. There are two main ways of dealing with third-party liability.

- When confidential information is passed to a third party he might be required to give a similar confidentiality agreement, perhaps in the third-party's letter of engagement or some similar document.
- There might be added to the confidentiality agreement an acknowledgement of confidentiality to be signed as a deed by the third party. The benefit of this is that the original discloser could then enforce directly against the third party in the event of breach. It is important that the acknowledgement is by way of a deed because, if given merely under hand, it would be lacking in consideration and therefore be unenforceable under English law.

It is important never to give an absolute undertaking that third parties will enter into confidentiality agreements because it will often be impossible to achieve this in many instances. The most that should be promised is for the disclosee to undertake to use his 'best endeavours' to do so.

Do not give an indemnity as part of the confidentiality agreement

It is sensible to have the confidentiality agreement as a straightforward term of the contract rather than by way of an indemnity provision. The benefits of this are as follows:

- damages for breach of condition are limited to the actual loss sustained as a result of the breach and which loss was within the contemplation of the parties; and
- a party claiming damages for breach must do what he can to mitigate his loss.

An indemnity, however, would cover all losses, including legal costs, emanating from the breach.

Anticipate situations where disclosure must be made

There are instances where, as a matter of law or other mandatory regulation, disclosure must be made (e.g. to the Stock Exchange in certain circumstances which might arise in the course of the takeover of a quoted company). Usually a confidentiality agreement will permit disclosure in such circumstances. It is sensible for such disclosure to be permissible without the need to notify the original discloser because of the potential criminality of so doing (e.g. under the money-laundering laws). Thus, an obligation to obtain prior consent before disclosure should always be avoided and any notification requirement should be stated to be 'as far as legally permissible'.

Consider limiting the length of the confidentiality agreement

There should usually be a limit placed on the duration of the confidentiality agreement. This might be expressed as a set period of time (e.g. one year or until completion of the contract).

In this regard, the following should be borne in mind:

- the longer the confidentiality agreement, the more difficult it will be to manage; and
- given that the value of the confidential matter will diminish as time passes, a long confidentiality period will rarely be necessary.

However, there might be information (e.g. personal information about individuals or a list of customers) which it may be appropriate to keep confidential indefinitely.

Use the promise of a confidentiality agreement as a bargaining tool to obtain exclusivity

Often a request for a confidentiality agreement may be used by the other party as a bargaining tool to seek exclusivity for the period needed for the completion of their due diligence. During such time, the discloser might be persuaded to agree that there should be no disclosure to or negotiations with a third party in relation to the subject matter of the contract.

Seek the right to enforce any other confidentiality agreements given by other potential contracting parties

If the confidentiality agreement is being given in the course of what is, in effect, an auction, it is sensible to ask that in the event of the giver of the confidentiality agreement's being successful, all other confidentiality agreements obtained from the other bidders will be assigned to the successful party on completion of the transaction. Of course, should the giver be unsuccessful, such a provision will work against them, but that is usually a price worth paying.

Be cautious regarding a promise to return information

Often a confidentiality agreement will be accompanied by a covenant to return information on the expiry of the agreement. When giving such an undertaking, it is crucial that the giver is able to uphold their side of the bargain. An undertaking to return information immediately should be avoided; rather there should be a promise to return the information within a reasonable time.

It is also worthwhile seeking an option to destroy, rather than to return, confidential information. Such information might, for example, be contained in private notes or in entries on a private laptop etc. Destruction rather than return in such circumstances would clearly be preferential to the covenantee.

Moreover, any such undertaking to return or destroy should expressly exclude certain matters such as:

- information set out in documents available to the board of a company such as board minutes, board papers etc;
- information in documents containing information which is subject to legal privilege;
- information contained in documents which cannot legally be destroyed, such as documents required to be maintained by law or other regulatory rules; and
- information stored on back-up systems or through other archive arrangements.

Make sure that the agreement is enforceable

As long as the confidentiality agreement is two ways, there will be consideration moving between the parties and it will thus be enforceable even where it is merely under hand. However, if the agreement is one way, it may need to be executed as a deed by the person to whom the information is given for it to be enforceable.

Freedom of Information Act 2002

When making disclosure to a public authority including a university, it should be borne in mind that the authority is under an obligation to make information available to the public pursuant to a request under the Freedom of Information Act 2002, the Freedom of Information (Scotland) Act 2002 or the Environmental Information Regulations 2004. It may be advisable to ask such authority to take advantage of the exceptions to such obligation contained in the legislation.[1]

Draft clauses

None of the parties hereto shall (except under compulsion by law or with the prior consent of the other parties or where required by the rules and regulations of [ ]), either before or after the termination of this agreement, disclose to any person not authorised by the other party or parties to receive the same, any confidential information relating to such party or parties or to the affairs of such party of which the party disclosing the same shall have become possessed during the period of this agreement, and each party shall use all reasonable endeavours to prevent any such disclosure as aforesaid.

The recipient of confidential information shall, at the request of the discloser, return all copies and records of such information to the discloser and undertakes not to retain copies or records of such information.

The undertakings contained in clauses [ ] hereof shall continue in force [for [ ] years from the date of the agreement's being executed] [indefinitely].

None of the parties hereto shall (except under compulsion of law or with the prior consent of the other parties or where required by the rules and regulations of [ ]) either before or after the termination of this agreement, disclose to any person not authorised by the party to which it pertains to receive the same, any confidential information relating to such party or to the affairs of such party of which the party disclosing the same shall have become possessed during the period of this agreement and each party shall use all reasonable endeavours to prevent any such disclosure as aforesaid.

All information disclosed by either party to the other in connection with the performance of this agreement, except such information as may be generally available to the public, shall be disclosed in confidence. Each party is obliged to keep any such information as it may acquire confidential and, save as required by applicable laws or regulations, not to disclose it to any other person or otherwise improperly use it while this agreement is in effect or after its termination except insofar as such information has entered the public domain otherwise than in breach of this clause.

Neither of the parties hereto shall, either before or after the termination of this agreement, disclose, to any person not authorised by the relevant party to receive the same, any information relating to such party or to the affairs of such party of which the party disclosing the same shall have become possessed during the period of this agreement and each party shall use its bests endeavours to prevent any such disclosure.

[X] recognises that the information already provided to it and to be provided to it by [Y] is commercially sensitive information and that it must be treated in the utmost confidence. Therefore [X] agrees that it shall maintain all such information as strictly confidential and shall not use it for its own purposes (other than for the assessment of the business of [ ] for the purposes of the transaction contemplated hereunder) or disclose such information to any third party without prior written consent of [Y].

The parties to this agreement will at all times respect and protect the confidentiality of information acquired in consequence of this agreement (except as may be otherwise required by law [or the rules and regulations of [ ]).

Neither [X] nor any associate is obliged to disclose to [Y] or, in making any decision or taking any step in connection with the management of [Y's] affairs under this agreement, to take into consideration any information:

(i) if any disclosure of the information by them to [Y] would or might be a breach of duty or confidence to any other person;
(ii) which comes to the notice of an employee or agent of [X] or of an associate but does not come to the actual notice of the individual or individuals making the decision or taking the step in question.

All parties to this agreement shall confidentially maintain any information given to them, whether directly or indirectly, by any party to this agreement either under the agreement or in anticipation of it, and shall take such reasonable security measures as are necessary to protect its own confidential information. They also agree to use such information for the purposes only of performing their obligations under this agreement and undertake not to disclose such information to any other person, other than to consultants or employees who need to have access to such information in regard to the performance of this agreement, and who have themselves accepted obligations of confidentiality and restriction of use in accordance with this clause.

The obligations referred to in this clause do not apply to information which the party receiving the information can prove:

- *was already lawfully in its possession before its receipt from the other party;*
- *was already within the public domain at the time when it was provided by the other party;*
- *subsequently entered the public domain other than through the default of the party receiving it;*
- *was acquired by the party receiving it from a source which is not a party to this confidentiality agreement;*
- *was acquired by the party receiving it through his own research;*
- *is required to be disclosed by any lawful order of the court or governmental authority or by the rules of any stock exchange; or*
- *is trivial or obvious or otherwise of a non-confidential nature.*

Confidentiality

It is desirable to define any information which is to be subject to obligations of confidentiality. It could relate simply to technical information (e.g. regarding the product being sold, to more general commercial information or perhaps, to all information).

The party who is to be fixed with obligations will wish to be as certain as possible as to what those obligations are.

If one party is likely to give more information than the other party they will want a wide definition of what information is subject to the confidentiality requirement. If they are likely to give less information, they will want a narrower definition.

If a wide definition is used, particularly one which includes oral information, proof may be difficult. When litigating, it is sometimes difficult to prove that information was ever in the possession of the other party. The wider the definition of confidential information used, the harder it will be to prove such possession.

A warranty of right to disclose will often be included. This is obviously sought by recipients but avoided by disclosers.

The parties may be concerned about the publicity surrounding the agreement. Provision should be made that any publicity requires the consent of both parties.

Care should be taken to ensure that secrecy extends to employees.

General restrictions

None of the parties hereto shall (except under compulsion by law or where required by the rules and regulations of [ ] or with the prior consent of the other parties) either before or after the termination of this agreement, disclose to any person not authorised by the other party or parties to receive the same any confidential information relating to such party or parties or to the affairs of such party of which the party disclosing the same shall have become possessed during the period of this agreement, and each party shall use all reasonable endeavours to prevent any such disclosure as aforesaid.

None of the parties hereto shall (except under compulsion of law) either before or after the termination of this agreement, disclose to any person not authorised to receive the same by the party to which it pertains any confidential information relating to such party or to the affairs of such party of which the party disclosing the same shall have become possessed during the period of this agreement and each party shall use all reasonable endeavours to prevent any such disclosure as aforesaid.

All information disclosed by either party to the other in connection with the performance of this agreement, except such information as may be generally available to the public, shall be disclosed in confidence and each party is obliged to keep any such information as it may acquire confidential and, save as required by applicable laws or regulations, not to disclose it to any other person or otherwise improperly use it while this agreement is in effect or after its termination except insofar as such information has entered the public domain otherwise than in breach of this clause.

Neither of the parties hereto shall, either before or after the termination of this agreement, disclose to any person not authorised by the relevant party to receive the same, any information relating to such party or to the affairs of such party of which the party disclosing the same shall have become possessed during the period of this agreement and each party shall use its bests endeavours to prevent any such disclosure.

[X] recognises that the information already provided to it and to be provided to it by [Y] is commercially sensitive information and that it must be treated in the utmost confidence. Therefore [X] agrees that it shall maintain

all such information as strictly confidential and shall not use it for its own purposes (other than for the assessment of the business of [ ] for the purposes of the transaction contemplated hereunder) or disclose such information to any third party without prior written consent of [Y].

The parties to this agreement will at all times respect and protect the confidentiality of information acquired in consequence of this agreement (except as may be otherwise required by law [or the rules and regulations of]).

Neither [X] nor any associate is obliged to disclose to [Y] or, in making any decision or taking any step in connection with the management of [Y's] affairs under this agreement, to take into consideration any information:

(i) if any disclosure of the information by them to [Y] would or might be a breach of duty or confidence to any other person;
(ii) which comes to the notice of an employee or agent of [X] or of an associate but does not come to the actual notice of the individual or individuals making the decision or taking the step in question.

Announcements

No announcements or information concerning this agreement shall be made or released before or after completion to the public or [to shareholders] or to the press by either party except in the agreed terms.

[X] shall not, and shall procure that any other member of the [X] Group shall not, at any time, use the words 'ABC' in any circular, promotion or advertisement without the prior consent of [Y] but this prohibition shall not apply to the use of the name in any fair or factual reference to the history of [the company] or of its former management.

Access by accountants and auditors

.... will allow [Y's] accountants or auditors such access to its accounts and, if necessary, provide certification from time to time in respect of such transactions, holdings, books, records and systems in so far as the same relate to the affairs of [Y] as [Y] or its accountants or auditors may reasonably require.

Note

1 A full consideration of the Act is beyond the scope of this work. However, see Part 2, Freedom of Information Act 2002 for the exceptions applicable to public authorities.

5 – Intellectual property rights

It is obviously necessary to define intellectual property rights in many commercial contracts.

Care should be taken with the term 'know how'. In its broadest sense it is simply information. As such, it cannot be a proprietary right. However, sometimes it is extended to include the material embodiment of the information (e.g. '*... includes all those patentable and non patentable inventions, discoveries and improvements and processes and copyright works'*).

In a contract where intellectual property is being transferred, warranties in regard to the accuracy and efficacy of the know-how are often sought, together with warranties as to the licensor's right to transfer and to licence.

In licensing or technology transfer agreements it is necessary to clearly define what is being transferred.

Sometimes a contract will speak of 'trade secrets' or 'proprietary information'. However, 'know how' is not an intellectual property right. Information cannot be owned.

Definitions

Intellectual property rights	These include patents, trade marks, service marks, design rights, copyright (including all copyright in any designs and computer software), inventions, trade secrets, know-how, confidential information, registrable business names and all other intellectual property rights and rights of a similar character in any part of the work (whether or not the same are registered or capable of registration), and all applications and rights to apply for protection of any of the same.
Confidential information	This means information which any party to this agreement (for whatever reason) might reasonably be expected to object to becoming generally known, for whatever reason.

6 – Warranties, guarantees and indemnities

Warranty of authority

An individual may give a warranty that he has authority to sign an agreement on behalf of the party that he represents. This, however, is usually implied under most legal systems. The individual will be personally liable for breach of either an express or implied warranty of authority.

Sometimes a party to an agreement will give a warranty that it has the capacity to enter into the transaction. In the context of registered companies this is now probably irrelevant since s. 35 Companies Act 1985 effectively abolishes the *ultra vires* rule as regards third parties. However, this only applies to registered companies. In the case of other incorporated bodies, a third party may want some remedy against the signatory for the persons controlling a defaulting party.

Care should be taken when dealing with employees and other agents of local authorities and public bodies.

With overseas companies, a warranty of good standing may be required.

Warranty of good standing

A warranty is sometimes sought that a party is duly incorporated and does exist as a properly functioning corporation.

Best and reasonable endeavours

It is very common for a provision within a contract to refer to a party using either his best or reasonable endeavours.

For example:

[X] shall at its own expense use its best endeavours to procure all necessary government and other consents as are necessary [ ] to implement this agreement and shall thereafter use its best endeavours on a continuing basis to ensure that all such consents remain in effect.

There is little doubt that a requirement to use 'best endeavours' imposes quite a substantial level of commitment upon the party with whom it is fixed. In *Sheffield District Railway v Great Central Railway*,[1] it was stated that '"best endeavours" *means what it says – it does not mean second best endeavours*'. A party fixed with such an obligation should leave '*no stone unturned*'.

This was further explained by the Court of Appeal in *IBM United Kingdom Ltd v Rockware Glass Ltd*,[2] where it was said that the person fixed must 'take all steps in their power which are capable of producing the desired results ... steps which a prudent, determined and reasonable [person], acting in his own interests and desiring to achieve that result, would take'.

In *Midland Land Reclamation Ltd, Leicestershire CC v Warren Energy Ltd*,[3] HHJ Bowsher QC stated: '"Best endeavours" *imposes a duty to do what can reasonably be done in the circumstances and the standard of reasonableness is that of a reasonable and prudent board of directors acting properly in the interests of their company.*' However, the learned judge rejected a submission that a 'best endeavours' obligation was the next best thing to an absolute obligation or guarantee.

In *Terrell v Mabie Todd & Co Ltd*,[4] there were two licence agreements relating to inventions and designs. The licensee was to use its '*all diligence*' to promote sales of the inventions and designs and then to use its '*best endeavours*' for their exploitation. It was held that this required the licensee to take at least reasonable steps to exploit the inventions and designs having regard to the interests of its shareholders. Having said this, it did not require the taking of steps in '*utter disregard for the interests of shareholders*' which would lead to the '*certain ruin of the company*'.

Monkland v Jack Barclay Ltd[5] concerned the purchase of a Bentley car. The seller was required by the contract to use its best endeavours to secure delivery on an estimated delivery date though a precise date was stated. It was held that this meant that the seller should use its best endeavours to secure delivery within a reasonable time.

More recently, the term was considered by HHJ Mackie QC in *Jet2.com Ltd*.[6] Jet2 is a low-cost airline which had entered into an agreement with Blackpool Airport. The contract stated that:

> *'Jet2.com and BAL will co-operate together and use their best endeavours to promote JET2.com's low cost services from Blackpool Airport and BAL will use all reasonable endeavours to provide a cost base that will facilitate Jet2.com's low-cost pricing.'*

Blackpool Airport had specified and published opening hours, but these were not referred to in the contract. For some time, Jet2 had operated some flights outside these hours. Blackpool Airport had, however, changed hands and its new owners had decided that they would no longer permit flights outside the standard opening hours because of the cost involved. The learned judge observed that in this particular case the parties viewed *'best endeavours'* as having the same meaning as *'reasonable endeavours'*. However, he felt that the meaning of the expressions were a matter of construction in each case rather than being a matter of extrapolation from other cases. The fact that the contract contained no express provision as to opening hours meant that it was *'too obvious to mention'* that JET2 would not be confined to standard opening hours.

Notwithstanding that, in this case, the learned judge found the parties to have regarded the two expressions as having the same meaning there is little doubt that they will always be interpreted synonymously. In most cases, the approach of the judiciary has been to view 'reasonable' as creating a somewhat lower obligation than 'best'. For example, in *UBL (Mechanical Services) Ltd v Standard Life Assurance,*[7] Rougier J found that a requirement to use *'reasonable endeavours'* created an obligation less burdensome than *'best endeavours'*. A lessee had undertaken to use his *'reasonable endeavours'*. Such wording allowed him to take into account other commercial considerations besides his obligation to the landlord.

In *Rhodia International Holdings Ltd v Huntsman International LLC,*[8] the claimant had agreed to sell its European chemical surfactants business to the defendant. Included in the sale was a site which was powered by a third party pursuant to an energy supply agreement. Both parties contracted to use their 'reasonable endeavours' to obtain novation of the supply agreement to the buyer. This was accompanied by an undertaking by the buyer to obtain a parent company guarantee should the third-party supplier require it. Some three years later, completion had still not taken place, largely because the buyer had failed to obtain the guarantee which the supplier had requested. The seller now brought proceedings for breach of contract. Mr Julian Faux QC, sitting as a deputy High Court judge, found for the seller. Failure to obtain the parent company guarantee was sufficient to put the buyer in breach of contractual reasonable endeavours obligations.

In *Yewbelle Ltd v London Green Developments Ltd,*[9] sellers agreed to sell land to a buyer. The intention was that the buyer would then develop the land and lease parts of it back to the sellers. The sale was completed prior to planning consent having been obtained from the local authority. Although the sellers could not guarantee that planning consent would be forthcoming, they agreed to use 'all reasonable endeavours' to obtain it. Subsequent to the signing of the sale contract it became apparent that the planning agreement would require the involvement of land belonging to a third party. The sellers would have either to buy the land or, alternatively, to make the third party a party to the planning consent. In either event, this would involve the sellers in considerable further expense. It was held by the Court of Appeal that reasonable endeavours did not require this further expenditure to be incurred.

In *Rhodia*, the learned judge suggested that the difference between best and reasonable might be found in a situation where there may be several different but reasonable courses of action which might be taken to obtain a specified result. A party required to use reasonable endeavours might follow just one of these courses of action until it is exhausted. Best endeavours meant that all reasonable courses of action should be pursued until they are exhausted.

Sometimes a contract refers to a sort of halfway house requiring a party to exercise *'all reasonable efforts'*. In *Jolley v Carmel Ltd*,[10] it was suggested that if *'best'* and *'reasonable'* constitute two ends of a spectrum, *'all reasonable'* falls somewhere between the two.

In *Baring Securities v DG Durham Group*,[11] the claimant was required to use all reasonable endeavours to obtain a landlord's consent to an assignment of a lease and to obtain a guarantee from a subsidiary company if necessary. This required the claimant to *'do its best'* to obtain the consent, but did not go so far as to require it to obtain the guarantee from its parent company should a subsidiary be unwilling to give it. It was suggested that *'all reasonable endeavours'* is *'probably a middle position somewhere between the two implying something more than reasonable endeavours but less than best endeavours'*.

In *Rhodia* it was suggested that *'all reasonable endeavours'* equated to *'best endeavours'*. However, in *Agroexport State Enterprise for Foreign Trade v Compagnie Europeene de Cereales*[12] and, at first instance, in *Yewbelle v London Green*,[13] it was suggested that *'all reasonable endeavours'* could be used interchangeably with both *'best'* and *'reasonable'*. However, it might be that this applies only to the number of courses of action which the party fixed with the obligation is required in law to take rather than to any other distinction such as to what degree it might be required to compromise its own commercial interests.

This approach seems to have support in the recent decision on *CPC Group Ltd v Qatari Diar Real Estate*.[14] The case arose out of the redevelopment of the Chelsea Barracks. An application for planning consent sought by Qatari Diar was withdrawn following an intervention by the Prince of Wales. CPC was a Guernsey registered company. Qatari Diar was a subsidiary of the Qatari Investment Authority, a sovereign wealth fund. A sale agreement had been entered into between the parties under which Qatari Diar was to use *'all reasonable but commercially prudent endeavours'* to obtain the planning consent. Vos, J had to consider whether the withdrawal of the planning application constituted a breach of this obligation. It was held that there had been no breach. Although it seems that the words *'but commercially prudent'* were not key to the decision, they did allow Qatari Diar to have regard to its own commercial interests. As the learned judge said: *'It seems to me, therefore, that the obligation to use "all reasonable endeavours" does not always require the obligor to sacrifice his commercial interests.'*

If it is possible to draw a conclusion at this point, it may well be that a contract should be specific as to what precise steps must be taken to for an obligor to fulfil his contractual obligations.

Warranty of compliance with laws

Such a warranty encourages both parties to act in a lawful manner. It also imposes an obligation on each party to obtain all necessary consents and permissions to enable him to carry out his part of the bargain. Export licences and similar regulatory consents would come within such a warranty.

Consents and authorisations

[X] shall at its own expense use its best endeavours to procure all necessary government and other consents as are necessary [ ] to implement this agreement and shall thereafter use its best endeavours on a continuing basis to ensure that all such consents remain in effect.

Each company shall, and [X] shall procure that each other member of the [X] Group shall comply with all laws and regulations applicable to it and which are necessary and material in relation to the conduct of its business generally and shall promptly obtain, maintain and comply with the terms of and supply to [Y] at its request certified copies of any authorisation required under any law or regulation to enable it to perform its obligations under or for the validity, enforceability and admissibility in evidence of, any document executed under this agreement and any authorisation which is necessary and material in relation to the conduct of its business generally.

[X] warrants to [Y] that it has all necessary authorities to enter into this agreement and to appoint [Y] as its agent for the purposes referred to herein.

You warrant and represent (if a body corporate, partnership or unincorporated body) to us while this agreement subsists that you are, by your memorandum and articles of association, deed of partnership, trust deed or other constitutional document, as the case may be, empowered (and not prohibited) to act as the agent of [X] and to enter into this agreement.

You warrant while this agreement subsists that you will obtain and maintain in effect and ensure that [X] will obtain and maintain in effect, in relation to all transactions, all necessary consents of any governmental or other regulatory body or authority applicable to each transaction and that you will comply, and ensure that [X] will comply, with the terms of the same and all applicable laws, regulations and directives of such bodies and authorities. You will, forthwith on demand by us, deliver to us copies of all such consents or such other evidence of any such consents and such evidence of compliance with such and with any such laws, regulations and directives as we may reasonably require.

You confirm and undertake that you have and will have during the term of this letter agreement, all necessary consents (and, if you are not an individual, powers in your constitution) and authorities to enable all transactions under this letter agreement to be effected.

Competition law notification

No provision hereof by virtue of which this agreement is subject to registration under the Restrictive Trade Practices Act 1976 (or such legislation which may have been introduced to replace such Act) shall take effect until the day after particulars of this agreement have been furnished to the Director General of Fair Trading pursuant to section 24 of that Act.

Duty of care

In carrying out his duties and functions hereunder [X] shall act for the benefit of [Y] and shall act with the care which a businessman reasonably devotes to his affairs.

Warranty of title and quiet possession

Many legal systems have such implied warranties. In English law they generally cannot be excluded by virtue of the Unfair Contract Terms Act 1977. Nevertheless it is sensible to set them out.

Warranties of quality

Again, most legal systems have such warranties, but it is nevertheless sensible to set them out expressly in a contract.

N.B. Traditionally, it has only been the parties to a contract who have been able to enforce rights under the contract. However, the Contracts (Rights of Third Parties) Act 1999 allows the enforcement of rights under a contract by a third party who is identified within that contract or is a member of a class identified within a contract. Such third-party rights may be expressly excluded by a contract.

Representations and warranties

[X] makes the representations and warranties set out in this Clause [ ] (Representations and warranties) to [Y].

All such representations and warranties shall be construed when made and deemed repeated, subject to matters specifically disclosed in a letter dated [ ] 2006 from [X] to [Y].

The representations and warranties set out in this Clause [ ] are made by [X] on the date of this agreement and are deemed to be repeated by [ ] on the [date of completion] [last day of each calendar month] with reference to the facts and circumstances then existing.

[X] warrants and undertakes that, subject to the provisions of this agreement, the assets which are the subject of this agreement from time to time are and will remain beneficially owned by [X] and free from any charge, lien, pledge or encumbrance.

General indemnities

A customer is concerned that he is compensated for loss or damage caused as a result of a defect in goods supplied or as a result of the failure of the other party to perform the contract properly. Such remedies are usually provided by way of an indemnity rather than a warranty.

Indemnity

[X] agrees to use its best efforts and judgement and due care in performing its duties and obligations hereunder provided that, in the absence of wilful misfeasance, negligence, bad faith or reckless disregard of obligations or duties hereunder on the part of [X], any member of the [X] group, its or their directors, officers and employees and any persons delegated by [X], [X] shall not be liable to [Y] or to any shareholder for any act or omission in the course of or in connection with the services or any loss whatsoever that may result to [Y] as a result of the performance of the obligations and duties of [X] hereunder (except as otherwise specifically provided for herein).

[X] shall not be liable for any consequential loss or damage arising from its functions under this agreement, including, without limitation, loss of profit.

[Y] agrees to indemnify and hold [X] and any member of the [X] group, its or their directors, officers, and employees and any persons delegated by [X] harmless from and against all liability, costs, claims, actions, losses, damages and expenses whatsoever arising directly or indirectly as a result of its or their lawful actions taken or omissions made in good faith pursuant to the activities contemplated in this agreement and neither [X] nor any member of the [X] group nor its directors, officers or employees and any persons delegated by [X] shall be held liable to [Y] or any of its shareholders, directors, officers or employees as a result of such lawful actions taken or omissions made in good faith as aforesaid or for any obligations or liabilities incurred by [Y].

[X] hereby undertakes to hold harmless and indemnify [Y] and each director, officer, employee or agent of [Y] against any losses, claims, damages or liabilities (including legal or other expenses reasonably incurred in investigating or defending against such loss, claim, damages or liabilities) to which such person(s) may become subject by reason of such persons performing their duties hereunder for and on behalf of [X] PROVIDED THAT this indemnity shall not apply to cases involving wilful default, bad faith or negligence by such person.

To the extent permitted by law, [X] will indemnify [Y] against any cost, loss, liability or expense whatsoever which may be suffered or incurred by them directly or indirectly in connection with or as a result of any service performed or action permitted hereunder, save to the extent that the same is due to its negligence, wilful default or fraud.

You agree to keep [X] and its employees indemnified against all costs, charges, liabilities and expenses whatsoever incurred by them pursuant to or in connection with this agreement unless due to their negligence, wilful default or fraud.

[X] shall indemnify [Y] against all actions proceedings claims or demands in any way connected with this agreement brought or threatened against [Y] except to the extent that [Y] is liable to [X] under this agreement.

Guarantee

In consideration of [X] entering into this agreement the guarantor hereby unconditionally and irrevocably guarantees to [X] the due and punctual performance and observance by [Y] of its obligations under this agreement and this guarantee will not be affected by the granting of time or other indulgence on the part of [X].

[X] irrevocably and unconditionally as principal obligator guarantees to [Y] prompt performance by [Z] of all its obligations under this agreement and undertakes to [Y] that whenever [Z] does not pay any amount when due under or in connection with this agreement [X] shall forthwith on demand by [Y] pay that amount as if [X] instead of [Z] were expressed to be the principal obligor and indemnifies [Y] on demand against any loss or liability suffered by it if any obligation guaranteed by [X] under this clause is or becomes unenforceable, invalid or illegal.

This guarantee is continuing guarantee and will extend to the ultimate balance of all sums payable by [Z] under the agreement and regardless of any intermediate payment or discharge in whole or in part.

Where any discharge (whether in respect of the obligations of [Z] or any security for those obligations or otherwise) is made in whole or in part or any arrangement is made on the faith of any payment, security or other disposition which is avoided or must be restored on insolvency, liquidation or otherwise without limitation, the liability of [X] under this clause shall continue as if the discharge or arrangement had not occurred.

The obligations of [X] under this clause will not be affected by an act, omission, matter or thing which, but for this provision, would reduce, release or prejudice any of its obligations under this clause or prejudice or diminish those obligations in whole or in part, including:

- *(a) any time or waiver granted to or composition with, [Z] or other person;*
- *(b) the taking, variation, compromise, exchange, renewal or release of or refusal or neglect to perfect, take up or enforce, any rights against or security over assets of, [Z] or other person or any non-presentation or non-observance of any formality or other requirement in respect of any instrument or any failure to realise the full value of any security;*
- *(c) any incapacity or lack of powers, authority or legal personality of or dissolution or change in the members or status of [Z] or any other person;*
- *(d) any variation (however fundamental) or replacement of this agreement or any other document or security so that references to this agreement in this clause shall include each variation or replacement;*
- *(e) any unenforceability, illegality or invalidity of any obligation of any person under this agreement or any other document or security, to*

the intent that [X's] obligations under this clause shall remain in full force and its guarantee be construed accordingly, as if there were no unenforceability, illegality or invalidity; or

(f) any postponement, discharge, reduction, non-provability or other similar circumstances affecting any obligation of [Z] under this agreement resulting from any insolvency, liquidation or dissolution proceedings or from the law, regulation or order so that each such obligation shall for the purposes of [Z's] obligations under this clause be construed as if there were no such circumstance.

[X] waives any right it may have of first requiring [Y] (or any trustee or agent on its behalf) to proceed against or enforce any other rights or security or claim payment from any person (save for any demand on the principal debt) before claiming from [X] under this clause.

This guarantee is in addition to and is not in any way prejudiced by any other security now or subsequently held by [Y].

Notes

1 (1911) 72 TLR 451.
2 [1980] FSR 335.
3 20 January 1997; [1997] ABCLR. 01/20.
4 (1952) 69 RPC 234.
5 [1951] 2 KB 252.
6 [2011] EWHC 1529 (Comm).
7 (1986) *The Times*, 13 November.
8 [2007] EWHC 292 (Comm).
9 [2007] EWCA Civ 475.
10 [2000] 2 EGLR 154.
11 [1993] EGCS 192.
12 [1974] 1 Ll Rep 499.
13 [2006] EWHC 3166.
14 [2010] EWHC 1535 (Ch).

7 – Joint and several liability

Several liability makes each promisor liable for his own obligations alone. Thus where A and B severally agree to pay £1,000 to C, while C is entitled to receive £2,000, neither A nor B is liable to pay the other's debt.

However, if A and B jointly agree to pay C £2,000, both A and B are jointly liable for the £2,000. If A has to pay the full £2,000 to C, he can recover £1,000 from B.

Is there a distinction between joint liability and joint and several liability?

As a general rule, if one party dies, his estate is not liable where he has entered into joint liability. In such a case the survivor assumes full liability. However, s. 9 of the Partnership Act 1890 makes the estate of a deceased partner severally liable for the partnership's debts in these circumstances. Also with joint liability, a plaintiff must generally join all those whom he seeks to make liable jointly with himself for a debt when suing for recovery. However, there are exceptions under s. 48, County Courts Act 1984 and there is no need to join in a defendant who is an undischarged bankrupt under s. 345, Insolvency Act 1986.

Joint and several liability

Unless otherwise provided, all representations, warranties, undertakings, covenants, agreements and obligations given or entered into under this agreement by the sellers are given and entered into jointly and severally by the sellers.

Several liability

Unless otherwise provided, all representations, warranties, undertakings, covenants, agreements and obligations given or entered into under this agreement by the sellers are given and entered into severally by the sellers in relation only to himself and the liability of each such person in respect of any breach of any such representation, warranty, undertaking, covenant, agreement or obligation shall extend only to any loss or damage arising from his own breach.

8 – Retention of title

The possibility of retention of title comes from ss 16, 17 and 19, Sale of Goods Act 1979 which allow the seller to delay the passing of title even though delivery has occurred until a specific condition has been satisfied. Invariably this condition is payment for the goods.

The first major recognition of the efficacy of such clauses in English Law was *Aluminium Industrie Vaassen BV v Romalpa Aluminium (Romalpa) [1976] 2 All ER 552.*

Such clauses are of considerable use when a purchaser becomes insolvent as the seller can recover the goods.

Care must be taken not to create something which might be perceived as a floating charge and thus be void for non-registration under s. 860, Companies Act 2006 (e.g. *Bond Worth [1979] All ER 919*). *See also Cosslett Contractors v Glamorgan CC [1997] BCC 724*, subsequently confirmed by *HL [2001] BCC 740.*

The court is unlikely to issue an injunction to prevent a receiver from dealing with goods subject to a retention of title clause where he gives an undertaking to account for the proceeds of such goods to the seller: *Lipe Ltd v Leyland Daf [1993] BCC 385.*

A seller can refuse to supply further goods to a receiver unless the receiver agrees to pay for goods already delivered to the company: *Leyland Daf v Automotive Products [1993] BCC 389.*

Where a retention of title clause purports to give the seller a right over the proceeds of sale of goods, care must be taken to ensure that it is not such as to create a charge over book debts which would again be registerable under s. 395.

However, it may be that a retention clause should provide that the buyer holds the proceeds in a fiduciary capacity or as trustee for the seller, combined with an obligation not to mix the moneys with his own, but rather to pay them into a separate bank account: see *Welsh Development Agency v Export Finance Co Ltd [1992] BCC 270.*

The rules governing floating charges apply only to companies and not to individuals. Accordingly, there is more scope for effective extended retention of title clauses where the purchaser is an individual. This is particularly so since the doctrine of reputed ownership under the Bankruptcy Act 1914 no longer applies generally under the Insolvency Act 1986. It should, however, be noted that it does still apply in the context of distress by a landlord for unpaid rent.

Seller's right to sue for the price

Under s. 49, Sale of Goods Act 1979, a seller can generally only sue for the price of goods when title has passed to the buyer.

The problems caused by this are avoided by providing that payment should be made on a specific day (e.g. 30 days after delivery of the goods).

Retention of title

Title to the goods shall remain with the seller and shall not pass to the buyer until payment in full for the same shall have been received by the seller.

If the buyer is overdue in paying for the goods, the seller may, if still the owner of the goods, recover and resell them. The seller may enter the buyer's premises for such purpose and may, if necessary, detach or remove the goods from other goods. This does not affect any other right of the seller.

Risk in the goods shall pass on delivery to the buyer.

9 – Notices

A proper provision for the service of notices is obviously an essential part of almost any agreement.

There is no legal requirement generally that a notice should be in writing. However, in practice, this should be required. Proof of delivery of a written notice is obviously easier than for an oral notice.

Provision should be made for notice to be deemed to have been given, say 48 hours after posting to a specified or ascertainable address.

Consideration should be given as to whether telex, facsimile or e-mail notices should be permitted.

Where a party to the agreement is outside the jurisdiction, it is often useful to appoint an agent within the jurisdiction who can validly be served in that party's place.

Any notice given pursuant to this agreement shall be in writing and shall be served by hand at or by being sent by telex, fax, e-mail or pre-paid post to the registered office for the time being of the addressee. Any such notice shall be deemed duly served at the time of delivery (if delivered by hand), at the time of receipt of confirmed answerback (if served by telex), at the time of receipt (if served by fax) or on the business day immediately after the date of posting (if served by pre-paid post). Evidence that the notice was properly addressed, stamped and put into the post shall be conclusive evidence of posting.

Any notice required to be given hereunder may be served by being left at or sent by special delivery to the registered office for the time being of the party on which it is to be served and any notice so given by post shall be deemed to have been served at the expiration of seven days after it is posted and in proving such service it shall be sufficient to prove that the envelope containing the notice was properly addressed and sent by special delivery.

Any notice given hereunder shall be in writing and shall be served by hand at or by being sent by pre-paid post or telex or e-mail or facsimile machine to the following addresses (or such other addresses as may be notified from time to time):

if to [X], to it at :
[address]

if to [Y], to it at:
[address]

Any notice or other communication to be given hereunder shall either be delivered personally or sent by first class post or telex or e-mail or facsimile transmission. The address for service of each party shall be the address stated at the head of this agreement or such other address as it may have previously notified to the other. All notices shall be deemed to have been served as follows:

(a) if personally delivered, at the time of delivery;
(b) if posted, at the expiration of 72 hours after the envelope containing the same was delivered into the custody of the postal authorities; and
(c) if communicated by telex or e-mail facsimile transmission at the time of transmission.

Provided that where, in the case of delivery by hand or transmission by telex or facsimile, such delivery or transmission occurs after 6pm on a business day or on a day which is not a business day, service shall be deemed to occur at 9am on the next following business day.

In proving such service it shall be sufficient to prove that personal delivery was made or that the envelope containing such notice was properly addressed and delivered into the custody of the postal authorities as a prepaid first class letter or that the telex transmission was made and the recipient's 'answerback' received or that the facsimile transmission was made after obtaining in person or by telephone appropriate evidence of the capacity of the addressee to receive the same, as the case may be.

Any instructions, notices, demands, acknowledgements or requests requiring to be served hereunder may be given by any party by delivery by hand, by pre-paid letter or by cable, telex or facsimile transmission (subsequently confirmed in writing) addressed to the other party or parties at its or their respective registered offices for the time being, and any such communication, if delivered by hand, shall be deemed to have been served immediately, and if sent by post, shall be deemed to have been served two days after the same is posted, and in proving service it shall be sufficient to prove that the envelope or wrapper containing the same was properly addressed, stamped and posted. Any such communication if given by cable, telex or facsimile transmission shall be deemed to have been served 24 hours after the same is dispatched.

For the avoidance of doubt, notice given under this agreement shall [not] be validly served if sent by e-mail.

Process agent

Without prejudice to any other method of service [X] irrevocably appoints [Y] as its agent for service of process in England, service upon whom shall be deemed completed whether or not forwarded to or received by [X].

Definitions – business day

'Business day' *means any day except Saturday and Sundays on which banks in the City of London are open for business.*

'Business day' *means a day (other than a Saturday or a Sunday) on which banks are open for business in London and (in relation to a transaction involving a currency other than Sterling) the principal business centre of the country of that other currency.*

Variations and whole agreement

[X] reserves the right to vary any of the terms of this agreement by written notice to you. The variation shall take effect five business days from the date of the notice and all orders placed thereafter shall be governed by the terms of this agreement as varied.

This agreement (together with the documents referred to herein) constitutes the entire agreement between the parties in relation to the transactions referred to herein or therein and supersedes any previous agreement between the parties in relation to such transactions.

No variation of any of the terms of this agreement (or of any other documents referred to herein) shall be effective unless it is in writing and signed by or on behalf of each of the parties hereto or thereto. The expression 'variation' shall include any variation, supplement, deletion or replacement, however effected.

Save as provided in clause [ ], no variation of this agreement shall be made unless made in writing and signed by or on behalf of each of the parties hereto.

This agreement contains the whole agreement between the parties relating to the subject matter of this agreement and no variation hereof shall be effective unless in writing and signed by or on behalf of each of the parties provided that [X] may at any time amend the terms of this agreement in accordance with clause [ ] hereof.

This agreement embodies and sets forth the entire agreement and understanding between [X] and you with respect to the services to be provided herein and supersedes all prior oral or written agreements, terms, understandings or arrangements relating to its subject matter.

This agreement applies to all transactions to the exclusion of any other terms which might otherwise apply. No departure from this agreement may be made without the written agreement of both [X] and [Y].

Except as specifically contemplated herein, this agreement constitutes the entire agreement between [X] and [Y] as to the matters referred to in this agreement and shall supersede any agreement, contract, understanding, undertaking or commitment which may have existed between the parties prior to the date hereof.

Any position of this agreement may be amended only if the parties so agree in writing.

This agreement contains the entire agreement and understanding of the parties and supersedes all prior agreements, understandings or arrangements (both oral and written) relating to the subject matter of this agreement.

Each of the parties acknowledges that it does not enter into this agreement on the basis of and does not rely upon any representation, warranty or other provision made or agreed to by any person (whether a party to this agreement or not) except those expressly set out in this agreement and in particular, without limitation, it has not relied on any representation, warranty or provision made, given or agreed prior to the entry into of this agreement and which is not expressly repeated in this agreement.

Except in the case of fraudulent misrepresentation, the only remedy available in respect of any misrepresentation or untrue statement made to it shall be a claim for breach of contract.

Insurance

[X] shall insure all its assets of an insurable nature against:

(i) loss or damage by fire;
(ii) other risks normally insured against by persons carrying on the same class of business as that carried on by it; and
(iii) any other risks which [Y] may reasonably require.

Any such insurance must be in a sum or sums not less than the replacement value of the assets. Any such insurance must be with an insurance company or underwriters acceptable to [Y].

[X] shall procure that a note of [Y's] interest is endorsed upon all policies of insurance maintained by [X] or any person on its behalf.

[X] shall not do or permit anything to be done which makes void or voidable any insurance in connection with any of its assets.

[X] shall promptly pay all premiums and do all other things necessary to keep all of its insurances in force.

[X] shall, on demand by [Y], produce to [Y] the policy, certificate or cover note relating to any insurance and the receipt for the payment of any premium for an insurance as [Y] may reasonably request.

[X] maintains [professional indemnity] [   ] insurance.

Governing law and jurisdiction

This agreement shall be governed by and construed in accordance with the laws of England.

The parties hereby submit to the non-exclusive jurisdiction of the courts of England in respect of any dispute arising out of this agreement or any transaction or act effected or carried on pursuant to this agreement.

This agreement is governed by English Law and the parties hereto submit to the non-exclusive jurisdiction of the English Courts.

This agreement shall be governed by and construed in accordance with the laws of England. In relation to any legal action or proceedings arising out of or in connection with this agreement ('proceedings'), each of the parties hereby irrevocably submits to the jurisdiction of the courts of England and waives any objection to proceedings in such courts whether on the grounds that the Proceedings have been brought in an inconvenient forum or otherwise. The submission of each party is made for the benefit of the other party and shall not affect the right of either of them to take proceedings in any other court of competent jurisdiction nor shall the taking of proceedings in any court of competent jurisdiction preclude any of them from taking proceedings in any other court of competent jurisdiction (whether concurrently or not).

This agreement shall be governed by and construed in accordance with English law and the parties irrevocably agree that the courts of England are to have exclusive jurisdiction to settle any disputes which may arise out of or in connection with this agreement.

[X] hereby submits to the non-exclusive jurisdiction of [ ] provided always that [Y] shall be at liberty to take proceedings against [X] in whatever jurisdiction [X] may from time to time be resident. This submission is for the benefit of [Y] and shall not limit its right to take proceedings in any other courts of competent jurisdiction.

This agreement shall be governed by and construed in accordance with English law. Disputes arising herefrom shall be subject to non-exclusive jurisdiction of the English courts to which both parties hereby submit.

Delegation

[X] shall [not] have power to delegate the responsibility for the whole or any part of its services hereunder to any other company, firm or person.

[X] shall be entitled to seek advice from and to delegate its functions, powers, discretion, privileges and duties hereunder or any of them to any subsidiary or affiliate or any other person firm or corporation approved by [Y] (hereinafter referred to as 'Z'; any such advisory arrangement or delegation will be on the same terms and conditions as are herein applicable to [X]). If [X] shall have delegated the whole of its functions hereunder, Y agrees that whilst such delegation remains effective, it shall no longer look to [X] for performance hereunder but to [Z] provided that, nevertheless, [X] shall continue to be liable for any [defaults].

Appointment of agents and sub-agents

[X] shall be entitled from time to time in its absolute discretion to appoint agents or sub-agents (including an associate) to perform any of its functions or of any of its powers, duties, authorities and discretions and remunerate such person.

Arbitration

Any dispute arising out of this agreement shall be referred to a single arbitrator (in default of agreement to be appointed by the President for the time being of [ ]) in accordance with the Arbitration Act 1996 or any statutory modification or re-enactment thereof for the time being in force.

10 – Assignment and change of control

It is not possible to assign the burden of a contract.

It is possible in equity to assign the benefit of a contract but not the burden.

By LPA 1925, there can be a legal assignment as long as it is given:

- under the hand of the assignor; and
- express notice in writing is given to the debtor, trustee or other person from whom the assignor would entitled to claim such debt of thing in action.

In *Tolhurst v Associated Portland Cement Manufacturers [1903] AC 414,* it was said that there cannot be an assignment of rights under a personal contract. There can only be an assignment 'in cases where it can make no difference to the person on whom the obligation lies to which of the two persons he is to discharge it'.

Thus it is possible to assign:

- the right to be paid a debt;
- the right to occupy land;
- the copyright of a written work;
- the rights under a contract for the sale of goods; and
- the proceeds of litigation.

But it is not possible to assign:

- the benefit of a motor insurance policy;
- the right to employ someone; and
- the right to sue for a non-proprietary tort (e.g. for defamation).

As a general rule it is acceptable for a person obligated to do something under a contract to employ a sub-contractor to fulfil his obligations. Note, however, that some contracts are too personal to permit subcontracting (e.g. a contract to paint a picture) and that subcontracting can never relieve the original contractor of his personal liabilities. Sub-contracting can be prevented by a properly drawn contract.

It may be possible for a party to a contract to declare himself to be a trustee of the benefit of the contract for a third party. Such a device can be used to circumvent a non-assignment clause. In *Don King Productions Inc v Warren [1999] 2 All ER 218,* the plaintiff company was owned by King, the leading boxing promoter in the USA. In 1994, King and Warren, the leading promoter in the UK, entered into two successive partnership agreements relating to the promotion and management of boxing in Europe. In the first agreement, Warren purported to assign to the partnership the full benefit and burden of all his existing management and promotion agreements with boxers. In fact, the agreements could not be assigned because they were for personal services and some also contained express provisions against assignment. Under the second agreement, Warren covenanted to hold all the agreements relating to the business of the partnership for the benefit of the partnership absolutely. It was held that the declaration of trust constituted an agreement relating to partnership property under s. 20 of the Partnership Act 1890 notwithstanding the covenants against assignment. Such declarations of trust can be prevented by a properly drawn contract.

Assignment

Your rights under this letter and/or transactions effected under it are not capable of assignment and your obligations shall not, without our consent, be capable of performance by anybody else.

No party may assign, transfer, novate or dispose of any of or any interest in, its rights and/or obligations under this agreement.

This agreement shall not be assigned by either party save with the prior written consent of the other party.

This agreement shall not be assignable by either of us unless the other shall have given express written agreement to such assignment.

Your rights and obligations under this agreement and any transactions entered into pursuant hereto are not capable of assignment.

This agreement is personal to [X] and [X] shall not be entitled to assign, sub-contract or in any other way part with its rights or obligations under this agreement without the prior written consent of [Y].

It is hereby agreed between the parties that neither party shall have the right to sub-contract or assign this agreement or any part thereof, except that [X] may assign this agreement to any member of the [X] Group.

[X] may assign all of its rights and obligations hereunder to any other person, firm or company and such assignee shall, upon serving on [Y] an instrument in writing whereby it shall assume the obligations of [X]

hereunder and agree to become bound by the provisions hereof, become the successor to the party hereto. Save with the consent in writing of the [X], [Y] may not assign its rights and/or obligations hereunder or any of them.

Either party may at any time assign, transfer, charge or deal in any other manner with all or any of its rights under this agreement or sub-contract any or all of its obligations under it.

The seller may procure that this agreement is performed by any parent, subsidiary or associated company of the seller, but no such procurement or assignment shall relieve the seller of its obligations to the buyer.

Costs

Each party shall pay its own costs, charges and expenses incurred in the preparation, completion and implementation of this agreement.

Glossary

Acceptance An agreement to accept all the terms of an offer.

'Business day' A day (other than a Saturday or a Sunday) on which banks are open for business in London and (in relation to a transaction involving a currency other than Sterling) the principal business centre of the country.

Breach of contract This occurs where a party to a contract fails to perform, precisely and exactly, their obligations under the contract.

Confidential information This means information which any party to an agreement (for whatever reason) might reasonably be expected to object to becoming generally known, for whatever reason.

Consideration The price paid for the benefit received.

Contract An agreement made in writing, orally or by conduct.

***Contra proferentem* rule** Where there is doubt about the meaning of the contract, the words will be construed against the person who put them forward.

Covenant A clause or term in an agreement restricting a person's freedom of contract to carry on in the future any trade or business that person wishes.

Deed A formal contract.

Discharge of a contract The contract has ended.

Equitable promissory estoppel 'Equitable' means that the doctrine applies only in equity; 'promissory' that it is based on a promise unsupported by consideration; and 'estoppel' is a rule of evidence preventing a person going back on their promise.

Express terms These state the basis of the contract.

Honour clause A clause that can be inserted into a commercial agreement if the parties to a commercial agreement do not wish it to be legally binding.

Implied terms Terms which are not agreed by the parties but which are automatically brought into the contract by custom or trade usage, statute or the courts at Common Law.

Intellectual property rights These include patents, trade marks, service marks, design rights, copyright (including all copyright in any designs and computer software), inventions, trade secrets, know-how, confidential information, registrable business names and all other intellectual property rights and rights of a similar character in any part of the work (whether or not the same are registered or capable of registration), and all applications and rights to apply for protection of any of the same.

Limitation clauses Express terms in a contract which operate in the event of a breach.

Misrepresentation A contract induced by a false statement of fact.

Offer A willingness to contract.

Operative mistake A mistake that is fundamental to the whole basis of the contract.

Penalty clause A sum which is not a genuine pre-estimate of the expected loss on breach.

Simple contract A contract based on the principle that each party must give something to the other.

***Solus* agreements** An agreement between a supplier and a retailer whereby the retailer agrees to sell only the products of the supplier in return for the supplier giving some benefit such as a reduction in the price charged for the goods.

'Subject to contract' This is generally taken to show that the parties do not intend to be bound until a formal contract is drawn up, especially if the contract is still unexecuted.

Undue influence A contract that has come into being because one party is in a position to dominate the other.

Void A contract that has no effect.

Warranty A term not vital to the main purpose of the contract.

Directory

Chartered Association of Certified Accountants (ACCA)
29 Lincoln's Inn Fields
London WC2A 3EE
Tel: +44 (0)20 7059 5000
Fax: +44 (0)20 7059 5050
E-mail: info@accaglobal.com

Chartered Association of Certified Accountants (ACCA)
Cymru/Wales
PO Box 2520
Cardiff
CF23 0GN
Fax: +44 (0)2920 263 700
E-mail: wales@accaglobal.com

Chartered Institute of Management Accountants (CIMA)
26 Chapter Street
London
SW1P 4NP
United Kingdom
Tel: +44 (0) 20 8849 2251 8am to 8pm Monday to Friday
E-mail: callback@cimaglobal.com

CMA consumer enforcement guidance
Collection of guidance on consumer protection and unfair terms from the Competition and Markets Authority, some of which was originally published by the Office of Fair Trading.

Contract law in Europe (Business Link)
A guide from *Business Link* covering contracts in the European single market, the validity of contracts in Europe, interpretation of terms in European contracts and other topics.

Contract law (European Commission)
Information on the EU proposals for harmonised European Contract Law for consumers and businesses.

Department for Business, Innovation and Skills (formerly the DTI and BERR)
1 Victoria Street
London SW1H 0ET
Tel: 020 7215 5000
E-mail: enquiries@bis.gsi.gov.uk
www.bis.gov.uk

Federation of Small Businesses (FSB)
Sir Frank Whittle Way
Blackpool Business Park
Blackpool FY4 2FE
Tel: 0808 20 20 888
www.fsb.org.uk

Financial Conduct Authority (FCA)
25 The North Colonnade
Canary Wharf
London E14 5HS
Tel: 0845 606 9966
www.fsa.gov.uk

Financial Reporting Council (FRC)
5th Floor, Aldwych House
71–91 Aldwych
London WC2B 4HN
Tel: 020 7492 2300
www.frc.org.uk

Health and Safety Executive (HSE)
Head Office
Redgrave Court
Merton Road
Bootle
Merseyside
L20 7HS
Tel: 0151 951 4000
www.hse.gov.uk

ICSA Publishing
Saffron House
6–10 Kirby Street
London EC1N 8TS
Tel: 020 7612 7020
E-mail: publishing@icsa.co.uk
www.icsa.org.uk/products-and-services/bookshop

Institute of Chartered Accountants in England & Wales (ICAEW)
Metropolitan House
321 Avebury Boulevard
Central Milton Keynes
MK9 2FZ
Tel: +44(0) 1908 248 050
www.icaew.com

Institute of Chartered Secretaries and Administrators (ICSA)
Saffron House
6–10 Kirby Street
London EC1N 8TS
Tel: 020 7580 4741
E-mail: info@icsa.org.uk
www.icsa.org.uk

International Association for Contract and Commercial Management
Kingston Lodge,
Canada Road
West Wellow
Hampshire
SO51 6DE
United Kingdom
Tel: +44 1202 553657
General Enquiries: info@iaccm.com

Jordans Secretarial Services
Jordan Publishing Limited
21 St Thomas Street
Bristol
BS1 6JS
Tel: +44 (0) 117 923 0600
Fax: +44 (0) 117 925 0486
E-mail info@jordanpublishing.co.uk
DX 78161 Bristol

Law Society of England and Wales
113 Chancery Lane
London WC2A 1PL
Tel: +44 (0) 20 7242 1222
Fax: +44 (0) 20 7831 0344
DX: DX 56 London/Chancery Lane
www.lawsociety.org.uk

The Legal 500
www.legal500.com

Privy Council
2 Carlton Gardens
London SW1Y 5AA
Tel: 020 7747 5310
E-mail: pcosecretariat@pco.x.gsi.gov.uk
www.privycouncil.independent.gov.uk

Index

Additional Content Online

This text comes with customisable, 'boilerplate' clauses for use in your own contracts.

To download your extra content, visit this link:

www.icsa.org.uk/commercial-contracts

Click 'download additional content' and enter this code:

39f0-c508-a6cb-62cf